PRINT MEDIA

PRINT MEDIA

N. Afaque Shamsi

ANMOL PUBLICATIONS PVT. LTD.
NEW DELHI - 110 002 (INDIA)

ANMOL PUBLICATIONS PVT. LTD.
H.O.: 4374/4B, Ansari Road, Darya Ganj,
New Delhi-110 002 (India)
Ph.: 23261597, 23278000
B.O.: No. 1015, Ist Main Road, BSK IIIrd Stage
IIIrd Phase, IIIrd Block,
Bangalore - 560 085 (India)
Visit us at: www.anmolpublications.com

Print Media

First Published, 2006

ISBN 81-261-2661-2

PRINTED IN INDIA

Published by J.L. Kumar for Anmol Publications Pvt. Ltd., New Delhi - 110 002 and Printed at Mehra Offset Press, Delhi.

Contents

Preface *vii*

1. **The Backdrop** 1
   - Dawning and Birth
   - The Founder
   - Players at the Beginning
   - Gigantic Pillars

2. **Development and Evolution** 39
   - Development in Straight Way
   - Significant Roles
   - The Dominance
   - Facility of Official Nature

3. **Promotion Movement** 59
   - Vital Angles
   - Major Links
   - Circle in Society
   - Action of Silent Nature
   - Lion's Chunk

4. **The Stalwarts** 87
   - Stout Heroes
   - Prominent Papers

5. **National Movement** 153
- Vital Contribution
- Primary Political Strength
- Force from Opposite Side
- Pivotal Players

6. **Academic Elements** 189
- Popular Case
- Leader of Immense Greatness
- Main Contributors

7. **Freedom at Last** 243
- Dawn of the Freedom
- Independent Print Media
- Anecdotes of Various Nature

8. **Post-independence Scene** 261
- Best Stage
- Age of Independence
- The Etiquettes

9. **New Phase** 327
- Slow Development
- Smooth-stage
- Novel Drifts
- More Promotion

Bibliography 347

Index 353

Preface

Media is the plural of 'Medium' and 'mass' means a large number. Thus, by mass-media, what is meant is 'the main means of communication at a large number' i.e., all those means, which are used to communicate with people on a vast level or at a great number, as, newspapers, magazines, radio and television, etc.

Though communication has always been an important need of life, it assumed the status of the most essential and one of the basics of life in the later half of the 20th century. As a result, a number of different and diverse forms of media emerged and institutions imparting their thorough knowledge mushroomed throughout the width and length of the country and world.

In this battle of survival and cut-throat comptetion, the one which won the greatest appreciation and applaud of the masses is the Electronic Media by virtue of its being capable of communicating to people, live and pulsating coverage of news and events occurring in every nook and corner of the world and in all the strata of the society ranging from the laymen to the top brass of Government, Semi-Government and non-Government administrations.

Given the above-discussed situation, there was an urgent demand for such an Encyclopaedia, which may cater to the maximum requirements of the seekers of knowledge in this regard. This series has been prepared with a view to encapsulating most of the stuff required by a media-lover.

Should we succeed in our attempt and get a favouring feedback excluding unnecessary brickbats, we would put a more enlightening, informative and comprehensive ocean of knowledge in the hold of your hands.

Editor

1

The Backdrop

Dawning and Birth

Broadly speaking, the functions of the press are to convey government policies to the public, keep government informed of public needs and reaction to.government policies and keep the public and government informed of events and happenings at home and abroad. Each of functions developed as the need for it was felt.

The history of the Indian press begins with the coming of the European. The Portuguese were the first European nation who brought a printing press to India and the first book published in India was by the Jesuits of Goa in 1557. In 1684 the English East India Company set up a printing press in Bombay. For about a century no newspapers were published in the Company's territories because the company's servants in India wished to withhold the news of their malpractices and abuses of 'private trading' from reaching London.

The first attempts to publish newspapers in India were made by the disgruntled employees of the East India Company who sought to expose the malpractices of private trade. In

1776 William Bolts, being censured by the Court of Directors for private trading, resigned his service under the Company and announced his intention to publish a newspaper and made it known that he had in his possession "in manuscript many things to communicate which most intimately concerned every individual".

The official quarters at once reacted and Bolts' scheme ended in embryo. It was left to James A gustus Hickey to publish the first newspaper in India entitled. The Bengal Gazette or Calcutta General Advertiser in the year 1780. For his outspoken criticism of Government officials and scurrilous attacks on the Governor-General and the Chief Justice, Hickey's press was seized in 1782. The following years saw the appearance of new publications like.

The Calcutta Gazette (1784), The Bengal Journal (1785), The Oriental Magazine of Calcutta or Calcutta Amusement (1785), The Calcutta Chronicle (1786), The Madras Courier (1788), The Bombay Herald (1789) etc. The promoters of these new publications profited from Hickey's bitter experience and avoided clash with the authorities.

The Circulation of newspapers during this early period never exceeded a hundred or two hundreds. These journals usually aimed to cater to the intellectual entertainment of the Europeans and Anglo Indians. There was hardly any danger of public opinion being subverted in India. What really worried the Company's officers in India was the apprehension that these newspapers might reach London and expose their misdoings to the Home authorities. In the absence of press laws, the newspapers were at the mercy of censorship, sometimes deported the offending editor for anti-government policies.

Through the Censorship of the Press Act, 1799 Lord Wellesley imposed censorship on all newspapers. Apprehending a French invasion of India and engaged in the struggle for supremacy in India, Wellesley could not tolerate the publication of any matter which adversaries or the French promoted. The Censorship of Press Act, 1799, imposed almost wartime restrictions on the press. The regulations required :

(a) The newspaper to clearly print in every issue the name of the printer, the editor and the proprietor; and

(b) The publisher to submit all material for pre-censorship to the Secretary to the Government.

Breach of these rules was punishable with immediate deportation. In 1807 the Censorship Act was extended to cover journals, pamphlets and even books.

Relaxation of press restrictions came under Lord Hastings. The Governor-General tried to put his liberal ideas in practice and succeeded in establishing in India some of the progressive views which were gaining ground in England. In 1818 pre-censorship of the press was dispensed with. However, the Government laid down some general rules for the guidance of newspaper editors with a view to prevent the discussion of topics likely to affect the authority of the Government or injurious to public interests. The Governor-General refused, much against the wishes of the members of his Council and particularly John Adams, to cancel the licence of James Buckingham, the editor of The Calcutta Journal or deport him.

The appointment of John Adams as acting Governor-General in 1823 gave him the opportunity to give a practical shape to his reactionary views. Press Regulations of 1823 proved more stringent than any that had been in force earlier. The new regulations required:

(a) Every printer and publisher to obtain a licence for starting a press or using it.

(b) The penalty for printing and/or publishing any literature without the requisite licence was Rs. 400 for each such publication or imprisonment in default thereof. Magistrates were authorised to attach unlicensed presses.

(c) The Governor-General had the right to revoke a licence or call for a fresh application.

From the arguments supporting the ordinance and its subsequent application, it is clear that Adams' regulations were directed chiefly against newspapers published in the Indian languages or edited by Indians. Raja Ram Mohan Roy's Mirat-ul-Akbar had to stop publication. After Adams' regulations only three Bengali and one Persian newspapers continued publication in Calcutta. J.S. Buckingham was also deported to England.

Lord William Bentinck adopted a liberal attitude towards the Press. Although Adams' press regulations were not revoked, considerable latitude of discussion was given to the press, Indian as well as Anglo-Indian. It was, however, left to Charles Metcalfe, officiating Governor-General (1835-36) to repeal the obnoxious ordinance of 1823 and earn the epithet of 'Liberator of the Indian Press'. Lord Macaulay, a true Whig, supported the case for a free press in India. He argued that since the Government possessed unquestionable powers of interference whenever the safety of the state was in danger, it was therefore unnecessary to keep the offensive form and ceremonial of despotism in times of peace.

A new Press Act required a printer and publisher to make a declaration giving a true and precise account of the premises of publication. It was open to a printer and publisher to cease to function as such by a similar declaration to that effect. The result of this liberal press policy which continued unchanged till 1856 was the rapid growth of newspapers all over the country.

The emergency caused by the Rebellion of 1857 led the Government to reimpose restrictions on the press. Act No. XV of 1857 reintroduced licensing restrictions in addition to the existing registration procedure laid down by the Metcalfe Act. The Act prohibited the keeping or using of printing press without a licence from the Government and the Government reserved the discretionary right to grant licences or revoke them at any time. The Government was also empowered to prohibit the publication or circulation of any newspaper, book or other printed matter. The act was an emergency measure and its duration was limited to one year. Charles Metcalfe's statute, however, continued in force.

The Press and Registration of Books Act XXV of 1867 replaced Metcalfe's Act of 1835 pertaining to registration of printing presses and newspapers. The Act was of a regulating nature and not a restriction on printing presses or newspapers. By this Act every book or newspaper was required to have place of printing. Further, within one month of the publication of a book and a copy of the book had to be supplied free of charge to the local government. This Act was amended in 1890 and again in 1914, 1952, and 1953.

An act to amend the Indian Penal Code, was passed which contained a sedition section. The revolt of the Wahabis (1869-70) alarmed the Government and impelled it to arm itself with wider powers to deal effectively and promptly with seditious writings and speeches Later on this section was incorporated in the Indian Penal Code as Section 124-A.

An unfortunate legacy of the Rebellion of 1857 was the growth of the spirit of racial bitterness among the rulers and the ruled. As a result the European press in India after 1858 was always ranged on the side of the Government in all political controversies. The vernacular press, which had developed and grown on an unprecedented scale since 1857 became more vocal and increasingly critical of governmental policies. This in turn created a strong public opinion critical of the imperialist acts of Lord Lytton. The terrible famine of 1876-71 which took a toll of over six million souls and the lavish expenditure on the Imperial Darbar at Delhi In January 1877 made the public opinion and the press restive. Lytton on his part considered the newly rising intellectual class in India as 'a deadly legacy from Macaulay and Metcalfe' and tried to stifle their views.

The Vernacular Press Act of 1878 was designed to 'better control' the vernacular press and to empower to Government with more effective means .of punishing and repressing seditious writings. The act empowered :

(1) a District Magistrate with the previous permission of a Local Government to call upon the printer and publisher of any vernacular newspaper to enter into a bond under-taking not to publish anything likely to excite feelings of disaffection against the government or antiparty between persons of different races, castes and religions among Her Majesty's subjects. The magistrate could further require a publisher to deposit security and to forfeit it if the newspaper contravened the regulation. If the offence reoccurred, the press equipment could be seized.

(2) The magistrate's action was final and no appeal could be made to a court of law.

(3) A vernacular newspaper could get exemption from the operation of the Act by submitting proofs for the paper to a government censor.

The act came to be nicknamed Gagging Act. The worst feature of the Act was that it discriminated between the English press and the vernacular press and no right of appeal to a court of law was given. Under the Act, proceedings were instituted against The Som Prakash, The Bharat Mihir, The Dacca Prakash, The Sahachar and a few other newspapers. The Act succeeded in its objective and the tone of the vernacular press became submissive and the vernacular newspaper of the period showed very little originality in thinking and more often largely borrowed from the English press.

Lord Cranbrook, the new Secretary of State, objected to the pre-censorship clause of the Act on the ground that the censors would have to the Indians and that they would have to, in point of fact, re-write the newspapers. Consequently in September 1878 the precensorship clause was deleted. At the suggestion of the Secretary of State, a Press Commissioner was appointed charged with the duty of supplying authentic and accurate news to the press.

The Vernacular Press Act was repealed in 1882 by the Government of Lord Ripon. Ripon, the nominee of the Liberal Government of Gladstone, held the view that the circumstances which justified the Act of 1878 no longer existed.

The misery caused by the famine of 1896-97 and the bubonic plague led to discontent in the Deccan and there were cases of violence. The newspaper press played its part in the political controversies. By Act VI of 1989, Section 124 of the Penal Code was restated and amplified and a new Section 153-A was added. Similarly, Section 505 of the Penal Code was amended to punish statements which might head to public mischief, cause disaffection among the armed forces or induce a person to commit an offence against the state.

The disaffection created by the unpopular acts of Lord Curzon resulted in the growth of an Extremist Party in the Indian National Congress and led to acts of violence. The newspapers of the time often commented adversely on the Government policies. The Government followed a repressive policy and enacted the Newspapers (Incitement to Offences) Act, 1908. According to this Act :

(a) The magistrates were empowered to confiscate printing presses' property connected thereto of newspapers which published objectionable material which served as incitement to murder or acts of violence.

(b) The Local Government was empowered to annual anaya declaration made by the printer and publisher of an offending newspaper made under the Press and Registration of Books Act of 1867; and

(c) The newspaper editors and printers were given the option to appeal to the High Court within fifteen days of the order of forfeiture of the press.

Under the Newspapers Act of 1908, the Government launched prosecutions against nine newspapers and confiscated seven presses.

The Government further sought to strengthen its hands by the Indian Press of Act 1910 which revived the worst features of Lytton's Press Act of 1878. The Act empowered the Local Government to demand at the time of Registration security of not less than Rs. 500 and not more than Rs. 2,000 from the keeper of a printing press or publisher of a newspaper and to forfeit the security and annual the declaration of Registration of an offending newspaper. The Government could allow fresh Registration and may demand a security of not less than Rs. 1,000 and not more than Rs, 10,000 and forfeit the fresh security and annual the fresh declaration of Registration as well as confiscate the Press and all copies of such newspaper, books etc. if the newspapers persisted in publishing objectionable material.

The aggrieved party could appeal to a Special Tribunal of the High Court against orders of forfeiture within two months. Further, the printer of every newspaper was required to supply to the Government free of charge two copies of each issue of the newspaper published. The Act gave powers to the Chief Customs Officer to detain all imported packages which contained objectionable material.

Under the Act action was taken against 991 printing presses and newspapers. Out of these 286 were warned, in 705 cases heavy securities were demanded. During the first five years of the Act the Government confiscated securities amounting to about five lakh rupees.

During the World War I, 1914-18, the Defence of India Rules were promulgated. The executive used the new powers not only for war purposes but also for purposes of repression of political agitation and free public criticism.

In 1921 a Press Committee was appointed under the chairmanship of Sir Tej Bahadur Sapru, then Law Member of the Viceroy's Executive Council, to review the working of press laws. On the recommendations of the Committee, the Press Acts of 1908 and 1910 were repealed.

The swift turn of the political movement in the thirties and the civil disobedience movement launched by Mahatma Gandhi moved the Government to issue a fresh Press Ordinance in 1930 'to provide for the better control of the Press'. This Act revived the provisions of the Press Act of 1910. In 1931 the Government enacted the Indian Press (Emergency Powers) Act which gave sweeping powers to the provincial 'governments in suppressing the propaganda for the civil disobedience movement. Section 4 (1) of the Act sought to punish "words, signs or visible representations which (a) incite to or encourage or tend to incite to or to encourage, the commission of any offence of murder or any cognizable offence involving violence, or (b) directly or indirectly express approval or admiration of any such offence, or of any person, real or fictitious, who has committed or is alleged or represented to have committed any such offence."

In 1932 the Press Act of 1931 was amplified in the form of the Criminal Amendment Act of 1932. Section 4 was made very comprehensive and expanded to include all possible activities calculated to undermine the Government's authority. During the Second World War (1939-45), the executive exercised exhaustive powers under the Defence of India Act, Pre-censorship was reinforced, the Press Emergency Act and the Official Secrets Act were amended and at one time the publication of all news relating to the Congress activities declared illegal. The special powers assumed by the Government during the War ended in 1945.

In March 1947 the Government of India appointed a Press Enquiry Committee and charged it with the duty of examination of the press laws in the light of the fundamental rights formulated by the Constituent Assembly of India. Among the recommendations of the Committee were the repeal of the Indian Emergency Powers Act of 1931, amendments in the

Press and Registration of Books Act, modification in Sections 124-A and 153-A of the Indian Penal Code, repeal of the Indian States (Protections against Disaffection) Act, 1932 and the Indian States (Protection) Act, 1943.

The new Constitution was adopted in January 1950. In 1951 the Government felt compelled to seek amendment of Article 19(2) of the Constitution and enactment of the Press (Objectionable Matters) Act. The new Act was more comprehensive than any earlier legislation affecting the press. It replaced the Central and State Press Acts which had been in operation till then. The Act empowered the Government to demand and forfeit security and demand further security from presses and newspapers for publication of 'objectionable matter'. The Government could also declare certain publication forfeited, prohibit transmission by post of objectionable documents, to seize and destroy unauthorised newspapers and to seize and forfeit unauthorised presses. The aggrieved owners of newspapers and printing presses were allowed the right to demand trial by jury. The Act remained in force till 1956.

The All-India Newspapers Editors Conference and the Indian Federation of Working Journalists opposed the Act and urged the Government to institute a comprehensive enquiry into the working of the Indian Press. The Government yielded to the demand and in 1952 appointed the Press Commission under the presidency of Sir Justice G.S. Rajadhyaksha.

The Commission which submitted its report in August 1954 recommended among other things the setting up of an All-India Press Council, the system of price-page schedule for newspapers, banning of crossword puzzle competitions, a strict code of advertisements by newspapers, and drew the Government's attention to desirability of preventing concentration in the ownership of Indian newspapers. In recent years the Central Government has passed the Delivery of Books and Newspapers (Public Libraries) Act, 1954 ; The Working

Journalists' Conditions of Services and miscellaneous provisions Act 1955, the newspaper (Price and page) Act 1956. The Parliamentary proceedings (protection and publication) Act 1960 etc.

> "The over-200-year history of the Indian press, from the time of Hicky to the present day, is the history of a struggle for freedom, which has not yet ended. There have been alternating periods of freedom and of restrictions on freedom amounting to repression. The pioneering works on the Indian press, like that of Margarita Barns, were stories of arbitrariness and despotism, of reforms and relaxation. The story of the Indian press is a story of steady expansion but also one of press laws."

The first newspaper meant for publication was 'announced' in 1776 by William Bolts. He asked those interested to come to his residence to read the news. This 'newspaper' had the twin function of informing the British community of news from 'home', and of ventilating grievances against the colonial administration.

But it was not until James Augustus Hicky dared to start his Bengal Gazette (also called Hicky's Gazette) in 1780 that the age of Journalism dawned in the country. England had already had a taste of the Spectator papers of Addison and Steele, and of lesser known periodicals as well, and learnt about the power of the periodical essayists, to laugh to scorn the manners and mores of society, and of those in high places.

Political and social corruption was rife among the British sent to rule the country when Hicky, a printer by profession, launched his Gazette in order to purchase freedom for my mind and soul. He described the Bengal Gazette (later called Hicky's Gazette) as a weekly political and commercial paper open to all parties but influenced by none. His venom was aimed at individuals like Mrs. Warren Hastings and their private affairs. He published announcements of marriages and engagements, and of 'likely' engagements. The Gazette was, in essence, no better than a scandal sheet. Barely a year later, Sir Warren Hastings denied all postal facilities to Hicky who hit back with these ringing words:

> 'Mr. Hicky considers the Liberty of the Press to be essential to the very existence of an Englishman and a free Government. The subject should have full liberty to declare his principles and opinions, and every act which tends to coerce that liberty is tyrannical and injurious to the community.'

In June the following year (1781), Hicky was arrested and thrust into jail, from where he continued writing for the Gazette. He was stopped from bringing out his weekly only when the types used for printing were seized.

Five newspapers made their appearance in Bengal in six years' time—all started by Englishmen. Some of these newspapers received government patronage. The Madras Courier and the Bombay Herald (which later merged with the Bombay Courier) were then launched in the two cities. They were subservient to the government, and therefore flourished. The total circulation of all these weeklies was not more than 2,000; yet, the government issued Press Regulations (1799) making the publication of the name of the printer, editor and proprietor obligatory. The regulations also ordered these to declare themselves to the Secretary of the Government; and to submit all material for prior examination to the same authority. Pre-censorship was to dog the Indian journalist for many years to come.

The pioneers of Indian language journalism were the Serampore Missionaries with Samachar Darpan and other Bengali periodicals, and Raja Ram Mohan Roy with his Persian newspaper Mirat-ul Akhbar. The object of Ram Mohan Roy, the social reformer, in starting the paper was to lay before the public such articles of intelligence as may increase their experience, and tend to their social improvement, and to indicate to the rulers a knowledge of the real situation of their subjects, and make the subjects acquainted with the established laws and customs of their rules. Roy ceased publishing his paper later in protest against the Government's Press Regulations.

The Bombay Samachar, a Gujarati newspaper, appeared in 1822. It was almost a decade before daily vernacular papers like Mombai Vartaman (1830), the Jan-e-Jamshed (1831), and the Bombay Darpan (1850), began publication. In the South, a Tamil and a Telugu newspaper was established with the aid of a government grant, and in the North—west Provinces, a Hindi and an Urdu periodical started off under the government's patronage. The Bengali press with as many as nine newspapers in 1839 had a circulation of around 200 copies each, even as the British press with 26 newspapers (six of them dailies) grew in strength and power, under the liberal rule of Lord Metcalfe, and later of Lord Auckland.

The year of what the British historians term 'the Sepoy Mutiny', however, brought back the press restrictions in the form of the Gagging Act, 1857. Lord Canning argued for them, stating that 'there are times in the existence of every state in which something of the liberties and rights, which it jealously cherishes and scrupulously guards in ordinary seasons, must be sacrificed for the public welfare. Such is the State of India at this moment. Such a time has come upon us. The liberty of the press is no exception.

The Mutiny brought the rule of the East India Company to a close, with the Crown taking over the 'colony', with the promise of religious toleration and press freedom. The main topics of discussion in the English and vernacular press before and after the Mutiny were sati, caste, widow remarriage, polygamy, crimes, and opposition to the teaching of English in schools and colleges. Bombay's Gujarati press, in particular, excelled in the defence of the Indian way of life. In 1876 the Vernacular Press Act was promulgated.

During the next two decades The Times of India, the Pioneer, the Madras Mail, and the Amrit Bazar Patrika came into existence—all except the last edited by Englishmen, and serving the interests of English educated readers. The English press played down the inaugural meeting of the Indian National Congress on December 28, 1885 in Bombay, but it was reported at length by the vernacular papers such as Kesari (founded by Lokmanya Tilak). "The Amrit Bazar Patrika and Kesari soon gained a reputation for opposing government attempts to suppress nationalist aspirations.

The Amrit Bazar Patrika, for instance, denounced the deposition of the Maharaja of Kashmir, and Kesari was foremost in attacking the Age of Consent Bill of 1891, which sought to prohibit the consummation of marriage before a bride completed the age of 12. The Kesari's stand was endorsed by the Amrit Bazar Patrika and Bangabasi of Calcutta on the ground that the government had no right to interfere with traditional Hindu customs. Tilak charged the government with disrespect for the liberty and privacy of the Indian people, and with negligence in providing relief during the countrywide famine in 1896-97, which resulted in the death of over a million people.

Such savage anti-government sentiments could not be allowed free play and so Lord Elgin added sections to the Indian Penal Code to enable the government to deal with promotion of 'disaffection' against the Crown, or of enmity and hatred between different classes. Also prohibited was 'the circulation of any reports with intent to cause mutiny among British troops, intent to cause such fear or alarm among the public as to cause any person to commit an offence against the State, or intent to incite any class or community to commit offences against any other class or community. The penalties for offences ranged from life imprisonment to short imprisonment or fines.

The man who became the most noteworthy victim of these new laws was none other than Bal Gangadhar Tilak, editor of

Kesari and its English companion, Mahratha. He was arrested, convicted and jailed for six years, but Kesari continued to build up its reputation and influence as a national daily, as India woke to the 20th century. Other champions of press freedom who were prosecuted at about the same time were Aurobindo Ghose of Bande Mataram, B.B. Upadhayaya of Sandhya, and B.N. Dutt of Jugantar.

In 1910, the Indian Press Act clamped further controls on newspapers in the wake of the partition of Bengal and violent attacks by terrorists in Ahmedabad, Ambala and elsewhere. The Act required owners of printing presses to deposit securities of Rs. 500 to Rs. 2,000, which were forfeited if 'objectionable matters' were printed. The threats of seizure of the printing press, and confiscation of copies sent by post were also included in the Act. The vernacular press suffered rigorous suppression during this period (1910-1914). The government banned 50 works in English and 272 in the vernacular, which included 114 in Marathi, 52 in Urdu and 51 in Bengali.

World War I introduced still more severe press laws, but there was no let-up in nationalist agitations. Annie Besant's New India became the mouthpiece of Home Rule advocates, ably supported by the Bombay Chronicle (edited by Benjamin Horniman), Maratha (edited by N.C. Kelkar) and other publications. The government reacted swiftly by exiling Annie Besant, deporting Horniman and imposing new securities on offending publications. The Rowlatt Act of 1919 infuriated Indian opinion, which now came under the leadership of Mahatma Gandhi. His Non-Cooperative Movement took the press by storm. Gandhi was to remain front-page news for years to come. His arrests and imprisonments were covered with relish by the English and the vernacular press, whose readership now rose dramatically.

The Swaraj Party led by C.R. Das, Vallabhbhai Patel and Motilal Nehru, launched its own publications—the Banglar

Katha in Calcutta, the Swadesh Mitram in the South, and Hindustan Times, Pratap and Basumati in the North.

The Indian Press Ordinance (1930), like the Press Act of 1910, and five other Ordinances gave added power to the government in dealing with acts of terrorism, and inflammatory literature. The Swadeshi Movement, covered prominently by the press, as in The Hindu (Madras) led to the imprisonment of leaders like Gandhi and Nehru, and of editors like S.A. Brelvi of Bombay Chronicle and Ganesh Shankar Vidyarthi of Pratap. The Indian Press (Emergency Powers) Act of 1931 raised deposit securities and fines, and gave Magistrates the power to issue summary actions. Several other Acts were made law during the thirties, forcing the closure of many presses and publications.

Meanwhile, the Free Press of India, which began as a news agency, started The Indian Express and Dhenamani in Madras, the Free Press Journal in Bombay, and Gujarati and Marathi journals. The news agency collapsed after it forfeited Rs. 20,000 security under the Indian Press (Emergency Powers) Act, but its publications continued under different owners, and the Free Press editors started a new agency called the United Press of India (U.P.I.)

Then came the Quit India Movement, and World War II, and the press in India, including the English language press and that in the Indian Native States played a commendable role in reporting the struggle for freedom fairly. It opposed communal riots and the partition of the country, and when partition did take place in the glorious year of independence, lamented it. Indeed, it could be said that the press played no small part in India's victory to freedom. Free India's Constitution upheld the citizens' right to freedom of speech and expression, which included the freedom of the press. While the obnoxious Press Acts were repealed or amended, the Official Secrets Act and Sections of the Indian Code dealing with disaffection, communal hatred and incitement of armed forces to disloyalty, were retained.

The Nehru Government passed in October 1951 the Press (Objectionable Matters) Act which was reminiscent of earlier press laws enacted by the colonial rulers. The 'objectionable matters' were quite comprehensive. So fierce was the opposition to it that in 1956, it was allowed to lapse, and the first Press Commission was formed.

The national and regional press covered the campaigns of the first national elections of 1951-1952 with professional skill. So were the other events of the Nehru era, like the formation of the linguistic States, the second and third general elections, the Chinese attack, and the take-over of Goa. Unlike her father, Mrs. Indira Gandhi had never been at ease with the press. 'How much freedom can the press have in a country like India fighting poverty, backwardness, ignorance, disease and superstitions?,' asked she in the first year of her regime.

The national dailies grew strident in their attacks on her government, especially on the question of nationalisation of banks, privy purses, the Congress split, but joined forces with her during the Bangla Desh war of liberation. The attacks reached their climax in the period prior to the emergency, with open accusations of rampant corruption, and demands for her resignation, followed by the Allahabad High Court's verdict of her being guilty of corrupt election practices.

During the British regime, Indian newspapers were not allowed to publish any material considered 'seditious'. Yet few printing presses were confiscated, and fewer journalists arrested. Complete censorship was imposed only on rare occasions as when Gandhiji's arrest led to countrywide disturbances and the detention of over 60,000 persons.

Though some papers like the Bengali weekly Jugantar, or the daily Sandhya (also Bengali) were banned in the thirties, they were published secretly. Restrictions were imposed on the press during the Quit India Movement of 1942. Yet major papers could publish the arrest of national leaders and reports of demonstrations and protests. Moreover, pre-censorship was never enforced and that explains why articles critical of the British Government were carried freely.

In 1975, however, an internal emergency was clamped on the nation, and pre-censorship imposed in a draconian manner. The government suppressed transmission of news by imposing censorship on newspapers, journals, radio, TV, telex, telegrams, news agencies and on foreign correspondents. Even teleprinter services were subjected to pre-censorship. The censorship was total and unparalleled. News agencies had to get all their material censored in Delhi prior to transmission. Further, newspapers had to submit already censored news for re-censorship in their respective headquarters. What is more, even advertisements, cartoons, and comic-strips were subjected to pre-censorship. Foreign papers and journals were confiscated if they carried criticism of the emergency; some issues of Time and Newsweek were banned outright.

The underground press was, however, very active. More than 34 printing presses were seized and over 7,000 people arrested in connection with the publication and circulation of underground literature. Small publications such as A.D. Gorwala's Opinion, A.B. Shah's Quest (now New Quest), were forced to close down. Underground literature flourished in Gujarat, Tamilnadu, Bihar and Maharashtra. Letters from Jayaprakash Narayan and George Fernandes were published regularly and distributed discreetly around the country. From Bihar alone more than 2,000 titles were circulated. The RSS distributed underground literature in the form of news-sheets which contained only news and quotations. They were published in English and the major Indian languages. Indians abroad published anti-emergency literature e.g., Swarajya (England), Satyavani, Indian Opinion (USA).

Among the few overground publications that opposed the emergency despite stringent censorship regulations were: Sadhana (Gujarati), Himmat (edited by Rajmohan Gandhi), Freedom First (owned by M.R. Masani), The Statesman, The

Indian Express, Daily Morosoli (Tamil), Tughlak (Tamil) and Radical Humanist. Most other major national dailies like The Times of India, The Free Press, the Hindustan Standard, and the National Herald "crawled when they were only asked to bend."

The post-Emergency period too was witness to attempts by the Congress Party to control the press. In 1984, Bihar's Chief Minister, Dr Jagannath Mishra, mooted the Bihar Press Bill, but protests by journalists forced him to withdraw it. Three years later, an Anti-Defamation Bill (1987), initiated by Prime Minister Rajiv Gandhi, also met the same fate. More recently, Veteran Congressman V. N. Gadgil introduced the Right to Reply Bill (1994), but this too had to be withdrawn.

Pick up half a dozen newspapers of different publishing houses on a single day, and scan through the news items on the front pages of the newspapers. What strikes you at once is that most of the same items ('news stories') appear in each paper, often with a similar headline and in a similar position on the front page. Stories appearing on the top half of the front page are considered to be more important than those appearing below the fold. Prominence and significance of stories is suggested by type-size of headlines, placement, and column centimeters of space; sometimes news items are 'boxed' to suggest their greater significance.

Clearly, there is a 'hierarchy' in the selection of news. Political stories receive more prominent coverage than say stories of heroism; disaster and crime stories get greater attention than social or civic problems. The focus, it becomes clear, is on 'events' rather than issues and processes; on eminent and elite people rather than the poor and the marginalised; on the exotic and the novel rather than the ordinary, the everyday and the usual. Evidently, certain 'values' are at work in the way some happenings, some people, some nations and some cities, are considered newsworthy and others not so. Numerous happenings are not reported; a strict selection process sifts out what is not newsworthy, and chooses to publish what is. From whose perspective and in terms of which value-system is this selection being made?

It appears that journalists in all newspapers think alike and work according to the same set of values. It is true that they use the same sources (the news agencies) for the majority of their news stories, but even where newspapers have their own special correspondents, say as in New Delhi or the state capital, one finds that exactly the same stories come to be selected for reporting. It appears that reporters hunt in packs; they have a similar sense of what makes for news. An earthquake takes place in Latur, and the world's press was there the next day in hordes; Anna Hazare of Ralegaon Siddhi threatened a fast unto death, and Maharashtra's reporters queue up outside his temple-residence. The Prime Minister come to town, even on a personal visit, and the press was busy sniffing around.

This approach to journalism is sometimes labelled 'Pack Journalism'. Further, how is it that journalists the world over swear by the 'inverted pyramid structure' when writing up the news? Such a structure came into existence with the telegraph; the electronic media and the internet have a potential for experimenting with other formats, but journalists cannot shed their old habits of thought and their old routines of working to deadlines. With round the clock news on news channels (such as CNN, BBC World, Star News and Zee India TV) and on the internet, the traditional forms of journalism and traditional routines of journalists have taken a thorough beating.

In India, the Press originated during British rule. The main players initially, were Englishmen. It was an Englishman who brought out the first newspaper, a weekly journal, on Indian soil in 1780. But it could hardly be described as an Indian newspaper.

The emergence of the Indian Press, properly so called, was at once the product and a stimulant of the process of national regeneration that began in the 19th century. The attainment of political independence in 1947 was a landmark in this process of regeneration, which continues in the striving for a better society. In trying to define and to promote it, the Press has been playing an important part alongside of the three other estates of India's democratic realm, the national and State legislatures; the executive and the judiciary.

The Founder

Printing presses were first brought to India in the 16th century by Christian missionaries for publishing evangelical literature. Their publications included such aids to conversion as a Tamil-Portuguese dictionary published in 1679 at Ambalakad, near Trichur in present-day Kerala. The presence of Christian missionaries increased along with growing numbers of European traders and soldiers.

The British East India Company also brought printing presses into India, augmenting those of the missionaries. A press was installed in Bombay in 1674, in Madras in 1772, and at Calcutta in 1779. But the Company's officials did not encourage the publication of newspapers. The last thing they wanted was the disclosure--specially in London--of their illegal accumulation of wealth through private trade, they dictated miserably low prices to Indian peasants and artisans and sold at a large profit.

Following the Battle of Plassey in 1757, the Company gained mastery over the large and rich province of Bengal. It gradually reduced the Mughal emperor in Delhi to a figurehead and began to rule the greater part of India. The appointment of Warren Hastings in 1774 as Governor-General at Calcutta, with a supervisory role in relation to the Governors of Madras and Bombay, marked the emergence of the East India Company as a territorial power. Calcutta was the seat of the 'Supreme Court', which had jurisdiction over British nationals.

It was also in Calcutta that the first printed newspaper, the weekly *Bengal Gazette* or *Calcutta General Advertiser*, made its appearance, on 29th January 1780. Its publication probably owed to in-fighting between two factions in the Governor General's Council. The opposition to Warren Hastings was led by Philip Francis, whose ambition was to become Government-General himself.

The publisher of this first newspaper was James Augustus Hicky. The journal claimed to be impartial. It proclaimed itself, under the masthead, as "A Weekly Political and Commercial Paper, Open to All Parties but Influenced by None." However, the journal in fact carried on a partisan campaign against Warren Hastings and his friend Elijah Impey, Chief justice of the Supreme Court. Hicky's *Gazette* would lampoon Impey as 'Poolbundy' (pul in Hindustani means bridge) in an obvious reference to a contract for maintaining bridges which the Chief justice had secured for a relative, Warren Hastings and his wife were also boldly satirised. In those days when inconvenient Britishers could be deported, Ricky could not have carried on his campaign against the Governor-General without the backing of a powerful patron in the administration. The types of Hicky's press were seized and his journal was suppressed in 1782 after Philip Francis decided to leave India.

The *Bengal Gazette* carried news of the fighting in various parts of the country between the Company's forces and those of Indian princes not yet subdued, lengthy accounts of parties and balls given boy European residents of Calcutta; advertisement notices of property and articles available for sale; a Poet's Comer for presenting amateur verse--and a large number of letters, which praised Hicky to the skies. Typical of these eulogies was one published on the front page of the 47th issue of the journal, dated 16th December 1780. The letter-writer speaks of the nausea experienced by him on exposure to a rival newspaper the *India Gazette* started by B. Messinck and Peter Reed who enjoyed support from Warren Hastings and secured postal facilities not available to Hicky, and of the cure effected by "Dr. Hicky's medicine".

The only item in this issue of the *Bengal Gazette* pertaining to a non-European is the announcement that a slave boy (a Kaffir, from southern Africa) was available for sale. It reads: "To be SOLD: A fine Coffre Boy that understands the Business of a Butler, Kismutdar and Cooking. Price four hundred Sicca Rupees. Any Gentleman wanting such a servant may see him, and be informed of further -particulars by applying to the printer." (A Sicca rupee was at that time equivalent to two shillings.) There were also repeated insertions about a slave boy who had run away from his European master, under the heading 'Eloped'.

In the ensuing years more journals--all British-owned out, several of them with official patronage, in Calcutta itself as well as in Bombay and Madras. Hicky was doubtless a pioneer but, considering the contents and context of his paper, it is hardly appropriate to regard him as the founder of Indian journalism-even less, as some have painted him, as a, fighter for freedom of the Press who paid the price of suppression by officialdom. He was merely the first in a long line of Anglo-Indian newspaper publishers (the term was used till the early part of the 20th century for Britons living in India, not for persons of mixed parentage.)

A half-way house to the emergence of an Indian Press was marked by the journals brought out, early in the 19th century, by Christian missionaries. Though published by foreigners, these journals were addressed to Indians, and some of them were in Indian languages.

With the rise of Protestantism in Europe and the establishment of the Anglican Church in England, the early Catholic missionaries were followed by many more of other Christian denominations. These missionaries undertook educational and humanitarian work including medical relief, but primarily as aids for converting 'heathen' Indians to their religion. If social service and not proselytisation had been their primary motivation, there was plenty of work for them to do right at home, in England, where illiteracy and ill-health were rampant. As in other European countries which were at that time passing through the phase of primitive accumulation of capital for industrialisation, workers in Britain, women as well as men, had to slog away for long hours in crowded and ill ventilated factories. More than the amelioration of the living conditions of their own countrymen, the prospect of saving the souls of non-Christians impelled the missionaries who came, out to India.

The first among missionaries to publish newspapers were the Baptists of Serampore (Srirampur) where a mission was founded in 1799 by Dr. Joshua Marshman and William Carey. Their attitude is illustrated by a pamphlet brought out in 1813 by Marshman on the 'Advantages of Christianity in promoting the Establishment and Prospect of the British Empire in India'. He wrote : "It is my opinion that to the very end of time, through the imbecility of their character which Christianity itself will never remove, they will be dependent on some other nation." Again: "Every converted Hindoo or Mahommedan is necessarily the cordial friend of the British, on the grounds of his own interest and security; for on the continuance of their empire in India his very existence depends."

The Serampore journals pursued these frankly stated dual objectives of promoting religion and empire. *Dig-Darshan,* a Bengali monthly magazine for youth, came out in 1818. It was soon followed by *Samachar Darpan,* a weekly in Bengali, and *Friend of India,* a monthly in English.

It was in order to counter the attacks on Indian religions which these journals carried, and to assert national self-respect, that the first truly Indian newspapers were established by Raja Rammohun Roy (1772-1833), the initiator of India's renaissance in the modem period. When the Baptist editor of *Friend of India* went so far as to say, that Hinduism owed its origin to the Father of lies Rammohun Roy reminded him that they were engaged in solemn religious discussion and not in an exchange of abuse.

The early missionaries thought nothing of holding out material inducements to secure conversions. Rammohun Roy wrote in the course of a letter to the Rev. Henry Ware of the Harvard College, U.S.A: "Several years ago there was a pretty prevalent report in this part of India that a native embracing Christianity should be remunerated for his loss of caste by the gift of five hundred rupees, with a country-born Christian woman as his wife; and while this report had any pretension to credit, several natives offered from time to time to become Christians.

The hope of any such recompense being taken away, the old converts find now very few inclined to follow their example. This disappointment not only discourages further conversion, but has also induced several Moosulman converts to return to their former faith; and had Hindoos with equal facility admitted the return of outcastes to their society, a great number of them also would , suspect, have imitated the conduct of their brother Moosulman converts." On the other hand there were also, over the years and specially in Bengal, instances of the acceptance of Christianity by educated persons belonging to notable families including Brahmins.

Broadly speaking, there were two contrasting reactions to the Western impact. Many educated Indians aped Western manners of dress and living, even if they did not change their religion. The conservatives, in contrast, both among Hindus and Muslims, withdrew into the shells, of their respective orthodoxies. But the most constructive response, which was receptive to the best elements of Western civilisation while wanting to retain the Indian cultural heritage and to purify it of the dress of superstition and harmful social customs, was typified by Rammohun Roy.

Born in a well-to-do family, Rammohun acquired proficiency in Persian and Sanskrit as well as English. Joining the East India Company's service, he assisted British officials in the revenue and judicial administration at district level. Though a Zamindar himself, Rammohun Roy urged that a limit should be fixed on the rent payable by cultivators. He initiated an intellectual and social resurgence by promoting the spread of modern knowledge through English education, and by fighting evil practices. He was principally responsible for securing the legal prohibition in December 1829 of Sati (the custom, promoted by male chauvinists, specially in Bengal where the local customary law of Dayabhaga gave a share of a deceased man's property to the wife, of the widow burning herself on the husband's funeral pyre).

Rammohun Roy was the first to advocate many of the reforms, which were to be demanded in subsequent decades by leaders of the nationalist movement, such as equality before the law and separation of the judiciary from the executive. However, he did not press for representative government. It was too soon for that, with an entrenched imperial power and a people, steeped in illiteracy and superstition and with little sense of a national identity; the affiliation of caste was, at that time, all that mattered. But Rammohun Roy's consciousness of India's unfortunate status as a subject country and his readiness to assert national self-respect are evident from his courageous criticism of the foreign missionaries' brash methods.

> "It is true", Rammohun Roy said, "that the apostles of Jesus Christ used to preach the superior superiority of the Christian religion to the natives of different countries. But we must recollect that they were not the rulers of those countries where they preached. Were the missionaries likewise to preach the Gospel and distribute books in countries not conquered by the English, such as Turkey, Persia, etc., which are much nearer England, they would be an esteemed body of men truly zealous in propagating religion and in following the example of the founders of Christianity. In Bengal, where the English are the sole rulers, and where the mere name of Englishman is sufficient to

> frighten people, an encroachment upon the rights of her poor; timid and humble inhabitants and upon their religion cannot be viewed in the eyes of God or the public as a justifiable act."

Because of the institution of army chaplains who were known as padre lat , and the aid and encouragement that the missionaries received from officialdom, they were widely perceived as limbs of the Company Raj. They were to be seen everywhere and gave most offence at the market-place where they poured ridicule on the beliefs and practices of Indians, both Hindus and Muslims. It required courage on the part of Rammohun Roy to criticise these tactics. And the criticism commanded respect because it came from one who wag himself deeply attracted by the humanist teaching of the gospels. Rammohun Roy published a tract on 'The Precepts of Jesus, the Guide to Peace and Happiness'. Monier Williams has described him as "perhaps the first earnest-minded investigator of the science of comparative religion that the world has produced."

Attacks on Hinduism were not confined to the Serampore Baptist publications. The *Bengal Hurkaru,* an English journal (whose title was based on the Indian name by which the mail runners, carrying the post, were known) carried an offensively worded, article, by a writer signing himself as 'Layman, on, a tract by Rammohun Roy entitled 'Second Appeal to the Christian Public'. Disagreeing With the Indian savant's understanding of Christ's life and teaching, the 'Layman' alluded to the existence of penal statutes, which made blasphemy a cognisable offence.

In a rejoinder which the *Bengal Hurkaru* declined to publish, Rammohun Roy said: "I am not at all surprised at the reference of the Layman to the penal statutes against those who deny the Divinity of Christ; for when Reason and Revelation refuse their support, Force is the only weapon that can be employed." On 14th July 1821, *Samachar Darpan* carried a sharply worded attack on the Vedantic religion. Inviting replies, the journal said : "Whoever writes a proper answer may have it printed and distributed everywhere by sending it to the Serampore printing office." Rammohun sent a considered reply under the name of Pandit Sivaprasad Sharma. *Samachar Darpan's* failure to print it offended Rammohun Roy's sense of fairness.

This incident probably impelled Rammohun Roy to become a publisher in order to propagate his ideas. He launched in or around 1821 three journals : *Sambad Kaumidi* and *Mirat-ul Akhbar,* weeklies in Bengali and Persian (the then language of the court of the nominal Mughal emperor in Delhi, and of law), and the *Brahmanical Magazine* in English. Through these, Rammohun endeavoured to counter the tirades of the missionaries on the one hand, and to, educate Indian public opinion on the need for social reform. The first among Indian owned newspapers of whose sustained publication there is evidence, Rammohun Roy's publications marked the true beginning of Indian journalism. They were addressed mainly to Indians, but also appealed to the better sense of Englishmen living in India.

Of the three journals, *Brahmanical Magazine* was in the nature of a series of tracts. Three issues appeared in the second half of 1821, and the fourth and last in 1823. More regular in publication, and closer in their contents to modern periodicals, were *Sambad Kaumidi* and *Mirat ul Akhbar*. They tried to meet a wide variety of reader interests. There were items of local news including births, marriages and deaths, as well as reports of events in India and the world; articles on themes of religious and social reform-- specially the need to end the inhuman custom of Sati as well as travelogues; and shipping and, commercial news. The fourth issue of *Sambad Kaumidi* gives an idea of the arrogant ways of Englishmen in Calcutta of that time. It appeals for "measures to restrain Christian gentlemen" from driving their carriages through Indian crowds, cutting and lashing them with whips, while they were assembled "to witness the images of their deities pass along Chitpore Road".

Sambad Kaumidi began under the editorship of Bhawani Charan Bannerji. After the 13th issue he left the paper on account of disagreement with Rammohun Roy's campaign against. Sati and for social reforms. Banerji started a rival weekly called *Samachar Chandrika* which espoused orthodox Hindu views and opposed the teaching of English. This was an early instance of the Indian Press reflecting the views both of the forward looking section of the intelligentsia and of conservative opinion.

Mirat ul Akhbar, the weekly in Persian, devoted much space to international affairs. The first issue carried an article on China and an analysis of the causes of tension between Russia and the Turkish ruler at Constantinople. A later issue solicited aid for the victims of the famine raging in Ireland, and gave the names of "a number of respectable gentlemen of liberal principles" who had, "for the love of God", subscribed for the starving Irish. The article is significant as an early expression of the sympathy and kinship felt by the Indian national movement with the Irish struggle.

The writer begins with a brief survey of the geography and political history of Ireland and refers to acts of British usurpation. 'The kings of England gifted away to their courtiers the estates of Irish noblemen, and levied taxes on the Irish Catholics to defray the expenses of the Church of England. The landed proprietors passed their time in England with a view to promoting their careers at the Court and to enjoy the luxuries of life. They spent in England vast sums of revenue derived from their Irish estates, which they collected through oppressive stewards; and consequently the trades people in England, instead of the people of Ireland, benefited.

Rammohun Roy received material and moral support in his journalistic and other public work from two close friends: Dwarkanath Tagore 1794-1846), grandfather of the poet Rabindranath; and James Silk Buckingham, an Englishman of liberal sympathies who was the first in a line of British friends of India.

Enlightened and affluent, Dwarkanath respected and liked his elder friend Rammohun Roy. Krishna Kripalani says in his biography : Without ever formally renouncing the family observance of, orthodox Hindu ritual, Dwarkanath actively supported every crusade of Rammohun Roy for social reform, religious tolerance and intellectual freedom. Dwarkanath regularly attended the meetings of the Atmiya Sabha (Friendly Society) formed by Rammohun Roy in 1815 and of the Calcutta Unitarian Committee, which replaced it in 1821.

The two friends and their close associates subsequently felt that if religious worship had to have a form, it was better that the weekly worship should have an indigenous form. This was the origin of the Brahma Samaj inaugurated on 20th August 1828. Dwarkanath contributed funds liberally for the activities of the Samaj. He also gave financial assistance to Rammohun Roy's publications as well as to other journals of a progressive hue. *The Bengal Hurkaru,* which began to adopt a liberal policy under the editorship of James Sutherland, published a statement on 30th June 1836, which is of interest both for the light it throws on Dwarkanath's munificence and on the emergence of India's first daily newspaper.

The first number of the daily *Hurkaru (being* likewise the *first* daily paper ever published in India) appeared on 29th April 1819. The interests and resources of several Calcutta journals have from time to time merged in the *Hurkaru,* and it received an important accession on 1st October 1834 when the oldest newspaper in India *(India Gazette),* with all its stock, having been sold by public auction, was purchased by a public spirited native gentleman, Dwarkanath Tagore, and united to the *Hurkaru* press which, by this important accession, now stands unrivalled in every respect its circulation being greater than that of any-Indian newspaper; the *Hurkaru* being the first daily journal published in India, and the only five-column newspaper."

While the first daily newspaper in English thus emerged

in Calcutta in 1819, Bombay accounted for the emergence of the first daily newspaper in an Indian language: *Mumbai-na-Samachar (Bombay Samachar).* Fardoonji Murzban, a Parsi entrepreneur, began by establishing a printing press in 1812 and brought out the Samachar as an annual *Panchang* or almanac. It began to be published as a weekly newspaper from 1st July 1822, and became a daily in 1832.

The circulation of newspapers was small during this early period. Rarely did a daily or periodical sell more than 200 copies. A contemporary estimate by Rev. J. Long, in 1855, places the number of those who read, or listened to the reading of, a newspaper copy at an average of ten. According to him, the newspapers published in Bengal had a to total sale of 2,950 copies and a readership (including listenership) of about 30,000. In the North-West Provinces (corresponding to the present Uttar Pradesh), there were 28 newspapers with a total circulation of 2,216 copies.

Rammohun Roy's other stalwart supporter, James Silk Buckingham, recorded his first impression of his Indian friend in these words : "In June 1818, the month of my first arrival in Calcutta, I was introduced to Rammohun Roy, and was surprised at the unparalleled accuracy of his language, never having before heard any foreigner of Asiatic birth speak so well, and esteeming his fine choice of words as worthy the imitation even of Englishmen." Buckingham started the weekly Calcutta journal with the help of some English mercantile interests and extended full support through its columns to Rammohun Roy's causes.

Buckingham described the object of his journal to be "To admonish Governors-of their duties, to warn them furiously of their faults, and to tell disagreeable truths." This is interesting as an affirmation, on Indian soil, of the adversary role which the Western Press has, by and large, tended to see for itself. And it is in contrast to the more complex role, of self-criticism as well as criticism, which was sought to be played by a large section of the Indian nationalist Press, starting with Rammohun Roy's papers.

On the one hand Rammohun utilised his journals to appeal to his countrymen to free themselves from the incubus of obscurantist traditions, to discard the rigidities of caste, to equip themselves with modem knowledge, and to cultivate thrift and industry. On the other hand he kept making demands on the authorities such as for the opening of schools for imparting modern education, curbing the haughty behavior of whites, improvement of conservancy services in Calcutta, and for making the services of European physicians available to Indians. In a later period this dual role of social self-criticism and political mobilisation was to be a feature of a large section of the nationalist Press. The journalistic activities both of Rammohun Roy and of Buckingham soon ran into difficulties. Lord Hastings, who had let the earlier Press regulations' fall into disuse, retired as Governor-General towards the close of 1822. John Adam, who officiated for six months till the arrival of Lord Amherst, was a bureaucrat who did not like the way Buckingham was running the Calcutta Journal. Buckingham's residential licence was revoked, and a deportation order was served on him. (Nearly a century later, another British journalist friend of India, Benjamin Guy Horniman, was to be deported in 1919 for his trenchant criticism of the massacre of unarmed Indians at Jalianwala Bagh in Amritsar.)

The Hastings-Adam contrast illustrates a swing between imposition and relaxation of restriction on the Press which characterized the period of British rule, and which was to persist in post-independence India. It comes naturally to a government, whatever its political complexion, to seek to protect and perpetuate itself. And the attitude to the Press depends to a considerable extent on the personality and values of the principal wielder of government authority at a given time.

When the *Asiatic Mirror*, European-owned, published some information regarding military affairs in the context of the

British-French contest for supremacy in India, the Governor General, Lord Wellesley, wrote to the Commander-in-Chief promising to lay down "rules for the conduct of the Whole tribe of editors". In May 1799, regulations were issued which required a newspaper to secure a licence--revocable at the Government's will--prior to publication and to carry the names of the printer, editor and proprietor. When the Baptist missionaries of Serampore published vicious attacks on the religions of India, which created disaffection among Indians, Lord Minto (forbear of the later and better known Governor General of the early 20th century) ordered them to move their presses to Calcutta so that they could be kept on a short leash. The missionaries appealed against the order on grounds of expense, and promised to submit the manuscripts of their pamphlets for scrutiny prior to publication.

Hastings, who had taken over from Minto, issued orders on 19th August 1818 abolishing pre-censorship and throwing on publishers and editors the responsibility for excluding matter likely to affect the authority of the Government or likely to be injurious to the public interest. Hastings regarded "the freedom of publication as a natural right of my fellow subjects, to be narrowed only by special and urgent cases... It is salutary for the supreme authority, even when its intentions are most pure, to look to the control of public scrutiny. While conscious of rectitude, that authority can lose none of its strength by its exposure to general comment."

John Adam took an opposite view. He objected, he said, "to the assumption by an editor of a newspaper of the privilege of sitting in judgement on the acts of Government and bringing public measures and the conduct of public men as well as the conduct of private individuals before the bar of what Buckingham and his associates miscall public opinion." Rammohun Roy's *Mirat ul Akhbar* was among the newspapers, besides Buckingham's, which attracted Adam's adverse attention. This was despite the fact that Rammohun Roy was known for his constructive attitude and moderation in language.. He had pledged himself to have due regard for truth and for the rank of persons in authority, his two-fold object being to enlighten the public and to "communicate to the rulers a knowledge of the real situation of their subjects and make the subjects acquainted with the established- laws and customs of their rulers, so that the rulers may more readily find an opportunity of granting relief to the people and the people may be pot in possession of the means of obtaining protection and redress from their rulers."

Rammohun Roy and some other public men appealed, in vain, to the Supreme Court of the East India Company in India. Equally fruitless was an appeal to the King in Council, drafted by him and signed by Dwarkanath Tagore and others, which said that a free Press had never yet caused a revolution, but revolutions had been innumerable where no free Press existed to ventilate grievances. In protest against the Adam 'regulations, Rammohun Roy ceased publication of *Mirat ul Akhbar*.

Rammohun Roy's vision of the future of India was expressed in these words : "Supposing that, a hundred years hence, the native character becomes elevated from constant intercourse with Europeans and the acquirement of general and political knowledge as well as of modern arts and sciences, is it possible that they will not have the spirit as well as the inclination to resist effectively any unjust and oppressive measures serving to degrade them in the scale of society."

Players at the Beginning

Raja Ram Mohun Roy (1772-1833) has been described by Jawaharlal Nehru as a founder of the Indian press. Another writer has said: "He was perhaps the first 'Modern Indian'. The incentive of Roy's example was to produce the greatest awakening of Indian India in the second half of the 19th century." He was the earliest champion of press freedom. He was a fighter for social reform and he wielded his pen in the many journals, he sponsored to achieve a social and cultural renaissance in Hindu society. Born in a Brahmin family, he learnt Persian, Arabic, Sanskrit and English. He entered the Company's service but later resigned to utilise his time and energy for social reform. He believed that Hindu gods and idol worship were accretions to the true Hindu scriptures.

He founded the *Sambad Kaumudi* (Moon of Intelligence) in 1821 in Calcutta; due to the success of another rival, *Samachar Chandrika*, Roy was forced to close it down in 1822, but it was revived the following year. Roy also started a newspaper in Persian, *Mirat-ul Akhbar* (Mirror of News) in 1822 but shut it down in 1823 in protest against the press regulations of 1823. The Chief Secretary to the Bengal Government, Butterworth Bayley, made frequent mention of Roy's Persian weekly to justify the restrictions on the press. Roy gave three reasons for closing down his paper. "(1) An Indian had no access to officials as English editors had to secure a licence as required under the new law. (2) To make an affidavit in open court in the presence of respectable magistrates is looked upon as very mean and censurable by those who watch the conduct of their neighbours. (3) After incurring the disrepute of soliciting and suffering the dishonour of making the affidavit, the constant apprehension of the licence being revoked by government which would disgrace the person in the eyes of the world, would create such anxiety as entirely to destroy one's peace of mind."

It was under these new press regulations that Buckingham had been deported in 1823. Ram Mohun Roy had presented a petition through his counsel, Fergusson, to the Supreme Court on behalf of the natives of India protesting against the regulations. But Justice Macnaghton ignored the petition, pointing out the anomaly of a free press under a system which was not free. From the very beginning, Roy provoked the opposition of the administration and the European community in general who did not want him to propagate his views on social reform and religion and were dismayed by the tenacity with which he persisted in his campaign as a social reformer.

Some of the Company's employees carried on an active tirade against him and persecuted some of the Indian employees for their kinship with him. It was said that the administration as a whole looked upon his activities with considerable misgivings. He was generally considered as "unrepresentative" of Hindu opinion.

Once he realised that his direct interest in journalism provoked opposition born from the Hindu reactionaries and Company officials, Ram Mohun Roy kept himself in the background and encouraged others who were progressing in the same direction as he wanted to. The newspapers with which he was associated strongly protested against the deportation of Buckingham and he was the inspiration behind many newspapers which dominated the newspaper world of Calcutta for a long time. It was his friend and collaborator, Dhirendranath Tagore who opened his purse to both English and Indian newspapers when they were under financial strain. Roy, with his varied interests and numerous activities, could not be shaken by his small-minded opponents whose campaign of vilification seemed to have stopped at nothing.

Ram Mohun Roy stood for a free press. He said: "Every good ruler must be conscious of the great liability to err in managing the affairs of a vast empire and, therefore, he will be anxious to afford to every individual the readiest means of bringing to his notice whatever may require his interference. To secure this important object, the unrestrained liberty of publication is the only effective means that can be employed". He said that Indians should be told of the excellent institutions of the English and the struggles in other countries to restrain despotism and avert anarchy and that the rulers should be made aware of the grievances of their subjects. He said the people looked up to the king of England to remedy the evils perpetrated by the administration in India. In his petition to the king against the rejection of his protest by the Calcutta Supreme Court against the press regulations, Roy referred to him as the "Liberator of Europe".

Gigantic Pillars

One writer described Roy as "Mohun Roy, Hindu reformer, searcher after truth, universalist and staunch champion of freedom everywhere and in all spheres." The newspapers which he sponsored or which followed him propagated his political philosophy which could be summarised as follows: he favoured a policy of "judicious colonisation" of India by Europeans with education and capital in order to expand India's contacts with the West, obtain England's technical knowledge, ensure closer contacts with England. He believed that independence of the American colonies had been brought about by bad administration and he saw no reason why with liberal administration, India should not be content to remain with Britain even if there was a large increase in the European element. Jeremy Bentham, the English writer, admired Roy's writing and said of his English "which but for the name of a Hindu, I should certainly have ascribed to the pen of a superiorly educated and instructed Englishman."

Ram Mohun Roy was fully conscious of the political transformation along national lines then taking place in Europe, but he was actually conscious of the extreme backwardness of India in just those areas which provided the basis for that transformation. He felt that until that process had reached an advanced stage, India should be governed by the wisdom of the English monarch and his Parliament acting through the East India Company's officers. He, however, felt that Indian opinion as voiced by newspapers and in direct petitions and in evidence before commissions should be given proper weight and attention. According to one writer: "His reliance on the British Parliament for arbitration of political conflict, redress of popular grievances and guidance on constitutional advancement was not widely challenged in India even at the end of the century. His genius lay partly in his ability to use arguments which met Western intellectual standards, thereby appealing to both the British and other newly influential groups of educated Indians."

Roy's high standard of political leadership and writing became the intellectual basis of later political activity. The standard was Western, not Indian. He founded no political party but his political doctrines were the keystone of liberalism and individualism in the 19th century. The beginnings of modern political thought and the struggle for individual rights were seen in his plea for political reform, an end to racial discrimination in court procedure, consultation with Indians before legislation, admission of Indians to higher jobs in the administration and most important, freedom of the press from arbitrary Government regulations. He was devoted to the principles of constitutional monarchy as obtained in Britain and he believed that political progress in India could be achieved by operating within the British system.

Indian leaders after him, however much they criticised it, found ample opportunities to fight for their aims without breaking out of the system. Indians did not want to end British rule but wanted, in the words of one writer, "to increase the advantages for themselves under it. Most of them believed there was no alternative system of administration that could possibly maintain the unity, security, and social progress which the British Government had undertaken to provide."

As a social reformer, Roy's aim was to provide a synthesis between the new liberal world of the West and Hinduism. In the words of one biographer: "He maintained that the core of Hindu thought was both moral and rational and, therefore, could come together with the moral rationalisms of the West. His main contribution was to show the way to the reconciliation of political aims that were Western in direction and inspiration with certain elements in the traditional Hindu pattern—to show, in fact, that it was possible to agitate for liberal democracy without ceasing to be an Indian. Such an apparently simple premise was to produce a nationalist movement based widely upon a continuing tradition yet forward looking and progressive, its political demands readily comprehensible to the rulers."

2

Development and Evolution

The print medium can be broadly divided into two parts-periodical publications including daily newspapers, and publications such as books and other printed material. Publicity in the press, particularly through the daily newspapers, is the most effective and popular mode of projection compared to publicity through any other medium. Newspapers occupy a commanding position as a medium of mass communication. This is so, despite widespread illiteracy and limited circulation of newspapers in India. The reasons are both physical and psychological. A newspaper can be read at the reader's own convenience. It can also be referred to as and when required. Newspaper reading is more or less a habit with most people. It is also generally presumed that, newspapers provide relatively impartial coverage of happenings compared to other media. Newspapers, therefore, make a greater impact on the public mind, particularly in urban and semi-urban areas.

Development in Straight Way

The Press in India has maintained a steady growth, reflected both in the number as well as in the circulation of newspapers.

The number rose to 22,648 at the end of 1985. Likewise, the circulation of newspapers advanced to 61,981,000 copies in 1985. The number of newspapers on RNI's live register in 1988 was estimated at 29,000.

The number of daily newspapers in 1985 increased to 1,802. The circulation of daily newspapers rose up to nearly 2 crore copies. The majority of Indian newspapers are periodicals. Out of 19,227 periodicals in 1983, as many as 7,232 (37.6 per cent) were monthlies, 6,122 (31.8 per cent) weeklies, 2,817 (14.7 per cent) fortnightlies, and 1,979 (10.3 per cent) quarterlies. There were 244 annuals, and 833 bimonthlies, half-yearlies, etc. Monthly journals led in circulation, too, with a share of 41.1 per cent, closely followed by weeklies with 40 per cent. Fortnightlies accounted for 13.0 per cent of the circulation. The remaining 5.9 per cent belonged to other periodicals. The share of periodicals in the number of newspapers was as high as 92.6 per cent, but their share in circulation restricted to 69.4 per cent.

Newspapers were published in as many as 92 languages during 1985. Apart from English and fifteen principal languages enumerated in the Eighth Schedule of the Constitution, newspapers were published in 75 other languages, mostly Indian languages or dialects, and also in a few foreign languages.

Hindi newspapers numerically constituted the largest group in the country in 1983. As in the previous years, highest number of newspapers were published in Hindi (5,936), followed by English (3,840), Bengali (1,582), Urdu (1,378), and Marathi (1,131). In circulation too, Hindi newspapers maintained their lead with 15,458,000 copies, followed by English with 10,627,000 copies, and the third position was claimed by Malayalam press with 4,918,000 copies. Likewise, in the matter of daily newspapers, the first place went to Hindi (470), Urdu (148) came second, and Marathi (127) third; English (123), Malayalam (112), and Tamil (106) were the other languages with more than 100 daily newspapers. As regards circulation, Hindi press continued to lead in 1983, claiming the top position with 4,537,000 copies (being 27.1 percent of total circulation of all dailies). English dailies claimed the second position, with a circulation of 3,349,000 copies (20.0 per cent).

In 1983, the largest number of newspapers were published from Uttar Pradesh (2,912). Maharashtra with 2,654 came next, followed by Delhi and West Bengal with 2,637 and 2,274 respectively. Other States having more than one thousand newspapers were Tamil Nadu (1,289), Rajasthan (1,142), and Andhra Pradesh (1,123), Kerala (1,085) and Karnataka (1,019) crossed the thousand mark during the year under review.

The press in Delhi maintained its top position in circulation with 8,176,000 copies in 1983. The press in Maharashtra (8,132,000) came second, and Tamil Nadu (6,552,000) was third. Uttar Pradesh took the fourth place with 6,025,000 copies.

As in the previous years, Uttar Pradesh continued to have the largest number of daily newspapers (192), Maharashtra occupied the second position with 177 newspapers. During 1983, Karnataka with 121, Kerala 116, Tamil Nadu 112 and Madhya Pradesh 111 had more than 100 daily newspapers. Rajasthan became the seventh state to have more than 100 daily newspapers. However, Maharashtra dailies continued to dominate in circulation with 2,350,000 copies. It was followed by dailies from West Bengal which had a circulation of 1,888,000 copies. Dailies published from Uttar Pradesh also had a circulation of 1,688,000 copies.

Delhi press has the distinction of publishing newspapers in 15 out of 16 principal languages. Tamil Nadu came next in position with publishing newspapers in 14 languages. Newspapers in more than ten principal languages were published from Maharashtra (13), West Bengal (12), Andhra Pradesh (11), and Uttar Pradesh (11). Another interesting feature of the press in India was that more than 2,000 newspapers in a single language were published from Uttar Pradesh (2,139) in Hindi. More than 1,000 newspapers in a single language were also published from West Bengal (1,452 in Bengali), Delhi (1,138 in English), and Maharashtra (1,091 in Marathi).

According to the circulation data available, there were 192 big, 427 medium, and 7,356 small newspapers. The big accounted for 22,843,000 copies, medium 11,561,000 copies, and small 20,987,000 copies. Percentage-wise, their share of circulation came to 41.2, 20.9, and 37.9 respectively. The big newspapers included 71 dailies. Among medium newspapers 165 were dailies. There were 651 small dailies. The big dailies had a share of 50.1 per cent in the total circulation of the daily press, and the medium accounted for 26.8 per cent. Remaining 23.1 per cent belonged to small dailies.

Significant Roles

Ananda Bazar Patrika, a Bengali daily from Calcutta, with a circulation of 402,491 copies, retained the place of pride as the largest circulated single edition in 1983. *Jugantar*, a Bengali daily from Calcutta which had a circulation of 327,549, came second.

Indian Express, published in English from ten centres, claimed the first position among multi-edition dailies, with a circulation of 5,67,801 during 1983. With three editions, *Times of India*, also in English, came second with a total circulation of 5,30,565 copies. The third position went to *Malayalam Manorama*, published from Calicut, Cochin and Kottayam, with a combined circulation of 5,27,657 copies.

Among periodicals, *Malayalam Manorama*, the Malayalam weekly published from Kottayam, was the largest circulated periodical during 1983 with 6,48,524 copies. Next came *Kumudam*, the Tamil weekly of Madras, which commanded a circulation of 5,88,350 copies.

The Dominance

Out of 20,758 newspapers in 1983 as many as 13,705 were owned by individuals, 3,456 by societies and associations,

1,009 by firms and partnerships, and 877 by joint stock companies. There were 612 newspapers brought out by the Central and State Governments.

Newspapers owned by individuals had the largest share in circulation with 36.7 per cent, followed by those owned by joint stock companies with a share of 36.3 per cent. In 1983, there were 106 common ownership units which brought out 423 newspapers. Newspapers belonging to these units had a circulation of 16,690,000 copies, which was 30.1 per cent of the total circulation commanded by the entire Indian Press.

Apart from dailies and tri/bi-weeklies, there were 7,604 periodicals which dealt with news and current affairs. There were 2,927 literary and cultural magazines. Apart from these categories, the Press in India had newspapers pertaining to religion and philosophy, commerce and industry, medicine and health, labour, engineering and technology, science, children film, sports and art, etc. Indian Press consists of 36 centenarians. *Bombay Samachar*, a Gujarati daily, is the oldest daily newspaper which came into existence in 1822.

Miscellaneous Data

- Nearly a third of newspapers (3,873), or 30.9%, are published from four metropolitan cities-Bombay, Calcutta, Delhi and Madras. The big, medium and small newspapers (over 50,000; from 15,001 to 50,000; and up to 15,000 copies respectively) number 107,240 and 7,567 with circulation of 34.8%, 19.1% and 46.11% respectively.
- Political parties own 82 newspapers including 9 dailies with a total circulation of 2.40 lakhs.
- Twenty-six, foreign Diplomatic Missions in India own and publish 111 papers. The USSR tops the list (50) followed by USA (10).
- Periodicals published by the Central and State governments number 268 and 202 respectively.

The Registrar of Newspapers for India, appointed under the Press Registration and Books (Amendment) Act, 1955, prepares an annual report on the press which is presented to Parliament. The Registrar also allots newsprint and recommends import of printing machinery for newspapers.

Facility of Official Nature

The Press Information Bureau (PIB) is the centralized agency of the Government of India to disseminate information on its policies, decisions, programmes and activities. The information put out by PIB goes to daily newspapers, news periodicals and news agencies, as well as radio and television organizations, both Indian and foreign. With a countrywide teleprinter network and airbag facilities, PIB reaches newspapers not only in Delhi but also in all other parts of the country. No other organisation in the country reaches out to such a large number of newspapers and other media. While about a thousand newspapers subscribe to the wire-news agencies, the PIB distributes its press material to over 7,000 newspapers.

The main functions of the Bureau are to put out information of Government policies, programmes and activities, and obtain feedback on how these policies, programmes and activities are received, and to apprise the Government of public reaction as published in the news and editorial columns of English and Indian language newspapers. The Bureau also advises the Government on its information policy.

Officers of the Bureau at its headquarters in Delhi are attached to different Ministries and Departments of the Government of India. These officers are in daily contact with their Ministries and Departments. They explain and interpret Government policies and disseminate factual information. The departmental publicity officer also performs the role of public reaction evaluator, keeping the Government in touch with public opinion, besides providing explanation and background to official pronouncements. He also acts as an adviser to the

Government on press relations and publicity. He maintains constant liaison with newspaper correspondents as weir as representatives of other mass media.

In dissemination of information, the Bureau employs a variety of means. Written material issued by the Bureau includes press communiques, press notes and handouts, backgrounders, features and newsletters. The material is put out in English, Hindi, Urdu and 15 other Indian languages. The Bureau also arranges press conferences and briefings to enable media representatives to get the news and clarifications at first hand.

The PIB arranges photo-coverage of Government activities. A large number of photographs on Government activities are supplied to dailies and periodicals all over the country to enable them to supplement written coverage by pictures. The Bureau has its telephoto equipment with which photographs are transmitted the same day to some of its Regional and Branch Offices. The Bureau supplies ebonite blocks to small and medium newspapers, which have no facility to make their own blocks. *Charbas* are supplied to Urdu newspapers for use in the litho process.

The Bureau provides professional facilities to correspondents, cameramen and technicians accredited to the Government of India. As on 31 July 1989; a total of 1,167 press correspondents, cameramen and technicians were accredited. The Bureau extends temporary accreditation facility to foreign correspondents and cameramen, coming to India on short visits. Special accreditation arrangements are made for important events.

The Bureau is the implementing agency for exchange of delegations of journalists between India and foreign countries under cultural exchange programmes and protocols.

The Bureau has a network of eight regional offices at Bombay, Madras, Calcutta, Chandigarh, Bhopal, Lucknow, Guwahati and Hyderabad, 27 branch office-cum-information centres, most of which are linked with the headquarters by teleprinter network. It also has two separate information centres located at Aizawl and Port Blair. Through the regional and branch offices, the Bureau supplies press material to newspapers and other news media of various Indian languages, besides Hindi and English in all parts of the country. Libraries are also attached to the information centres, which serve as repositories of information on various developmental matters.

To speed up the information flow, the Bureau has computerised a part of its operations. A data bank is being set up linking the headquarters with regional and branch offices. This will make available information about Government policies, programmes and activities to the press and other media all over the country simultaneously. The expansion programme envisages the use of FAX services for instant transmission of press releases. For faster transmission of photographs, additional telephoto transmitters and receivers are being procured.

The Bureau has established at its headquarters in Delhi a NATIONAL PRESS CENTRE for press both national and international with all modern infrastructural facilities.

The PIB's counterpart in States, to disseminate information on State governments' activities, are Public Relations and Information Directorates. They keep close liaison with the local press and representatives of other papers stationed at the State capitals.

Information to the press is also disseminated by PR Information Department of public sector undertakings. They maintain close liaison with the PIB and utilize its services for dissemination of news to the press.

Similar activities are undertaken by Public Relations Departments of commercial and private organizations, including chambers of commerce and industry and political parties. They have their own machinery for dissemination of news and information to the press.

The Outcome : Despite the phenomenal progress made recently by other mass media, books continue to remain the most effective means of education and mass communication.

The six largest book-producing countries in the world are the USA, the USSR, Federal Republic of Germany, Japan and the United Kingdom. The USA tops the list with 81,000 titles, closely followed by USSR with 80,000 publications.

India has made significant strides in recent years in the publication of books, not only in numbers but also in quality and variety. India is now the seventh largest producer of books in the world. The country produces over 25,000 titles. India is next only to the USA and the UK in respect of production of books in the English language.

Imported books significantly supplement the output of the domestic book industry. The import of books is now placed under OGL. Not only new firms but also individuals can import books without any import licence. Export of books is comparatively a recent phenomenon in India. Indian books, including journals and periodicals, are exported to nearly 100 countries in the world.

UK is the largest buyer of Indian books followed by USA, Singapore, Malaysia,. Bangladesh and Nepal. Books on indology, arts, culture, yoga and current topics of general interest are imported by the developed countries, while the developing countries import Indian books on science and technical subjects. A sustained effort is being made to promote export of Indian books through exhibitions and fairs.

UNESCO has defined the book as 'a non-periodical publication of at least 49 pages, excluding the cover page, published in the country and made available to the public'. As per this definition, the number of books published in India is reduced nearly by one third.

The largest number of books are published in Hindi followed by English and Bengali. India is far behind in the field of book publishing as compared to other countries, or in terms of its population. With 15% of world population, India produces only 3% of the world book titles. The print order is also very limited. If text books are excluded, the average print-run is about 2000, which is far below world average 16,000 copies.

The main elements in book-production work are: the author, the publisher and printer, and the distributor and bookseller. The author is the starting point in any book-production work. The publisher is the planner, financier and entrepreneur. The distributor and bookseller promotes sale of books and handles the actual selling operations.

The condition of the author, who is the basis of all publishing activity, is not very happy in India despite many steps taken since Independence to improve his lot.

Government of India now grants the author tax-exemption of income from royalties/writings by way of expenses without the production of any documentary evidence.

Under section 180 of the Income-Tax Act, the remuneration received by the author in lumpsum, as income from writings or royalties received during the first year of the publication of the work, can be spread over to three years before the taxable income is calculated, provided the time taken in writing the work is more than twelve months.

If the income is received from abroad by the author in the exercise of his profession, a deduction of 25% of such income is made while computing his taxable income.

To look after their profession and economic interests, an organized body of Indian authors, Authors Guild of India, was set up in 1974. It has more than 300 members representing English and Indian languages. The Guild has set up a Good Offices Committee of authors and publishers to settle disputes amicably. A Litigation Committee of the Guild assists authors to recover legitimate royalties from the defaulting publishers.

The Guild has prepared a draft of model agreement between the authors and the publishers. It also brings out a quarterly journal. The Guild has also set up an Authors' Publishing House to bring out books on cooperative basis.

The Indian Copyright Act, 1957 protects the literary works of Indian authors. According to the Act, the writer remains the owner of his writings during his lifetime and his successor can enjoy the benefits for 50 years after the death of the author. The author is always the proprietor of his writings and owns the copyright. He assigns or licenses his copyright to a publisher for exploiting his writings in consideration of royalty. The royalty usually ranges from 5% to 15% depending on the type of the book. In some cases, the author gives his manuscript for lumpsum payment. In this case, he foregoes his right on the manuscript. This practice is considered unfair, as it amounts to distress sale by an author due to his economic plight. The lumpsum payment, however, in the case of particular category of books (such as children books, translations, where the remuneration is small) or where the author is keen to get full benefit immediately, falls in a different category.

A number of organizations award prizes to authors for outstanding works. The Bharatiya Jnanpith, a private trust, gives every year an award of Rs. 1 lakh for the best creative writing in Indian languages. The University Grants Commission grants fellowship worth Rs.10,000 for writing a quality book of university level in English or in any Indian language. The Ministry of Education, in cooperation with the State governments, provides substantial financial assistance for production of university level books in Indian languages to facilitate smooth change-over of the medium of instruction in higher education from English to Indian languages. The Sahitya Akademi gives every year an award of Rs.5,000 each for outstanding works in the languages recognized by the Akademi.

According to the Directory of Indian Publishers, India has over 11,000 large, medium and small publishers. They publish books in all languages. A number of government and non-government institutions also bring out publications. There are more than 300 well-known publishers in the country.

The publisher transforms the written text into printed word, and puts it into the market for sale. To make his enterprise a success, the publisher needs the expertise and experience of both the profession and the business. Before accepting any manuscript from the author, the publisher has not only to make professional evaluation of the work but also a survey of sales prospects in India and abroad. The accepted work must fall within the editorial competence and specialized field of the publisher. Some publishers have their own printing presses, while others get the work printed under their own supervision.

The role of distributor and bookseller is of no less significance. They generally handle sales promotion and actual sale of books. The trend now is that the publishers concentrate on publication of books, the distributors determine the market potential and take care of sales promotion and the actual sales. The share of distributor is roughly about 40% to 45% of the price of the book. This includes expenses on production of sales promotion literature, displays and exhibitions, stocking of books and trade discount.

The different elements which go into the cost of publication of a work vary a great deal. According to a rough estimate, the cost of printing and paper comes to about 25% of the total cost. The sales promotion roughly works out to be about 5% to 10%, while the distributor's commission is of the order of 45% including about 33% trade discount. The publisher is thus left with about 20% to 25%, and this amount is shared between the publisher and the author.

India has been organizing National Book Fairs, under the auspices of National Book Trust, in different parts of the country to promote interest of the people in the book-world. The first World Book Fair was held in New Delhi in 1972, the

International Book Year. The second and third World Book Fairs were held in New Delhi in 1976 and 1978 respectively. The Fairs ace organized by the National Book Trust in cooperation with the Federation of Indian Publishers and Federation of Publishers and Book-Sellers Association in India and other organizations.

The Government of India has set up various organizations for producing books at low prices, and for fostering book industry in the country.

The National Book Development Board, set up in 1967, is the principal advisory body for the development of the book industry and trade in the context of overall requirements of the country. The Board, as reconstituted in 1970, has representatives of different sectors of book industry-publishers, authors, printers, booksellers, as well as various governmental and non-governmental agencies.

The National Book Trust, set up in 1970, produces and encourages production of good literature in different languages and makes it available at low prices to libraries, educational institutions and the public. The Trust also subsidizes the publication of university level books. It organizes book fairs and regional book exhibitions.

The National Book Trust produces and encourages production of good literature. This includes classical literature on India, outstanding works of Indian authors in Indian languages and their translation from one Indian language to another, and also translation of outstanding books from foreign languages. It also encourages outstanding books which provide modern knowledge on a variety of subjects.

The National Book Trust organizes exhibitions and seminars, as a part of its effort, to make people book-minded. It also encourages formation of regional book trusts in different parts of the country. The Trust has published large number of books in English and Indian languages including books for children.

Books on diverse aspects of national life, culture and teachings of national leaders, and 21 magazines are brought out by the Publications Division of the Ministry of Information and Broadcasting.

The Publications Division is responsible for production, distribution and sale of books and journals on all subjects of national importance, with a view to providing up-to-date and authentic information to public at home and abroad. In the process of discharging this responsibility, it has emerged as the largest bureau of publishing and marketing in the public sector. Originally set up in 1941 as the foreign branch of Bureau of Public Information, the Division acquired its present name and identity in 1944.

The aims of the Division are:

(1) to disseminate information about various spheres of national development activities;

(2) to promote national integration by creating greater awareness and understanding among the people of different regions, adhering to different faiths and beliefs; and

(3) to stimulate interest in, and to generate appreciation of, and respect for, the variegated pattern of life and culture of India.

The books, albums and journals brought out by the Division cover a wide spectrum of subjects ranging from art and culture, flora and fauna, travel and tourism, biographies of the builders of modern India, speeches of national leaders to subjects of children's interest. The publications also include books on popular science, education, history, besides reference works.

By far, the most momentous assignment is the compiling and editing of the speeches and writings of Mahatma Gandhi, both in English and Hindi. Ninety volumes in English, which constitute the main series, and eighty volumes in Hindi have been published so far.

The Division has so far brought out about 6,200 books and volumes in Hindi, English and other major regional languages of the country. On an average, it publishes about 100 titles every year. The Division has started a new series of low-priced books titled "Books for Millions" under which it has released 13 titles so far; of these 9 are in Hindi, 3 in English and 1 in Punjabi.

The Division publishes 21 journals of varying periodicities. These journals are being published in English, Hindi and ten other regional languages. The foremost among these journals is *Employment News* published in English, Hindi and Urdu, which commands a paid circulation averaging above 3.90 lakh copies per week. They seek to project not only the largest assortment of job vacancies in Central/State government departments/ undertakings, private organizations and educational institutions but also to provide guidance material to enable prospective candidates to prepare for various kinds of tests/ interviews. Other important journals are *Yojana, Kurukshetra, Indian and Foreign Review, Aaj kal* and children monthly *Bal Bharati.*

The books and journals are sold through a network of over 3,600 authorised booksellers and departmental sales emporia located at New Delhi, Bombay, Calcutta, Madras, Patna, Trivandrum, Lucknow and Hyderabad. The sales emporia of the Division also market the publications of 21 other Government and autonomous organisations, such as the National Museum, Sahitya Akademi, National Book Trust, etc. It is also sells and distributes textbooks produced by the National Council of Educational Research and Training (NCERT).

Books for children are published, among others, by Children's Book Trust, National Book Trust, National Council of Educational Research and Training and Publications Division.

The Department of Tourism and several other government,

departments, the State governments, other organizations and private agencies bring out publications on a variety of subjects.

Under the Delivery of Books, Newspapers to Public Library Act, 1954, the copyright libraries are entitled to receive a copy of every new book and magazine in the country. There are four such libraries, namely, National Library, Calcutta; Central Library, Bombay; Connamara Public Library, Madras; and National Central Library, Delhi.

The *Indian National Bibliography*, published monthly, with author, subject and title index, by the National Library, Calcutta lists all publications published in India. It is an important source for the location of published literature on India.

The Sahitya Akademi, New Delhi, set up in 1954 for the development of Indian literature, translates and publishes literary works and popularizes the study of literature among the people. The Akademi has regional offices at Bombay, Calcutta and Madras. The Akademi also awards prizes to works of outstanding journals in English and major Indian languages. An important publication of the Akademi is *National Bibliography of Indian Literature (1901-1953).*

Apart from newspapers, periodicals and books, the printing and publishing industry in the country also brings out publications such as posters, folders, calendars, diaries, packaging labels, stickers, greetings, invitations and visiting cards, etc.

The Recognition : To provide encouragement and incentives to those engaged in graphic arts and to improve the techniques and standards of printing, the Directorate of Advertising and Visual Publicity, Ministry of Information and Broadcasting conducts annual All India Competition for the National Award for excellence in printing and designing of books and publications. Prizes are awarded in several categories of publications, and in each category a prize is given to the printer, the publisher, the advertiser and the designer. The categories are grouped into divisions, namely, books, newspapers, display advertisements, periodicals, publicity booklets, annuals, souvenirs and annual reports, posters, folders, calendars, diaries, type faces, packagings and miscellaneous. The first such competition was held in 1955.

Other awards in the field of journalism are:

1. The Rajendra Prasad Institute of Communication and Studies awards eight prizes every year to the best student in the following fields-reporting, study paper in radio and television journalism, writing, editing, study paper in journalism and industrial management.
2. The Chandrakant Vora Memorial Award consists of three annual cash prizes-one each for the best report published in Gujarati, Marathi and English newspapers.
3. The Durgadas Ratan Devi Trust also gives five awards:
   (i) The editor whose advocacy of a cause has made greatest impact on the public mind;
   (ii) Outstanding columnist;
   (iii) Best investigative report;
   (iv) Outstanding news story;
   (v) Outstanding portrayal of an event through pictorial reproduction, or cartoon.

India has more than 50,000 printing presses, big (employing 150 and more workers), medium (50 to 100 workers), and small (5 to 10 workers). About 90% of these presses are in the last category.

The Government of India has its own printing presses including three textbook presses at Chandigarh, Bhuvaneshwar and Mysore, and one Litho Press at Faridabad. The State governments, and in many cases, the public sector undertakings also have their own printing presses.

***The Training*:** There are five Printing Schools-two at Madras, and one each at Bombay, Calcutta and Allahabad-which impart training in printing technology at degree level. Elementary training in printing technology is also given at the Industrial Training Institutes in different parts of the country.

Though Press in India since Independence has grown vastly in size and circulation, it suffers from many ills. It has yet to identify its true post-Independence role, so as to ensure against haphazard growth and directionless expansion.

The role of the Press in India need not be that of adversary, or of blind support, to the government. The Press should be the watch-dog and act as a catalytic agent to hasten the process of social and economic change, and thus secure people's participation and involvement in the country's development.

The reasons for the present state of affairs in the Press are not far to seek. There are a few in-built handicaps such as the vast geographical area, illiteracy, poverty, multiplicity of languages, and absence of adequate communication facilities. The linking of ownership of newspapers with other industry or commerce enterprises, limited newspaper ownership with closely-held share interest, urban-oriented expansion of newspapers leaving the vast countryside population untouched, inadequate and expensive availability of newsprint, and lack of local advertisement support are some other bottlenecks.

The Press in India today is too much obsessed with politics. The country needs creative reporting, particularly on non-political themes such as unemployment, malnutrition, population growth, etc. The emphasis should be not on what the public 'wants', but what it 'needs'. Reporting should provide adequate local coverage and cover human activities in factories, farms, schools and universities. All this can be accomplished, if the Press is able to evolve a philosophy of mass communication and code of ethics through consensus.

There is great scope for regional, local and small papers in India, and they should receive all encouragement and support. In the present stage of country's development, there is also need for economic and development journalism, which is still in its infancy. The Press, in order to function efficiently, also needs well-paid and well-trained journalists to report events, particularly from small towns and rural areas.

Credibility is the life-blood of communication. Whatever is given out by the media is believed only if dissent is permitted, otherwise any message received through oral communication would be more acceptable.

It has been argued by eminent journalists in the profession that the present system of accreditation of journalists, government's allocation of newsprint and fixation of advertisement rates, favours to journalists in the form of perquisites such as subsidized housing, medical facilities, etc., and heavy dependence of the Press on official releases, etc. stand in the way of making the Press in India an independent and impartial instrument of communication of news and views.

Finally, there is a need for having a dialogue to consider amendment to the Constitution in order to provide constitutional guarantees against suppression of freedom of the Press. This is necessary to ensure that the Press functions without fear in all times to come.

3

Promotion Movement

Roy's campaign against Hindu society as he saw it and his appeal for purification of Hinduism which culminated in the founding of the Brahmo Samaj echoed throughout the century after his death from the lips and pages of his followers. In a letter he wrote to a friend in 1828, he said: "I regret to say that the present system of religion adhered to by the Hindus is not well calculated to promote their political interest. The distinction of castes introducing innumerable divisions and sub-divisions among them has entirely deprived them of patriotic feeling and the multitude of religious rites and ceremonies and laws of purification have totally disqualified them from undertaking any difficult enterprise. It is, I think, necessary that some change should take place in their religion, at least for the sake of their political advantage and social comfort."

In the second half of the century and in the decades when Indians were striving to organise a nationalist movement, the social revolt grew in intensity and led to social reform campaigns in the press and platform. Political reform occupied much less importance in the public and private lives of Indians than religious and social reform movements. In the words of historian of this period: "Religious and social reform movements represented two of the main areas of intellectual and practical endeavour for educated Indians. These movements were preoccupied with revolts against existing religious and social institutions and efforts to reform them according to the needs of individuals and small local groups."

The infant Indian press of this century reflected this trend among the intellectuals and leaders of the community. Political agitation did not assume that urgency and expansion as it did towards the closing decades of the century when the priorities were reversed and political ideas and goals became paramount. Nationalist political thought then came to exert a moulding influence on religion and social ideas and the methods of political organisation and propagation began to be evolved on an all-India basis.

The first Indian-owned English daily, the *Bengal Gazette* was published in Calcutta in 1816 by Gangadhar Bhattacharjee, a teacher who was influenced by Ram Mohun Roy's teachings. It is not quite certain how long it lasted. Some have claimed it continued to be published for four years, but the generally accepted view is that it did not last more than a year. According to one writer: 'The first Indian journalist seems to have represented a school of thought-progressive Hinduism—rather than commercial or individual interest. It is probable that Ram Mohun Roy was responsible for the venture but he may have avoided open association with it for various reasons.'

The *Sambad Kaumudi,* the Bengali weekly conducted by Ram Mohun Roy followed the *Bengal Gazette* but controversy surrounds its editor and the year of its publication. According to James Buckingham, it was stated in December, 1821, and shut down by its proprietor for want of encouragement in May, 1822. But it was kept alive by another native till the following September, when its publication was suspended, to rise no more. Many writers assert that the first 13 issues of

Sambad Kaumudi were edited by a man called Bhawani Charan Bannerjee, but a contemporary journalist, Dutt, dismissed the claim as "wicked and malicious fabrication of falsehood." The generally accepted view is that Mohan Roy was the moving spirit behind the weekly and that Bannerjee had worked with him for some time before joining the anti-reformist camp among the Hindus who started a weekly, *Samachar Chandrika.*

Mohan Roy, as we have seen, launched a Persian weekly, *Mirat ul Akhbar* for the benefit of Indians not conversant with English or Bengali. He also brought out a religious periodical, the *Brahminical Magazine,* to counteract the missionaries' propaganda. In April, 1818, William Corey and John Clark Marshman established *Friend of India,* an English monthly, which was later bought by Robert Knight, founder of *Statesman.* The same proprietors were the owners of the Bengali newspaper, *Samachar Darpan* which besides being a vehicle for missionary propaganda, specialised in publishing district news which made it popular among officials and educated Indians. And it also had official support.

First Phase : Ram Mohun Roy's campaign against sati which provoked Hindu orthodoxy into opposition gave a fillip to language journalism, but most of the journals which sprang up during this period were short-lived primarily because of the abolition of *sati* by Lord Bentinck. In 1855, an English writer noted that the *Samachar Chandrika,* which was exposing the orthodox causes, "occasionally barks, but is toothless now, having lost to the reformers." Three journals, all connected with Ram Mohun Roy, *the Reformer,* the *Inquirer* and the *Gyan Auneshun,* representing the school of progressive Hindu journalism held the field in Bengal till as late as 1891.

Language journals in Bengal carried articles and views on Hindu social customs, on government, on need for medical education and philanthropy along with local and foreign news, shipping intelligence and market prices. There were editorials against rival newspapers, criticism of government and ventilation of public grievances. There was less of news from other parts of India than from abroad. Company officials continued to fret and fume against what they called the "licentiousness of the press". They would not tolerate an Indian editor criticising the government even as they disapproved of European journalists indulging in it. Their chagrin, however, was that while the offending Europeans could be deported the Indians could not be proceeded against. Up to 1816, there were no Indian proprietors or editors of newspapers. Between 1816 and 1820, there was only one Indian-owned weekly in Calcutta. The Europeans controlled the press during the first 40 years of its existence.

The Indian press in Bengal and Bombay continued to function in the face of official harassment and hostility. Between 1831 and 1833, there were 19 new journals published in Bengal. According to one writer there were during this period, 33 English newspapers and 16 Bengali journals. Among the factors which helped the growth of newspapers were the extension of English education among Indians and the increasing interest taken by British journalists in Indian affairs.

A notable personality in Bengal journalism was Dwarkanath Tagore who started the *Bengal Herald*, an English weekly and *Banga Doot* in Bengali. He gave financial assistance to a number of newspapers, among them the *Englishman*, when a crisis overtook them in 1830 and he was responsible for saving many from extinction. An English weekly, the *Hindu Patriot* started in Calcutta in 1853 by Girish Chandra Ghosh, which had profound influence on latter day events in Bengal, began shakily. Harichandra Mukherjee, a clerk in a government office, took it over two years later and the journal began to prosper under his care. Mukherjee was a forceful writer and he published articles on the deplorable conditions in indigo plantations which led to the government appointing an enquiry commission.

After Mukherjee's death the *Patriot* passed into the hands

of the social reformer, Iswarchandra Vidyasagar who appointed Kristo Pal, a well remembered name in early Indian journalism, as editor in 1861. Pal served the paper until his death in 1884. Another well known journal of this period, *Indian Mirror*, an English fortnightly, was, started by Manmohan Ghosh in 1861. Keshub Chunder Sen who took over the Mirror in 1871, converted it into a daily, the only such newspaper to be owned and conducted by an Indian. Keshub Chunder Sen also owned a Bengali journal, *Sulabh Samachar* which was priced at one paise and had a circulation of 4,000 which must be considered phenomenal for that time.

The Indian language press was slow in growing outside Bengal and Bombay before the Mutiny of 1857. What journals there were, were run by missionaries. In Madras, there were two weeklies and a quarterly in Tamil, one weekly in Telugu and one in English. These were subsidised by the government partly for educational and partly for administrative reasons.

What was the attitude of the Indian press to the alien rulers at this stage of its development? It was clear that while some sections of it might have been anti-government, it was not anti-British and there was no suggestion that British rule must be ended. As we have seen, an important group led by Ram Mohun Roy actively campaigned for British contacts and support to British parliamentary institutions. Typical of the Indian faith in the British sovereign was this editorial in a Bengali newspaper: 'Henceforth... if any evil befall us we shall not sit down in silence but weep so loud that our cries may reach our sovereign. And if we live in happiness we shall so tumultuously make known our gladness that the praises of our benefactors may sound throughout the world.'

A staunch friend of the press during this period was Sir Charles Metcalfe, senior member of the governor-general's council and later acting governor-general. He stood for the freedom of the press and was instrumental in shaping the views of Lord Bentinck, governor-general, on this question.

Thanks to Metcalfe, Bentinck not only followed a policy of tolerance towards the press but also actively assisted it. When leaders of the Indian and European press in Calcutta submitted to him a petition in 1835 seeking the repeal of the restrictions on the press, Bentinck assured them that a system would be evolved which, while it gave security to every person engaged in the fair discussion of public measures, would effectively secure the government against sedition and individuals against calamity. He told them that the government had no intention of restricting the liberty which they already enjoyed.

Metcalfe, when he succeeded Bentinck for a short period, directed his Law Counsellor, Macaulay, to frame an appropriate law changing licensing of press to registration. Macaulay favoured a uniform law for all the Company's territories which leave the journalist free to print without permission, but still render him liable for punishment for printing seditious or defamatory material. A law on these lines was passed by Metcalfe and he earned the gratitude of the press. Metcalfe said: "Do what we will, we cannot prevent the progress of knowledge and it is undoubtedly our duty to promote it whatever be the consequences." He spurned the advice of his counsellors for special vigilance over the Indian language press and said there would not be any discrimination, as between Indian and English newspapers. He held that an administration which depended on attempt to suppress public opinion could not be lasting both because "such a tenure must be rotten and because such attempts must fail."

By promulgating the law relaxing the restrictions of the press which continued to be in force till 1856, Metcalfe earned the disapproval of the Board of Directors at home who charged him with going back on past directives. But Metcalfe would not relent and thereby he lost the chance of being the governor-general permanently. One writer has described him as "the great liberator of the Indian press who sacrificed his career, but who launched Indian journalism on its long and eventful journey."

Transit Period : A great transformation came in the official attitude to the Indian press after the Mutiny (also called the first War of Independence) in 1857. The Indian press in Bengal, Bombay and Madras took little interest in the Mutiny and there was no indication of unrest that was seen in the Company's army. In the words of a writer: "The Mutiny was of little significance for the press but what was far more important was its consequences." The English-owned press went crazy and blood thirsty and displayed the worst forms of racialism. The newspapers denounced the policy of conciliation pursued by Lord Canning, governor-general and indulged in intemperate abuse of Indians. There was nothing comparable to their virulence on the side of the Indian press.

The Mutiny drove a wedge between the English-owned and Indian-owned newspapers and created a distinction between English language anti Indian language journals. The gulf widened thereafter year after year between the Anglo-Indian press (as it came to be called) and the nationalist press and reached its climax in the freedom movement launched from 1920 onwards by the Indian National Congress under the leadership of Gandhi. George Trevelyan wrote six years after the Mutiny: "The tone of the press was horrible. Never did the cry for blood swell so loud as among the Christians and Englishmen.... Because the pampered Bengali sepoys had behaved like double-eyed rascals, every Hindu and Musalman was a rebel, a traitor, a murderer; every newspaper column teemed with invectives which at the time seemed coarse and tedious, but which we must now pronounce as wicked and blasphemous."

One historian of this period noted that long after the last rebel had laid down his arms, been hanged or vanished into the jungles, the Calcutta English-owned press continued its ferocious tirades. "The non-official population was encouraged to believe in a maudlin government, pre-rebel in sympathy, unpatriotic and radical." When for five years "this chorus of abuse and these cries for blood" had continued, it so happened that an Englishman was arrested for murdering one of his employees. And when he was tried and duly convicted, the English- owned press "burst out into a deafening scream". The *Bengal Hurkaru* suddenly became a champion of abolition of capital punishment. It organised processions and mass meetings of Europeans "to achieve the gain of a human life, an existence which is forfeit to the public strangler". When the government refused to yield to the clamour of the white press, the newspapers turned their guns on the officials who they alleged were devotees of the Goddess Kali to whom they wanted to sacrifice the "wretched" life of the man convicted for murder.

Here is another description of the English press reaction in Calcutta: "The most peaceful and charitable gentlemen fell into conclusions of race hatred. Everywhere retribution torture was advocated. The English press discussed the situation with a ferocious hysteria compared to which Gen. Geering's most unbalanced outbursts would seem polite commonplaces." Hymns of hate usurped the Poet's Corner of the *Englishman*. Cried one poet:

Barring Humanity-Pretenders
To Hell of none are we the willing senders
But if to sepoys entrance must be given
Locate them, Lord, in the back slums of heaven.

Legal Aspects : When Lord Canning, governor-general, promulgated a press law in 1857 imposing restrictions on the entire press (that is, both English-owned and Indian- owned) there was a hue and cry in the English press in Calcutta. But it was not only his profound sense of justice and his antipathy to racial discrimination which prompted Canning to include the English-owned press under the new law but his own disquieting observation that the English press was not free from the things which the Indian press had been accused of. He said: "While I am glad to give credit to the conductors of the European press for the loyalty and intelligence which mark their labours, I am bound by sincerity to say that I have seen passages in some of the papers under their management which though perfectly innocuous as far as European readers are concerned, may in times like the present, be turned into the most mischievous purposes in the hands of persons capable of dressing them up for the native ear."

Referring to the Indian press in a letter to the president of the Board of Directors at home. Canning said: "As regards the native press I shall be surprised if even in England there are two opinions as to the propriety of the measure. The mischief which such writings as these which I send you do amongst the ignorant and childish but excitable sepoys and the fanatical Mohamedans will be easily understood; especially when it is known that they are eagerly sought and listened to by the native soldiers. I consider this evil is one which cannot in the present state of India be allowed to continue without positive guiltiness on the part of the government. Therefore, I have not hesitated to take the power of arresting it by the only means which will be summary and efficient.

As to the English press, it has no claim to exemption. If it were read only by English readers something might be urged in its defence.... But the articles of the English newspapers are translated into the native languages and read by all." Lady Canning noted in her diary; "The English press has been very bad; civil enough to see himself but running down others—but that is not the mischief—it points out all sorts of imaginary reasons and grievances as causes for Mutiny; it spreads alarms and shows up weakness and gives information which, translated, may do untold mischief among the natives.

The *Friend of India*, weekly paper that thinks itself as great here as the *Times* of London, one day gave a long detailed account of the position of the whole of the English troops and the tracks of unprotected country and told exactly how vulnerable we were and must be until such and such reinforcements arrive.... Now this was put forth at the most ticklish moment three weeks ago and no doubt was instantly circulated and studied all over the country by the seditious. Treachery is not worse than such exceeding folly."

There was a spirit of revenge in the air among the British and Canning remarked: 'There is no doubt that many of the commissioners and commissions acted in a spirit of zeal or revenge which transcended any ordinary canons of justice and evidence. These emotions were often aroused by stories of outrages by rebels which had no basis in fact."

An editor of a Calcutta English-owned newspaper got hold of a secret circular of Canning to his officers and dashed off an editorial. "Leniency towards any portion of the conspirator," he wrote, "is misplaced, impolitic and iniquitous and is calculated to excite contempt and invite attack on every side by showing to the world the Government of India so powerless to punish mutiny or so indifferent to the sufferings which have been endured by the victims of the rebellion that it allows the blood of English and Christian subjects of Her Majesty to flow to torrents and their wives and sisters and daughters to be outraged and dishonoured without adequate retribution."

In desperation Canning wrote to a friend in London: "For God's sake raise your voice and stop this. As long as I have breath in my body I will pursue no other policy... but because it is just I will not govern in anger." In a letter to the Queen he said: 'There is a rapid and indiscriminate vindictiveness abroad even amongst many who ought to set a better example, which it is impossible to contemplate without something like a policy of shame for one's fellow countrymen... nor does it occur to those who talk and write most upon the matter that for the sovereign of England to hold and govern India without employing, and to a great degree, trusting natives both in civil and military service, is simply impossible. It is no exaggeration to say that a vast number of the European community would hear with pleasure and approval that every Hindu and Mohamedan had been proscribed and that none would be admitted to serve the government except in a menial capacity." Canning said that the constant vilification of the government by the European press had a mischievous effect on the natives and was leading them by degrees to lose all respect for authority.

According to an English writer, the native (Indian) press throughout this period "though viewing affairs from an oriental than an English standpoint, has maintained, on the whole, a moderate tone.... We have frequently observed with natives that read English newspapers a feeling of indignation against Europeans which exist only in a modified degree amongst natives whose reading is in vernacular channels." The same writer said that Indian language journals gave a picture of the issues that were warmly contested in Hindu society, of the grievances of the people, of the disadvantages of having a foreign language as the language of the courts, of the atrocities of Indigo planters and the blunders of young magistrates.

While the fears of the rulers about the Indian press were not based on facts, they failed to see that protection was required from the provocative writings of the English press. The *Friend of India* and the Englishman in Calcutta, and the *Bombay Times* in Bombay had, in fact, been issued warnings by the authorities for their virulent attack on the natives but the English editors were excused after assurances had been given by the proprietors, and the only Bengal newspaper whose licence was revoked was the *Bengal Hurkaru*. The concessions given to the European community by Canning's government and the bias in the practical implementation of the policy of conciliation estranged Indian feelings still further, and the gulf between the native and the European press grew wider and wider, never to be bridged.

The Indian press far from being regarded as an instrument for progress was regarded with suspicion by the authorities and these newspapers which were organs of progressive opinion were specially suspect. According to an Indian historian: "The Queen's Proclamation (1858) gave new hope but soon gave rise to disappointment and disillusion when British implementation lagged behind the promise.... Indian opinion was forming slowly. This period saw a national awakening and this was the beginning of the era of the great national newspaper."

Gandhi and Jayaprakash Narayan occupied the centrestage in two epoch-making periods of Indian history. While Gandhi moved millions during his struggle against the mighty British Empire, Jayaprakash Narayan stirred many souls in his campaign against the authoritative regime of Indira Gandhi. Gandhi in colonial times and Jayaprakash Narayan in independent India represent two of the most versatile and powerful mass leaders in the Indian tradition. Viewed superficially, however, they may represent two different models of leadership as well as ideologies. This is partly due to "the contexts in which they separated" and partly due to "their personal predilections and endowments."

In the beginning it is important to give an outline of the conceptual issues on which the following discussion is based.

Firstly, both Gandhi and Jayaprakash Narayan were communicators who well understood the basic processes of the mass media. They both had their own newspapers, and seemed to conform with the classical description of the way the press enables discrete individuals to join together in purposeful groups, as given by Tocqueville. "The effect of a newspaper is not only to suggest the same purpose to great number of persons, but also to furnish means for the execution of the designs which they may singly have conceived.... A newspaper then takes up the notion or the feeling that had occurred simultaneously, but singly, to each of them. All are then immediately guided toward the beacon; and these wandering minds, which had so long sought each other in darkness, at length meet and unite." This common action, believed the two great leaders, was made possible because of instrumental political participation, which is essentially directed towards the achievement of concrete goals. "

Though leading from the front in two different eras, both Gandhi and Jayaprakash Narayan relied heavily on public opinion. They agreed with Bailey who says that public opinion "has a giant's strength and we may use it with frightful effects". Like students of communication they saw the public as a semi-organised entity that in some way or another moves through stages of initiation and debate, and reaches a recognisable collective decision on an issue. To them the public was an organic entity linked together by means of mass communication.

Further, while Gandhi conducted his dialogue both with the 'mass public' and the 'attentive public,' a distinction suggested by Almond, JP communicated mostly with the 'attentive public'. The mass public informed by the mass media pays heed to the tone of discussion and issues and responds through moods of apprehension or complacency. The attentive public, a far smaller group, follows public issue in an analytical manner, is relatively well-informed and constitutes a critical audience for the discussion of public affairs. However, the size of the attentive public varies from time to time as new issues and problems arise. Again, at times, the attentive pubic may be large and quickly responsive to events and actions. At other times and on other questions, public discontent may be generated rather slowly. It may require years or decades for a public sentiment to develop. But whatever segment they may be targeting, both Gandhi and JP as communicators believed that an opinion has a bearing on groups of people and political mobilisation takes place on the basis of groups and associations.

Vital Angles

There are two main aspects to what occurs. On the one hand, there is the provision of a consistent picture of the social world, which may lead the audience to adopt this version of reality, a reality of facts and of norms, values and expectations. On the other hand, there is a continuing and selective interaction between self and the media, which plays a part in shaping the individual's own behaviour and self-concept. We learn about our social environment and respond to the knowledge that we acquire. In greater detail, we can expect the mass media to guide us about different kinds of social role and the accompanying expectations in the sphere of work, family life, political behaviour and so on. We can expect certain values to be selectively reinforced in these and other areas of social experience. We can also expect the mass media to give an order of importance and structure to the world they portray, whether fictionally or as actuality.

There are several reasons for the expectations listed above.

Firstly, there is a good amount of patterning and consistency in the media version of the world. Another is the wide range of experience, which is open to view and to vicarious involvement, compared to the narrow range of real-life experience available to most people. Third, there is the trust with which media are often held as a source of impressions about the world outside direct experience. Gandhi and Jayaprakash Narayan were quite methodical when it came to the content of their journals. Their content broadly fell in Eisenstadt's three main classes of communication content: technical content, which provides instruction and information; general cognitive content, which covers news ranging from gossip to politics; and normative content, which defines what is proper behaviour and is oriented to the transmission and maintenance of social norms.

Besides, both strongly believed in the agenda-setting function of the media. This function was pointed out by Bernard C. Cohen who says that "the press may not be successful much of the time in telling people what to think, but it's stunningly successful is telling its readers what to think about." Political scientists too have been most alert to the process and McCombs and Shaw have given the term 'agenda-setting' to it.

What follows is a comparative study of Gandhi and Jayaprakash Narayan with regard to the style of leadership of the two, particularly on how they both made use of the press in political mobilisation. A large part of the analysis is based on interviews and content analysis.

Major Links

Both Gandhi and Jayaprakash Narayan were great communicators. They knew the importance of getting their messages across to the people, that would in turn prompt them to action. "Both were masters of communication."

Though rooted in a mix of saintly and traditional languages of Indian politics in their discourses, both Gandhi and Jayaprakash Narayan were operating in two different time periods, a fact that makes this comparative analysis quite interesting.

"Gandhi belonged to that generation when media was an instrument of articulation of public opinion." Even the authorities in the Gandhian era used to rely on the contents of the newspapers upto a large extent. This was possible because of two reasons, as pointed out by G.S. Bhargava. "A kind of moderation with which the complaints were aired, and the restraint shown by them." Gandhi was quite logical and sharp in his writings. Thus he wrote about a movement and the British response to it: "Every good movement passes through five stages: indifference, ridicule, abuse, repression, and respect. We had indifference for a few months. Then the viceroy graciously laughed at it. Abuse, including misrepresentation, has been the order of the day.

The provincial Governors and the anti-non-cooperation press have heaped as much abuse upon the movement as they have been able to. Now comes repression, at present yet in its fairly mild form. Every movement that survives repression, mild or severe, invariably commands respect which is another name for success. This repression, if we are true, may be treated as a sure sign of the approaching victory. But, if we are true, we shall neither be cowed down nor angrily retaliate and be violent. Violence is suicide. Let us recognize that power dies hard, and that it is but natural for the Government to make a final effort for life even though it is through repression. Complete self-restraint at the present critical moment is the speediest way to success."

On the other hand, Jayaprakash Narayan was operating at a time when the mass media were fairly well developed. Newspapers in different languages had proliferated and the increased literacy rates facilitated the wide reach of the media. No wonder, as both Ajit Bhattacharjee and G.S. Bhargava observe, his *Everyman's* had a specific focus of readership. "It was more for political readership than for mass consumption," observes Bhattacharjee. He further elaborates that unlike Gandhi's journals *Young India, Harijan* or *Navajivan,* the *Everyman's* "was conceived in a very specific setting and was primarily aimed at the educated class and policy makers and was not meant for the masses."

The journals of Gandhi were meant for a wide range of readership. The very fact that he brought out his journals in different languages drives home the point that Gandhi's publications were meant for mass readership.

Circle in Society

However, both Gandhi and Jayaprakash believed in the process of shaping public opinion through the use of the press. Both relied on the technique of conducting dialogue on various issues by creating a public sphere (as suggested by Habermas), for it. As communicators, both subscribed to the media-centred view of communication theories that focus on the means of communication as a force for change.

Thus apart from writing on issues that concerned their immediate agenda like non-cooperation and total revolution, Gandhi and Jayaprakash Narayan would also touch upon issues of wider relevance in their journals and other writings. Gandhi wrote on education in his weekly *Harijan* in the 8 May, 1937 issue: "I hold that true education of the intellect can only come through a proper exercise and training of the bodily organs e.g. hands, feet, eyes, ears, nose, etc. In other words an intelligent use of the bodily organs in a child provides the best and quickest way of developing his intellect. But unless the development of the mind and body goes hand in hand with a corresponding awakening of the soul, the former alone would prove to be a poor lopsided affair. By spiritual training I mean education of the heart." According to him, a proper and all-round development of the mind, therefore, could take place only when it proceeded along with the education of the physical and spiritual faculties of the child. He continued, "They constitute an indivisible whole. According to this theory, therefore, it would be a gross fallacy to suppose that they can be developed piecemeal and independently of one another."

Similarly, Jayaprakash Narayan's weekly would highlight various social issues, despite being highly political in tone and tenor. In the thick of JP Movement, the April 12, 1975 issue of *Everyman's* carried an article 'Crimes against Harijans and Adivasis' written by Madhu Limaye. "Untouchability has no sanction of law," read the page seven story, "but it still rules the innermost recesses of the human heart. Unless men's hearts are purified, unless the pernicious principle of dividing people into higher and lower castes based on birth is abolished, unless the youth of the country are inspired by a burning hatred of this inequality, and unless a genuine sympathy for the lot of the oppressed is created, how could one expect a change in the mental outlook of the common people? Harijans and Adivasis constitute 21.53 per cent or more than one-fifth of India's total population. And they are the most oppressed of the citizens. Twenty seven years of freedom has neither altered their living standards nor their social status. There is an urgent need to transform the living conditions of these oppressed millions."

Thus, even in politically volatile times, Jayaprakash Narayan would not relegate social issues. Gandhi was, in fact, a step ahead of him in this regard. All the issues of his weekly newsletters would have some 'human interest' articles. Later on, Gandhi started *Harijan* solely for the purpose of propagating his campaign against untouchability.

It is also possible to argue against the contention that both the leaders used the press for conducting dialogues on various issues. According to a Gandhian journalist the element of dialogue was "missing in JP's approach, while it is more prominent in that of Gandhi's." He points out that "Gandhi had different target audience when he wrote in different languages." Thus for the English version of the *Young India* he had one kind of readership in mind and so on.

Gandhi even kept the sentiments of a particular section of readership in mind while bringing out various editions of his newspapers. In the Gujarati edition of the *Indian Opinion* of December 21, 1913, the following remarks were made, that substantiate the argument: "The Satyagraha campaign, as carried on this time and still continuing, has hardly a parallel in history. The real credit for this goes to the Hindi and Tamil speaking brothers and sisters living in this country. Their sacrifice has been the highest of all.

Some of them have even lost their lives: killed by the bullets of the white soldiers. As a tribute to their memory, we have decided to give Hindi and Tamil news in this paper. Some years ago we used to bring out this paper in these two languages as well, but we had to discontinue the practice owing to some difficulties. Those difficulties are not yet over. And yet, we resume publication in these languages for the duration of the struggle, that being, in our judgement, the least we must do, even at some inconvenience to ourselves, in honour of communities whose members have made such sacrifices in a struggle of this kind." So sensitive Gandhi was to the sentiments of his readers!

Jayaprakash Narayan too cared about the sentiments of his readers. He too had due respect for his readership, but as pointed out by Ajit Bhattacharjee, his focus was limited largely to the politically active and educated class or the 'attentive public'.

In addition to considering newspapers as the "most

powerful vehicle for transmitting pure ideas in a concise manner..." and making them a tool to educate public opinion, Gandhi had equal regard for opinions expressed by his readers. Jayaprakash Narayan came quite close to Gandhi in this respect. In fact a large part of page two of *Everyman's* was devoted to letters to the editor, that at times spilled over to page three also. And both of them gave proper display to letters representing dissent and the opposite point of view. Another quality of a great communicator.

Gandhi published a letter by CF. Andrews criticising 'The Growth of Intolerance' at the peak of the non-cooperation movement on the front page of *Young India* even at the risk of irking many: "I wish to make every allowance for mere boyish enthusiasm and for any juvenile ebullition of feeling; but these and other previous acts have gone far beyond this. They amount to persecution and cruel humiliation. I have watched, for a long time, with greatest pain, that in spite of all that Mahatma Gandhi has done to condemn the evil, it has increased, and it is not confined to one part of India only.

As it is entirely opposed to the principle of non-violence, which attracted me so strongly to the Movement, and drew me out of the retirement of Shanti Niketan to take part in it, I feel that the time has come for me to declare publicly and openly my detestation of these practices."

Jayaprakash Narayan too provided space to his readers to air their opinions. One of the letters on page two of the 18 May, 1975 issue of *Everyman's* titled 'The Movement and the Men Behind' reads: "JP's Movement started with its main target being the elected representatives who have been constantly betraying the people who elected them. But how is it that these MLAs and MPs who are elected for a specific, brief period, are able to sit over the heads of the administrative and bureaucratic executives who are there to guard the system?

What has happened to the sanity, morality and integrity of these people? JP relies too much on student power to achieve his goals. I feel that the students are generally not mature to be worthy of this faith. There may be a few individual students who think on the lines of JP, but as a force they cannot be relied upon.

How can we depend upon our students to achieve higher ideas in the larger canvass of society when they tend to be corrupt in their small sphere? Can we expect a student, who claims copying in the examination hall to be his right, to turn out to be a worthy product? Students have generally impressed the common man as an irresponsible lot. The majority of our present day students are incapable of any useful service to the illiterate masses. The so-called education successfully makes them snobs, devoid of any human sympathy and stern moral attitude."

There was no editing even of the harsh criticism. This shows the high degree of professionalism adhered to by both Gandhi and Jayaprakash Narayan. In fact Gandhi went a step further and would reply to "almost all the letters personally", as pointed out by Bhargava. "He wrote endlessly and made his point very sharply." Gandhi is specially recognised for his letters. His letters, small or big, official or personal, were pure gems. These were worded appropriately and spoken from the heart. "Many are playful; some loving.

Many administer a paternal rebuke; some with describable restraint, hit, and hit well; a few are intimates; scarcely any throbs with the impulse of an unguarded moment. The author adjusts the tone, the language and the perspective of every letter with uncanny precision so as to have the desired effect on the addressed. These letters have provided him with his greatest instrument of controlling the conscience and conduct of his friends and adherents. No man has wielded so great an influence through his letters; and few literary men have written theirs with such art."

Jayaprakash Narayan too wrote letters. But they used to be mostly political in nature. The available accounts do not indicate to his indulging in personal correspondence with the readers of his journal, as did Gandhi.

Commenting on the overall content of their journals, Ajit Bhattacharjee observes that while the content of the *Everyman's* was "basically political, criticising the politics and action of the government of the day, Gandhi covered broader national agenda as he had a much broader area to appeal to." He further points out that while Gandhi was fighting an alien government and anti-imperialist forces, the focus of Jayaprakash Narayan was much different. "He was fighting a native anti-democratic government, and hence the intensity differed." Rajiv Vora, in fact, goes a step further and sees very little role of the latter's journal in the Bihar Movement." It was primarily an organ informing the educated class about the various developments of JP movement," opines Vora.

Another factor that marks Gandhi as distinct from Jayaprakash Narayan is the fact that the former used to manage time to write even in the thick of movements. JP, on the other hand, did not write for mass consumption; however, "he did produce party documents and theses," informs G.S. Bhargava, who was an associate of Jayaprakash Narayan.

On the other hand, even when the call for Quit India Movement had been given in 1942, Gandhi wrote a letter to his "American friends" in the August 9, 1942 issue of *Harijan.* "I invite you to read my formula of withdrawal or as it has been popularly called 'Quit India'. I claim to be a votary of truth from my childhood. It was the most natural thing to me. My prayerful search gave me the revealing maxim 'Truth is God' instead of the useful one 'God is Truth'. That maxim enables me to see God face to face as it were. I feel him pervade every fibre of being.

With this Truth as witness between you and me, I assert that I would not have asked my country to invite Great Britain to withdraw her rule over India, irrespective of any demand to the contrary, if I had not seen at once that for the sake of

Great Britain and the Allied causes it was necessary for Britain boldly to perform the duty of freeing India from bondage. Without this essential act of fair justice, Britain could not justify her position before the unmurmuring World Conscience, which is there nevertheless.

Singapore, Malaya and Burma taught me that the disaster must not be repeated in India. You have made common cause with Great Britain. You cannot therefore disown responsibility for anything that her representatives do in India. You will do a grievous wrong to the Allied cause, if you do not sift the truth from the chaff whilst there is yet time. Just think of it. Is there anything wrong in the Congress demanding unconditional recognition of India's independence?"

Action of Silent Nature

Another factor on which Gandhi and Jayaprakash seem to have been at par is their dislike for "any form of propaganda". "They would both make out their cases quite logically, convincingly and with great conviction even when there was scope of propaganda. They would never resort to cheap techniques of writing for mobilising the masses," says G.S. Bhargava.

Gandhi was guarded in his writings. Thus he wrote on Khilafat: "In my humble opinion attainment of Swaraj is the quickest method of righting the Khilafat wrong. Hence it is that for me the solution of the Khilafat question is attainment of Swaraj and vice-versa. The only way to help the afflicted Turks is for India to generate sufficient power to be able to assert herself. If she cannot develop that power there is no way out for India and she must resign herself to the inevitable. What can a paralytic do to stretch forth a helping hand to a neighbour but to try to cure himself of his paralysis?

Mere ignorant, thoughtless and angry outburst of violence may give vent to pent-up rage but can bring no relief to Turkey. Nor can it increase the power of India to assert herself. And the measures taken to put down violence may well lessen the speed with which we are marching to our goal."

Jayaprakash Narayan was equally cautious and judicious in use of words. "It is interesting to note," he wrote in the November 16, 1974 issue of *Everyman's* "that the Prime Minister made a casual reference to the injuries inflicted on me by the police on November 4, saying that there was no intention to hit me and that I was injured in a stampede. There is however a crucial question involved concerning the role of law in the country including that of discrimination between two groups of citizens.

The entire machinery of the state was deployed on November 4 and the days preceding it to forcibly prevent the people of Bihar from coming to their capital city for a peaceful demonstration and dharna... The constitution provides that there shall be no discrimination in the application of law.

However, just a week after armed security forces did everything short of killing to prevent a peaceful demonstration, the CPI has not only been given permission to stage a rally in Patna but official agencies have gone out of the way to provide all possible facilities to help the CPI. The people do not want any facilities from the Government, but they certainly have the right not to be obstructed in activities of peaceful assembly and expression.

What is a matter of great concern to all democrats is that if this is repeated then the people will have no chance to give expression to anything that goes against Government policies and actions however bad or evil such policies might be. If this policy continues during election time democracy would be destroyed in our country."

Similarly, Gandhi did not cross the limit while writing even against the harsh treatment of the South African administration against the Indians residing there. *Indian Opinion* was the spearhead of the struggle in South Africa. Gandhi continued to inspire and infuse a spirit of passive resistance through his writings, which were sharp, straight and effective. Thus Gandhi wrote: "Of the many accomplishments that passive resisters have to possess, tenacity is by no means the least important. . They cannot and must not lose faith in themselves or in their mission because they may be in a minority.

Instead, all reform has been brought about by the action of minorities in all countries and under all climes. Majorities simply follow minorities." Then he wrote: "Brute force will avail against brute force only when it is proved that darkness can dispel darkness." And, "Death should cause no fear in us if we have .... done nothing in violation of the voice of our conscience. Then, indeed, is death but a change for the better, and therefore, a welcome change which need not evoke any sorrow.

And resisters must learn not only not to fear death, but must be prepared to face it and welcome it when it comes to use in the performance of our duty.... I wish for no better end, and I am sure no other passive resister does." This reflects Gandhi's ability to put an event as emotive in a style that will not amount to propaganda.

No wonder a large section of the mainstream press relied heavily on Gandhi's journals, when it came to picking up issues. Almost all the issues discussed by Gandhi figured prominently in all the major newspapers of the day, informs Bhargava. However, the situation was a little different in Jayaprakash Narayan's case. In fact, he was already getting a good publicity through the wide coverage of his movement in the mainstream newspapers. And given the wide reach of the newspapers in the 1970s, as compared to the colonial decades, the impact was much greater. There were, however, cases when issues were picked up by the mainstream media from Jayaprakash Narayan's journal.

Despite this, both the communicators had to face the brunt of the respective regimes. While Gandhi's *Young India* was forced to close down during the Civil Disobedience Movement, Jayaprakash Narayan's *Everyman's* was gagged during the peak of emergency. Both the journals were perceived to be creating a great impact on people's mind and propagating the movements. Similarly, Gandhi's *Harijan* was closed down forcibly during the peak of the Quit India Movement.

The British rulers had studied the penetration and power of Gandhi's journals. As has been said, the journals used to guide the masses about the various moves made by Gandhi and his workers. Similarly, Jayaprakash Narayan's journal, though meant primarily for the politically conscious educated class, was becoming a vehicle of ideological and moral debasement of Indira Gandhi's dictatorial regime. "There have been attacks on the freedom of press, the worst and most sustained occurring during the emergency when censorship was imposed and publications perceived to be hostile to the government were harassed legally and illegally."

Lion's Chunk

Gandhi and Jayaprakash Narayan both made the press partners in their campaign and mobilisation efforts. They would not only inform their readers about the development of movements and ideological moorings behind them but also chalk out a programme for future action.

While talking about his stay in Musahari block in Bihar and his programme of *Gramdan,* Jayaprakash Narayan wrote: "I should make it clear that we are fully aware that the implementation of our present programme would certainly not mark the completion of our work here. In fact, it would be only the beginning: Gramdan will only prepare the necessary socio-psychological conditions for the direct democracy of the village to function properly. But much will still remain to be done to make the democracy work.

> "The Gram Sabhas will have to develop the strength and moral resources to be able to resolve conflicts

> from being committed, and see that the Gram Kosh is collected regularly and utilized for the purposes laid down. The Sabhas will have to learn to prepare their own plans of development, to husband their own resources for their execution, and to obtain available help form Government agencies, credit institutions and other sources.... There are other future tasks too.
>
> The Gram Sabhas we are establishing are of an ad hoc nature, so they will have to be confirmed according to the provisions of the Gramdan Act. That is a tedious and time-consuming process. Then again, when Gram Sabhas have been set up in all, or at least in 80 per cent of the villages of the block, the next higher tier, or concentric circle as Gandhiji would have it, the Prakhand (Block) Sabha, will have to be organised. In that manner the structure of the communitarian policy of Sarvodaya will have to be raised tier by tier from the very grassroots of the primary community."

Again in the middle of this famous Bihar Movement, he wrote a signed letter titled 'Come with me to Parliament' in the March 2, 1975 issue of *Everyman's:* "I have made an appeal to the countrymen to hold at least a million-strong demonstration at the Parliament in support of the people of Bihar. The National People's Action Coordinating Committee has fixed March 6 for the demonstration."

Similarly Gandhi informed "How to Boycott Foreign Cloth" during the non-cooperation movement through his journal *Young India:* "The proposed boycott of foreign cloth is not a vindicative measure, but is as necessary for national existence as breath is for life....

It is of the highest importance to know how it can be brought about even before the first day of August next. To arrive at the boycott, it is necessary:

1. For the mill-owners to regulate their profits and to manufacture principally for the Indian market.
2. For importers to cease to buy foreign goods. A beginning has already been made by three principal merchants.
3. For the consumers to refuse to buy any foreign cloth and to buy khadi wherever possible.
4. For the consumers to wear only Khadi cloth, mill cloth being retained for the poor who do not know the distinction between Swadeshi and Pardeshi.
5. For the consumers to use, till Swaraj is established and Khadi manufacture increased, Khadi just enough for covering the body."

Gandhi, in fact, was more elaborate in his writing about the steps, style and strategies of movements than Jayaprakash Narayan. The reason is pointed out by Ajit Bhattacharjee. He says that "while JP used the mainstream media during the Bihar movement, Gandhi had to rely mostly on his own journals for popularising his ideas." Ajit Bhattacharjee was the editor of *Everyman's* weekly for a large part of its life before it was shut down during the Emergency.

Additionally, Gandhi was multi-lingual (his journals were brought out in many languages) that enabled him to appeal to a much wider audience than Jayaprakash Narayan could. The latter could only write in Hindi and English, while Gandhi wrote prolifically in Hindi, English and Gujarati besides being conversant in languages like Sanskrit and Tamil.

A major difference between the two was the way they ran their newspapers. While Gandhi was directly involved in the production of all his journals and wrote for most of the issues, Jayaprakash Narayan appointed a group of journalists to run his journals: *Everyman's* in English and *Prajaniti* in Hindi.

Gandhi observed that during his association with the *Indian Opinion*, until 1914 "excepting the intervals of my enforced rest in prison, there was hardly an issue of Indian Opinion without an article from me."

Another contrast appears in the different role that the media played during the two time periods. The media played the role of mediator during the times of Gandhi; it changed its role to that of a messenger during the JP Movement in independent India. This was possible because literacy rates were significantly higher and the growth of press made it possible for a large number of people to access it in the later period. In Gandhian era it was a marginal motivator while during Jayaprakash Narayan's era it was playing the role of a monitor. It was a monitoring instrument for assessing the development of the JP Movement.

In the end, it can be said that both Gandhi and Jayaprakash Narayan, despite differences in their style of leadership and their ways of life, are likely to be seen more and more as belonging essentially to the same genre of leaders, who devoted their whole life to political activities and brought about major changes in politics without ever aspiring to hold state power in their own hands. And, in this endeavour, they used the press with dramatic results.

4

The Stalwarts

Stout Heroes

Horniman : The battle for freedom was fought as much with the pen as with the weapon of *Satyagraha*. Editors of Indian newspapers used their pens like sharp swords to harass the alien government and to make deep thrusts at their vulnerable points to expose their oppression and exploitation. They inspired and encouraged freedom fighters and gathered support for them. They were patriots and their patriotism bordered on fanaticism. They were crusaders in the fight for independence and they made sacrifices and suffered privations (including imprisonment) unheard of in the annals of journalism of any country in the world.

There were giants among them who have found a place in the roll of honour of India's freedom. There were two foreigners in their ranks, one an Englishman who made India his home and was called a traitor by his countrymen, and the other an Irishman who edited a British owned newspaper and proved a great embarrassment to the British rulers. One of them, B.G. Horniman is the subject of this chapter.

Horniman came to India in the early years of this century as an assistant editor of the *Statesman*. He was the son of a former paymaster-in-chief of the British navy and the brother of a rear-admiral and a famous actor. He was a staunch advocate of Indian independence and was soon disgusted with the uncongenial atmosphere of Chowringhee (Calcutta) where the *Statesman* was printed. He resigned his job in 1912. Recommending him to Sir Pherozeshah Mehta who was in search of an editor for his newly started *Bombay Chronicle*, Surendranath Bannerjee wrote: "I may assure you that Horniman is as good an Indian as myself. During the days of the partition of Bengal he used to walk with us barefooted through the streets of Calcutta with a shawl on his broad white shoulders."

Before Horniman arrived in Bombay and took charge of the *Bombay Chronicle* in 1913, vigorous, dynamic public life was unknown. What public activity there was centred round the chambers of Mehta and Sir Chimanlal Setalvad. One commentator says: "Bombay got inspiration, advice and drive from the new editor who wrested for her a permanent position in Indian politics." An Englishman as editor of an Indian newspaper necessarily had to work under great strain but Horniman had the advantage of professionalism which made him an expert.

There had been British champions of the Indian cause before and after Horniman but none as eminent for personal identification with the causes he took up and for the vigour with which he pursued them. To his qualities as a trained journalist he added emotional involvement in the fight for Indian freedom. He was an indefatigable worker active in public life and in movements for relief to the people.

By his incessant attacks on the British owned press he shook the *Times of India* (which virtually enjoyed a monopoly until the arrival of the *Chronicle)* out of its smugness and exposed its anti-Indian views and race prejudice. It soon became a habit for the citizens of Bombay to read the *Chronicle* the first thing in the morning. As one writer remarked: "It supplied them their war cry. The fascination lay in the editor's nationality. A radical outlook, a consciousness and feeling born of right and a ruthless exposure of evil were the dominant features of Homiman's writings." An European bureaucrat said of him: "I hate Horniman though I can't help admiring his articles which are a tonic." The officials branded him a traitor to his motherland.

Referring to this, Horniman said: "They (his enemies) read every line I write. They read between the lines and above them, underneath them and in all sorts of positions but they couldn't catch me." Horniman, as president of the Bombay Journalists Association led a deputation to the viceroy early in 1916 to protest against the misuse of the Press Act of 1910. Other members of the deputation included C.Y. Chintamani, S.N. Bannerjee and Pandit Malviya. The viceroy's reply was not satisfactory but the deputation had the satisfaction of utilising the occasion to give wide publicity to the misdeeds of the government (central and provincial). Homiman's relations with the Board of Directors of the *Chronicle* were not happy and he was in frequent conflict with it.

It was dominated by Moderates but as long as Mehta was alive, things went on smoothly; with his passing away, Horniman began to feel the strain much more. Although he protested again and again against the interference of the Board with editorial policy, he was unable to make his voice felt. Annie Besant wrote to him that it was wrong to allow his independence of expression to be curtailed by a "stupid Board of Directors". "In your place", she said, "I would tell them frankly that either I edit as I like or I resign." Horniman had close relations with Besant and when she was interned in 1917 he went to Madras to edit her paper, *New India,* until P.K. Telang, acting editor took over. The Board of Directors of which Sir Chimanlal Setalvad was the chairman did not approve of his support for the Home Rule Movement started by Besant.

When Edwin Montagu, Secretary of state for India, visited India in 1917 in connection with constitutional reforms, the Viceroy, Lord Chelmsford, had made arrangements to accommodate his party in tents on the grounds of the Viceregal Lodge in old Delhi instead of offering rooms in the Lodge itself. Horniman protested in the columns of the *Chronicle* against what he called "this snobbery" of an English aristocrat who, Horniman said, thought it below his dignity to put up in his house a commoner who happened to be a Jew, Homiman's protest was taken up by other papers throughout India. Chelmsford offered an apology and said that no insult was meant. He said owing to lack of accommodation in the Viceregal Lodge and for Montagu's own convenience, he had decided to give him separate quarters.

Horniman refused to be convinced by this explanation and did not abate his criticism of the viceroy. Later, when Horniman met Montagu in the presence of Chelmsford, Montagu defended Chelmsford and chided Horniman for taking up the cudgels on his behalf. Horniman replied: "I admire your extreme courtesy to your not very cordial host, but I still I maintain that respecting the traditions of India, he had better given you, even at some personal inconvenience, accommodation in the Viceregal Lodge."

In 1919, Horniman wrote almost daily on the Punjab atrocities under Martial Law and exposed the abuse of power and the humiliation imposed on the people. As one observer of the scene remarked: "His articles struck terror in the hearts of bureaucrats as they read them morning after morning. One reader described the *Chronicle* as an appetiser to a hearty meal for the public and a paper which destroyed the appetite of the government and its sycophants. It was inspiring in its candid criticism of both the government and the Moderates.

Every time they read the *Chronicle* they could not help jumping in their chairs." Horniman's tussle with the Board became acute and one day it reached the crisis point. The board tried to dictate to Horniman what he should write and what he should not. Horniman refused to be dictated to and resigned. He announced the resignation in the paper itself. His resignation created a commotion among his readers and angry crowds invaded the *Chronicle* office and demanded the recall of Homiman.

The Board asked N.M. Samath, a leading Moderate, to reorganise the paper and he called in Pathan Joseph, a talented writer who had earlier served as assistant editor in a number of papers, to take charge. The circulation of the paper began to fall rapidly and the Board resigned. Setalvad relinquished control of the paper and a new Board was formed with M.A. Jinnah as chairman. Horniman was recalled. Pothan Joseph remained as assistant editor and Syed Abdullah Brelvi, who was a sub-editor, was made an assistant editor. Horniman was, however not to be in the *Chronicle* for long.

The Bombay Government was out to take action against him for his articles on the Punjab. In his own words: "Lord Lloyd (government) and his secretariat gang pored and pored over every *Chronicle* file until DORA (Defence of the Realm Act) came to their rescue and I was bundled off." Horniman was deported in April 3919. He was then recovering from an operation. He was removed to a ship in the harbour and sent back home.

Gandhi presided over a protest meeting of Bombay citizens in June, 1919, which urged the government to revoke the deportation order. Gandhi said: "Mr. Horniman is a very brave and generous Englishman. He has given us the *mantram-Liberty*. He has fearlessly exposed the wrong wherever he has seen it and thus has been an ornament to the race to which he belongs and rendered it a great service. Every Indian knows his services to India.

The continuance of the *Chronicle* without Mr. Horniman would be like an attempt to sustain the body when the soul has departed. The national cause will certainly feel hurt to find that one who presented it with a daily draught of Liberty is no more in its midst." Gandhi said he did not agree on many occasions with that Horniman wrote and said, he thought the language used by him was more suited to a Western than an Eastern country. But the question was one of liberty of the press and liberty of public speech and it was for this reason that they wanted the deportation order to be revoked.

Defending the action against Horniman Montagu said in the House of Commons: "We have been very patient with Homiman. In no case has there been a better example of our reluctance to interfere with mere eccentricities of political belief. But when this gentleman began to use his paper in the middle of the riots resulting in loss of life to spread and fan the flames and opened his columns to an accusation that British troops had been using soft-nosed bullets in the streets of Delhi and when his paper was being distributed free to British troops in Bombay in the hope of inciting disaffection and insubordination, why, then, I say, it was high time he left India." He added: "An Englishman, upon whom far greater responsibility certainly rests, cannot be tolerated in India if he is responsible for the occurrences which we associate with Mr. Homiman."

Horniman defeated himself through the columns of the *Manchester Guardian*. He wrote: "Though the government was strongly criticised as it deserved and the strongest protest was made in my paper regarding the public flogging of people in streets, the dropping of bombs on unarmed crowds, machine gunning of demonstrators without adequate provocation, the whole of my personal influence and that of my paper— neither of which is inconsiderable—were used in support of restoration of order and the inculcation of the doctrine and practice of *Satyagraha*—the very negation of violence—both before and during the disturbances that occurred."

In a letter to the *Chronicle* in September, 1919, he related the circumstances under which he was deported. He was ill, he said, and under doctor's orders after an operation not to leave the house, when the police came and asked him to pack up. He was carried from his house to an ambulance and placed on board the ship. Horniman returned to India early in 1926, defying a government order, by way of Colombo and according to one writer: "His journey from Dhanushkodi to Bombay was a triumphal march."

He became the editor of the *Sentinel*, a sister evening daily of the *Chronicle*. He also wrote a column in the *Chronicle* under the pseudonym, Atropos, which he used to attack the government and the Moderates. He called the *Times of India* "the Old Woman of Bori Bunder" which became famous. As editor of the *Sentinel* he became the *bete noire* of the police for his exposures of gambling in the city. He was trapped in a police raid while investigating and was hauled up before a magistrate like an ordinary felon.

The chief Presidency magistrate acquitted him and took the police to task for their treatment of him. Even the *Times of India* was forced to condemn the police action and demand an enquiry. In 12 articles after his acquittal, titled, "I accuse the police", Horniman charged the police with deliberately staging the raid and organising mass arrests merely to trap him and parade him before the public as a gambler. He had an amazing knowledge of the law and of "lawless laws" and this helped him to keep out of trouble. He always appeared in court without a lawyer and conducted his own defence. His articles in the *Chronicle* and the *Indian Daily Mail* during the *Satyagraha* movement in 1932 resulted in security being demanded from these papers by the government.

> "Horniman has done the work of 100 leaders", said a prominent Congressman. His sense of news was disconcerting to his opponents, in the profession. He was the *guru* of over a dozen journalists who have made good in Indian journalism. He was temperamental and this created several crises in his career. In the words of a writer: "He became at once the proud master and pitiless slave of his

temperament. It also invested him with a uniqueness of strength unknown to the majority of men." K. Rama Rao, who was one of his disciples, wrote: "He was a great chief. In a few words he would give instructions that illumined the sub-editor's or the reporter's path. Sitting in his room he gathered Bombay's political strings in his hands and knew all that was happening politically, noble as well as ignoble."

"I shall not set down my pen, he said on the occasion of the golden jubilee of his entry into the profession, until the freedom of India is achieved." "He was a school of journalism himself; taught many aspirants and saw several of them seated in editorial chairs. Stem and unbending were his political convictions, whatever his weakness otherwise. He had a genius to make history, not merely record it, whether he was participating in the Bengal anti-partition demonstrations in the early decades of the century or throwing out a reactionary Board of Directors and replacing them by men of his choice; whether he was being deported from his sick bed or was returning to India to a hero's welcome; whether he was founding, editing or killing newspapers or defying the tin gods of bureaucracy; whether he was defying the High Court needling a home member. He had a positive genius for lampooning the government and its overzealous minions and yet circumventing the law cleverly. He was justly proud of his sound judgment which the gods give only to their favourites. He was a lovable, adorable person and his colleagues called him, 'Governor'. He could rifle our pockets at leisure and we his. He ate no salt and only beetroot sugar for the sake of his throat. He argued his own cases

> and once expounded in court the startling doctrine that he had a right to travel first class on trains because no accommodation was available in the second. He dressed like a peacock, whoever paid the bills. He occasionally wore the *dhoti.* He spoke brilliantly on the platform and he wrote like an angel but could not, unlike some of us smaller fry, dictate an article. He invariably wrote it out. He spent money faster than he earned it and innumerable were the pirates and parasites around him."

After Horniman was deported in 1919, the *Bombay Chronicle* was placed under official censorship. The directors asked Gandhi to take over the conduct of the paper but before he could do so, the paper suspended publication following the forfeiture of the security of Rs. 10,000 deposited when the pre-censorship was imposed. When the paper resumed publication, S.A. Brelvi was appointed editor.

The *Chronicle* went through a financial crisis which was aggravated when a libel suit was filed against the company which owned the paper and heavy damages were awarded. The company went into liquidation. The paper was purchased by Belgaumwala who sold it to N.M. Cama who formed the Associated Paper Company. Brelvi brought a measure of stability to the paper and it played a notable part in the freedom movement. Both *the Chronicle* and *Sentinel* closed down in 1959.

Arthur Moore : Arthur Moore belonged to that rare species of editors who have a mind of their own and do not care what others think about it. Moore enjoyed in letting people in high positions in government or in politics know what he thought, and what he thought and wrote was not always palatable to the parties for whom it was intended. He was an unconventional editor and the Statesman which he adorned for 10 years from the editorial chair was not always happy with him. K.P.S.

Menon, the veteran diplomat, said: "Arthur Moore was no respecter of persons. Some VIPs disliked him and he reciprocated their sentiments cordially. On the whole, he was regarded by the Establishment as a difficult person to deal with."

Moore succeeded Alfred Watson as editor of the *Statesman* in 1932. Watson was the target of terrorist attack twice and he was injured in the second attempt when he was shot at by a young terrorist. The attacks were a sequel to some articles published in the *Statesman* and according to Muggeridge who had just then joined the paper, as an assistant editor, they had been written by Moore. Watson resigned his job and returned home.

> "Moore's mercurial temperament", Muggeridge wrote, "look him from the out and out imperialist position which might have cost Watson his life and did cost him his job, to one of close affinity with the Swarajists. He was a gifted, unstable, northern Irishman fated to make a mess of his career, not through being too rigid—which is one way of doing it—but through being flexible— which is another."

Muggeridge found that Moore "disliked the view I expressed in my leaders no less than Wordsworth (who acted as editor in Moore's absence) did. So it was exiling to all the three of us when it was decided, that I should go to Simla and represent the paper during the summer months when the Government of India functioned there." Before he came to India, Moore had worked as a reporter on the *Times* of London and was considered an authority on Balkan and Persian affairs. He served as the *Times'* correspondent in Persia (Iran) for some years. He came to India in 1924 and joined the *Statesman* as an assistant editor.

His most famous brush with authority was during the vice-royalty of Lord Linlithgow to whom he was like a red rag to a bull. In 1937 there was a constitutional deadlock in the provinces where the Congress had been returned in a majority in the elections to the Legislative Assembly. The Congress refused to accept office unless assurances were given that the governors would not use their reserve powers under the Constitution. The viceroy supported by the Home Government was unwilling to give any such assurance. It was at this time that an article appeared in the Statesman with the heading, "Indian impasse deplored—Unofficial anxiety. Viceroy's silence unhelpful." The article said that the House of Commons was critical of the government's attitude to the deadlock, that the viceroy's advisers in India were unwilling to help the Congress extricate itself from the impasse and that considerations of prestige on both sides could not be overlooked.

The article said the viceroy's prolonged silence was increasingly noticed and regarded as unhelpful. Parliamentary opinion, it said, was most impatient of this attitude and held that unless the legislatures in the Congress provinces were summoned, officialdom would incur some share of the responsibility for any further deterioration in the situation. The dispatch was purported to have come from Reuter's news agency but Reuter denied it. The viceroy found that the evidence suggested that the Message was sent from the *Statesman's* London office and inspired by the editor, Arthur Moore.

Linlithgow had met Moore from time to time and he had considered him to be an impulsive Irishman but read his editorials with particular care. He thought him markedly short of ability and extremely slapdash and impetuous in his methods. The article in the *Statesman,* he told Lord Zetland, secretary of state, might have very embarrassing reactions. If it really had been sent by Moore, he said, it would justify strong pressure on the Board of Directors of the *Statesman* in London to bring him under control. Zetland confirmed to Linlithgow that Moore was indeed the author of the dispatch. He said he had met Moore before his departure for India and "found it difficult to understand his mind." Moore told Zetland that he believed that with tactful handling, Jawaharlal Nehru could be led into the cooperation fold. Zetland hoped for the support of Lord Cato, chairman of the *Statesman's* Board of Directors, in dealing with Moore.

The *Statesman* again fell foul of the viceroy when in a leading article it said that there were many in the British Government who were to be profoundly mistrusted; they would be capable of Petain's conduct in comparable circumstances and they had their British counterparts in India. "We do not speak entirely without knowledge," the editorial said. Linlithgow was wild with rage. He wrote to L.S. Amerly, secretary of state, that "this gross and damaging libel came as a climax to a long series of damaging indiscretions". He said he had little doubt that the editorial was written by Moore "whose removal alone could correct the situation". But Moore did not go until 1942 by which time, according to the Establishment, he had done more damage to British prestige and authority.

On August 10,1942, Moore wrote an editorial, after the arrest and detention of Gandhi and other Congress leaders, criticising the government's action in terms which were considered by the government as "demoralising and defeatist". Members of the Viceroy's Executive Council were angry and wanted that action should be taken against the paper and the writer. However, to the great relief of Linlithgow, the Board of Directors decided to relieve Moore of his post and appointed Ian Stephens to replace him.

On the eve of Linlithgow's departure from India, the *Statesman,* while remembering the occasions on which it had criticised him, expressed in a generous leader its gratitude for his "courageous services" to India. Ian Stephens wrote in his memoirs that for two years after he became editor in August, 1942, "I suffered much embarrassment from his (Moore's) activities. He kept on revisiting our offices in Calcutta, Delhi or London or making speeches or issuing press statements and writing articles several of which by implication affected my shaping of the paper's policy.... His conduct then seemed inconsiderate."

Maulana-Abul Kalam Azad, the Congress leader, mentions in his autobiography, that when Gandhi went on a fast unto death in Delhi in 1947, following communal disturbances, Moore who was staying in the Imperial Hotel, also began a fast. The Hindu-Muslim riots had moved him deeply. He told Azad that if the disturbances did not end he would also fast unto death. He had been in India for many years and had adopted it as his home. As an Indian he regarded it as his duty to put a stop to the human misery and degradation that were taking place. Death, he said, was preferable to "this terrible tragedy" that had overtaken India. Azad sent him a message after Gandhi broke his fast and requested that he should do the same.

Moore served as a member of the Legislative Assembly in Delhi for a term as a member of the European Group and his presence and frequent interjections made the proceedings lively. At one time he crossed swords with the President, Vithalbhai Patel, and was admonished. He was a fearless critic and did not spare anyone, friend or foe if he thought he was in the wrong. Although a supporter of the nationalist cause, the Congress and especially Gandhi, had been at the receiving end in many of his by-lined editorials. He was a brilliant writer and commanded a simple style which at the same time was forceful and effective. He served India and her oppressed people in his own way and made Indian journalism the richer by his contribution to its vitality and strength.

S. Sadanand : In the history of Indian journalism S. Sadanand has an important place as an able editor, an innovator and a fearless patriot. Born in Tamil Nadu, he made Bombay his headquarters for his multifarious ventures in journalism. That was where he held sway during the *Salt Satyagraha* of 1930-33 when his newspaper, *Free Press Journal*, was a rage and eclipsed all other nationalist papers. He was a pioneer of popular journalism in English, who sold his papers at six piece a copy, an unheard of thing in those days when the minimum price of a newspaper was one anna (6 paise). He created a mass base for himself by espousing popular causes and airing public grievances in a big, spectacular way which caught the imagination of the educated masses. He, more than any other journalist, strove to instil pride and devotion among the people for their country and for the epic battle for freedom waged by the Congress under the leadership of Gandhi. He was a powerful, wholehearted supporter of the Congress movement and the *Free Press Journal* paid the penalty for it when the alien government persecuted it by demanding securities and forfeiting them and demanding fresh deposits.

Sadanand did not flinch and survived the ordeal even after paying Rs 70,000 in one year alone. He revolutionised editorial writing. Instead of the long and meandering editorials, very often going above the head of the ordinary reader, which were a feature of the nationalist newspapers then, Sadanand introduced the sharp, telling and pungent editorial paragraphs which, with their mythical *or Puranic* allusions and anecdotes, went straight to the heart of the readers and enabled him to grasp with ease what was being conveyed to him. The reader became emotionally involved in whatever was suggested and his cooperation was assured. And that was how the Congress gained its supremacy in Bombay. His right-hand man on the *F.P.J.* was "Stalin" Srinivasan who was an able and experienced journalist. The sobriquet, "Stalin", was given to him by his colleagues in the profession because of his moustache which closely resembled that of the Russian dictator.

Sadanand started his career as a journalist in Burma in the 1920s when it was part of India. He worked on the staff of a Rangoon newspaper and later came to India. He purchased the *Indian Express* from Dr. P. Varadarajulu Naidu in 1932 who had started it a year earlier. Sadanand ran it for some months and soon got tired of it for all his concentration was on the

E.P.J. in Bombay. He went to C. Rajagopalachari in April, 1932, and urged him to take over the *Indian Express.* ajaji told him that the man who could help him was K. Santhanam, who had just been released from prison where he had undergone imprisonment as a *Satyagrahi.* Santhanam had lost his wife while in prison and had declined the offer of the authorities to release him. When he came out of prison he had decided to renounce politics but fate willed it otherwise.

Rajaji advised him to take over the *Indian Express* as its editor. For Santhanam, Rajaji's words were a command and he started a new life as a journalist For him editing and running the *Indian Express* was a national service and a mission. The *Indian Express* became a morning paper and spokesman for the Congress. It was sold at half an anna in line with Sadanand's innovative seal. Very soon a sister Tamil daily was added and the *Dinamani* in a short time outstripped its rivals. The *Indian Express,* however, fell into a financial crisis and it finally passed into the hands of Ramnath Goenka who later became a newspaper baron and the owner of the largest chain of newspapers.

Sadanand was a man of great ambition. He wanted to start a paper in every province of India. As a nationalist he felt that was the only way to promote the integration of the country. In 1932, he started an evening newspaper, *Free Press Bulletin,* in Bombay and Gujarati daily, *Nav Bharat.* As we have seen, he bought the *Indian Express* in Madras in 1932, and started the Tamil daily, *Dinamani,* in 1934. He also started a Marathi daily in Bombay, *Navasakti. Free India,* an English daily which he began in Calcutta, had a very short life. In anticipation of establishing newspapers in other major cities, he purchased machinery and appointed editors but unfortunately he was not successful in his efforts. According to a close associate of his, hundreds of linotype machines which he had bought for the proposed newspapers lay idle in the godowns. "He was too ambitious", one of his friends said, "and he aimed at too much."

Sadanand's notable failure was the Free Press News Agency which he formed in 1927 as a rival to the Associated Press of India (A.P.I) which was a subsidiary of Reuter's Agency and enjoyed the patronage of the Government of India. Sadanand's objective was to survey news from a nationalist angle and to cover areas neglected by the semi-official news agency and also to provide Indian commercial news. He also had an ambition of appointing correspondents abroad to supply international news of interest to nationalist opinion in India. He was backed by big industrialists like Sir P. Thakurdas, G.D. Birla, Walchand Hirachand and M.R. Jayakar. But the nationalist news agency failed to evoke the sympathy and support of the Indian-owned press from the beginning and this was a great disappointment to Sadanand.

For over three years he made brave efforts to stabilise the news agency but the reluctance of the established Indian newspapers to subscribe to its service and the sustained pressure of the rival and more influential news agency to kill it proved too overwhelming and the Free Press News Agency steadily lost ground. Also, Sadanand had to fight against official censorship both at the distribution and receiving ends. The agency's speciality was supply of news about *Satyagraha*, of police firings and beatings of volunteers and these could not be carried by the newspapers as they were afraid of retaliatory action by the Government. Pressure from the Government forced the resignation of four directors of the agency in 1926 and the fifth in 1931. The government came down heavily on newspapers which published news from the agency and the Press Ordinance of 1930 signed its death warrant. Most of its clients shied away.

It was stated that the A.P.I. also applied pressure by insisting that its services would not be available to newspapers which subscribed to a rival news agency. Adding to Sadanand's troubles, his financiers withdrew support and the most grievous blow was his failure to win the support of influential Congress leaders. Sadanand's dream was to establish a world news agency. He had a talented correspondent in London who collected the important dispatches of foreign news agencies, selected the choicest among them and they were cabled to India and often Reuter was left standing. But the agency's scoops were of no avail. The Free Press News Agency died in 1935, unsung and unwept.

Sadanand was a builder of newspapers. His forte was management and improvisation. He was a competent news getter but it was always difficult for him to resist the temptation to transform news into brash publicity and propaganda. His news agency suffered from this foible of his and lacked credibility. One of his admirers called him "a man with a giant's energy." He had the capacity to get more out of man and machine than most others. He could produce a newspaper single-handed. It was nothing for him to sit before a linotype machine and compose copy or to sit at a news desk and edit telegrams. Once when there was stoppage of news supply owing to arrears of payment, he made up the pages with news he had written in his own hand. He could write a dispatch as lobby correspondent sitting in his chair in Madras about what took place in the Central Legislative Assembly in Delhi. He was a workaholic with a restless mind. He did not have patience with lazy people. He commanded the absolute loyalty of his workers.

And when creditors pressed him for payment he would tell them: "I am doing a national service. Give me credit for that." He looked upon journalism as a sacred calling which combined the highest ideals of nationalism and of public service. His motto and that of his papers was "Free and Fearless." In the words of a writer: "He had a rugged individuality, an embarrassing independence and a fierce possessiveness. He made lasting friends in the profession but his colleagues were overwhelmed by his exacting demands and his haunting suspicions. He combined a strange predilection for adventures on the side with an almost fanatical dedication to journalism."

A colleague who worked with Sadanand in the *F.P.J.* has written: "The honours of the freedom fight of 1930-33 went equally to Sadanand and the *F.P.J.* on the press front. The paper was waging an epic fight against the Government. In fact, it was the head and front of the journalistic onslaught. Sadanand was in high mettle and in more affluence too then. The *F.P.J.* was the dauntless bark he sailed and he was the pilot who weathered a myriad storms. The bark was often near going down but he somehow held it on course. He has left behind him a legendary fragrant reputation for a gallant courage and enterprise, and undying tradition of editorial audacity and several institutions firmly established and exceedingly useful to the country. He started life with a broken typewriter and died in a blaze of glory."

K. Rama Rao who joined the *F.P.J.* in 1932 wrote: "The combination of two mercurial minds and two devil-may-care spirits like us lasted long enough to cause surprise in friendly as well as in unfriendly quarters. We all appreciated Sadanand's superb courage, his capacity to plan like a genius and to execute like a giant. Made of tempered steel, he did not have an atom of fear in him. He was courageous to the point of being reckless, resourceful to the point of being inventive and original to the point of being unpredictable. Security after security was forfeited for defiance of law, blow after blow fell, but he did not bat an eyelid; he did not budge an inch from the firing line. With head bloody but unbowed, he went on attacking. No risk was too big, no adventure too reckless. He revelled in crises, some self-created. A soldier in every inch of him, how he fought and won; now he fought and lost; but he never ran away from danger or difficulty. His faith in his stars was unassailable."

Sadanand, who passed away in 1933, was a fighting editor, a great organiser, a powerful writer and a gentleman of extraordinary calibre.

Frank Moraes : The story is told that when Frank Moraes was a student at Bombay's St. Xavier's College in the 1920s, he was bored by the droning voice of a lecturer. As he slowly started sliding on his bench towards the door, the lecturer noticed it and shouted: "Moraes, what does that slow movement to the right indicate?" "Departure, Sir," said the nonchalant Moraes as he left his seat and made for the exit. True or not, it exemplifies Moraes' spirit of independence and his ready wit and humour. He was a journalist who did not suffer fools gladly and called a spade a spade. Long training and apprenticeship in a British-owned and edited newspaper had given him a discipline and keen sense of what was right and what was wrong, and integrity and clear thinking, so that when he came to assume positions of responsibility in a newspaper he commanded great respect and authority.

He asked himself once: "What did England give me?" and provided the answer: "Primarily, I think, a sense of tolerance combined with a habit of evaluation which while enabling one to listen to the other man's point of view did not necessarily imply that one necessarily accepted it. I suppose this attitude of mind really adds up to democracy. England also laught me to recognise the importance of standards in human relationship and individual conduct which in a way spells civilisation. I think the most valuable gift England gave me was a sense of proportion."

It is this sense of proportion which marked his editorship of the *Times of India* and later of the *Indian Express*. He occupied the editorial chair of India's two leading newspapers at a time when the country was facing enormous problems of reconstruction and survival. He was a constructive critic whose writings were valued in the highest quarters of Government and paid the greatest attention. A close associate described him as "one of the most straightforward journalists and a gentleman." He was of a reserved nature and a man of few words. He had the advantage of moving with the leaders of government on an equal footing which developed intimacy and trust and he established high level contacts in all spheres of public life. His close friendship with Jawaharlal Nehru and

Indira Gandhi was a great asset. His involvement with, and appreciation of, Nehru were such that he became his biographer.

Son of an Indian government servant, Moraes was born in Bombay in 1907. He graduated from St. Xavier's College, Bombay, and later took a degree from Oxford. He was also a barrister of Lincoln's Inn, and practised law for some time before he entered journalism in 1934. He worked first on the *Times of India* as a junior assistant editor. Of this period Moraes writes: "*The Times of India* then on the eve of its centenary was a British newspaper whose senior editorial and production staff were exclusively British and I was at the time the only Indian assistant editor. The editor, Sir Francis Low, was a competent Scotsman who had worked his way up through various departments of the paper. Outwardly he appeared to be reticent and diffident but he was not easily overawed or taken in."

The *Times of India* then was a firm supporter of the government since it was British-owned. "Its political policy, though more liberal than that of the Raj, moved broadly in step with it," Moraes wrote. "Its antennae were sensitive to New Delhi but less sensitive to London which failing led it occasionally to trip on British foreign policy, most noticeably as the war drew nearer. It approved the Italian invasion of Ethiopia only to make a quick about turn when Whitehall's reaction came over the wires. Its thinking was perhaps too overcast by the colonial smog."

Moraes said the system suffered "from a few imperial hangovers". He was, for instance, not invited to use the senior staff canteen which was exclusively British. "Nor was I proffered a key to their exclusive lavatory." He was also excluded from the daily morning conference which the other assistant editors, all British, attended. "In accordance with government office routine and the practice of European commercial establishments, the senior staff worked by the clock and only very rarely round it. Our daily office hours were from 10 a.m. to 5.30 p.m. with an hour and a half for lunch and in my 19 years on the *Times of India* I do not believe I came more than a dozen times to the office at night."

It was common in those days to think that every Indian who worked on the staff of a British-owned newspaper was anti-nationalist. "For an Indian to work as a senior member of the staff of any one of these (British-owned) newspapers was to be tarred with a semi-official brush," Moraes said. "Yet like most Indian officials who were part of the British bureaucratic machine, the majority of Indian journalists even on British newspapers were nationalistic in outlook. From my own experience, there is no denying that this conflict produced something of a split personality." Writing about the Indian press under British rule, Moraes said: "The Indian press could not be described as a free press in British days for though British-owned papers like the *Statesman* and *Times of India* rarely drew official frowns and a certain latitude of expression was permitted even to Indian-owned newspapers the Raj could, and did, descend heavily on the latter."

Moraes was not anti-British. He was conscious of the benefits of British rule. "Fairness compels the admission," he once wrote, "that whatever Britain's sins of commission and omission might have been in India, the credit side of the ledger overweighs the debit. Britain, opened for India new windows on the West. In a sense she helped India also to rediscover herself for until the researches of European scholars little or nothing was known of the pre-Islamic period nor of Hindu culture and civilisation. The British association made Indians familiar with the marvels of Western science and technology and with concepts like democracy and Parliamentary Government."

Moraes went out as a war correspondent to Burma in 1943 and his dispatches were prominently displayed in the *Times of India*. They were exhaustive and Moraes was able to meet all the top brass and wrote with authority and precision on allied strategy and of the victories and defeats. He particularly dwelt on the heroism of the Indian troops and their commanders. Moraes later went to China to cover the war on that front. After the war he took over as editor of the *Times of Ceylon* in 1946 and remained in that post for two years.

The *Times of India* changed hands at the end of the war and its new owner was Ramakrishna Dalmia. Moraes was appointed editor of the *Times of India* in 1950. It was the high watermark of his career and during the seven years he adorned the editorial chair he brought it much prestige and influence. His term as editor was marked by a brush with Bombay's Chief Minister, Morarji Desai, and he was hauled before the State Legislative Assembly on a charge of contempt of the legislature.

An editorial comment on certain proceedings in the Assembly during question hour had provoked Chief Minister Morarji Desai. The question and answer which led to the comment related to prohibition and involved issue of permits to judges. In his editorial Moraes pointed out the impropriety of the Assembly questioning the conduct of the chief justice of a High Court or the chief justice of the Supreme Court or his colleagues which could be done only by Parliament. The Assembly appointed a committee to decide if Moraes had committed contempt of the Legislature. The chairman of the committee after some hearings advised him to apologise, which he refused. He was then arraigned before the House. Moraes read out a statement justifying his comment. The Assembly decided to withdraw the press cards of the paper's Parliamentary correspondent.

Moraes thereupon issued instructions that the *Times of India* should use only the slender agency reports of the proceedings of the Assembly. "In less than three months", Moraes wrote, " an emissary approached me with a plea to forget, I forgot. So did the State Assembly. The press cards of our Parliamentary correspondent were returned." On another occasion, Morarji Desai, angry over an editorial of Moraes, withdrew all government advertisements to the *Times of India.* "Had we been a small provincial journal his action could have brought us to our knees," Moraes said, "but we were sufficiently affluent to continue defying him and his policies. In time the advertisements were restored."

Moraes became the editor-in-chief of the *Indian Express* in 1957. He scored many triumphs and his editorials carried great weight and influence both with government and the people. At times of national bereavement or disaster or when problems of great magnitude confronted the nation, Moraes wrote his editorial on the front page to focus attention and to convey the importance and seriousness of what was being written. He was a fearless critic of the government regardless of the personalities involved and his criticism was unbiased and free from taint of vindictiveness. He was a responsible journalist who weighed his words and did not criticise for the sake of criticism. He was an intellectual who was also author of many books, including an autobiography and a biography of his favourite Indian leader, Jawaharlal Nehru. Moraes believed in a free press as an essential corollary of a vibrant democracy.

> "In a colonial country", he said, "there can be no independent press but in an independent country dedicated to socialism and democracy a free press is a natural concomitant." He said Jawaharlal Nehru, always "conscious of democracy in democratic socialism scrupulously respected the freedom of the press;... So did his successor, Lal Bahadur Shastri."

Moraes thought that the political columnist or commentator had still to come into his own in India "where the newspaper reader more often than not takes opinions from the editorials which are perhaps more widely read and discussed in our country than in any other land. It does not follow from this that the average Indian reader's opinions are automatically moulded by his newspaper for most educated or even literate Indians tend to have definite political views even if these are sharper and more defined at local or state levels than at the national level."

K. Rama Rao : C.P. Scott, the great editor of the *Manchester Guardian,* said this of journalism: "What a work it is! How multifarious, how responsive to every need and incident of life! What illimitable possibilities of achievement and excellence!" Kotamaraju Rama Rao, a giant Indian journalist, drank deep the nectar of journalism, jumping from one flower to another, never satiated, ever humming and searching for more drops of honey. His was a restless spirit which sought adventure and excitement and did not mind the cost. He was in revolt not only against the British rules but also against the system which they perpetuated, the injustice and exploitation and sycophancy which they generated. He was a fierce patriot who used his pen like a sword and he made no bones about it. His words were meant to kill, to destroy the opponent if words could do so. He did not believe in soft language, in expostulations and arguments, in legalistic terminology and quibbling. Not for him what was said of another great editor, A. Rangaswami Iyengar, the quality of moderation and use of sober language which marked his editorials.

Mild language, however, direct or uncompromising in import, was with him a betrayal of timidity. He was blunt and outspoken and he used his pen with vitriolic effect. He was not happy with the proprietors whom he served for he kept them in perpetual fear of penal action against the paper. He moved from one paper to another, almost all of them espousing the national cause but his ebullient aggressive spirit could not be contained and the proprietors who believed in the stability and safety of the newspapers, although appreciating his patriotic fervour, were chary of entrusting him with the fortunes of their papers. He worked on the staff of more than 25 papers (including two weeklies) and was sent away in three places. It was said that Rama Rao, who hailed from Andhra Pradesh, always worked with a resignation letter in his pocket.

Rama Rao had his early training as a reporter under T.L, Vasvani of *New Times*, Hyderabad (Sind) like his brother, K. Punniah, who was editor of the *Sind Observer*, did much to promote the nationalist cause. Rama Rao later came to Bombay and joined the staff of the *Times of India*. After some years he left that paper to seek new pastures. When the editor asked him the reason for his resignation he said: "I have been long enough here and have learnt my work pretty well. I have my own ambitions. Can I ever be the editor of the *Times of India?"*

Then began Rama Rao's adventurous journey in journalism. He joined, as we have seen, Sadanand in the *Free Press Journal* during the crucial years of 1932-34 when the paper was a frequent victim of the rulers' persecution and fury, then moved on to T. Prakasam's *Swarajya* in Madras where he spent 100 days struggling to inject vigour and stamina into a paper which was dying for lack of resources. He was with the *National Call* in 1934 and with the *Hindustan Times* for a brief period of six months in 1938. He became the editor of the *National Herald*.

Lucknow, the same year and spent there the longest period he had served any newspaper. The founder of the paper, Jawaharlal Nehru, liked him although he was not always in agreement with his writings and language and style. The two, one a great national leader and considered as a leftist by the alien rulers and the other a firebrand who believed in fire and brimstone in the attack on colonialism in the press, easily established a rapport and friendship which was to transcend the boundaries of journalism.

Rama Rao was a crusading editor. Day after day he wrote with passion and zeal and his writings played a great part in rousing the masses to follow the leadership of Gandhi in the freedom struggle. The *National Herald* under him became a symbol of the nation's fight against tyramny and exploitation and against repression and denial of human rights. It was in the vanguard of the freedom struggle and became a propaganda forum for the leaders of the movement.

Rama Rao was defiant and fearless of authority and he slashed the opponents of freedom, be it British officialdom or the sycophantic moderates who flourished under the favours bestowed on them by the alien regime, with his pen which he used like a sword. He exposed abuse of power, and police brutality in language which made the blood boil in Indian hearts as it made the rulers sit up and vow vengeance. The officials involved him in a defamation case when the jailor of a prison where *Satyagrahi* prisoners were kept sued him for libel for an editorial on the treatment of political prisoners.

Rama Rao was convicted and sentenced to six months' imprisonment. The *Herald* stopped editorials from 1940 as a protest against the pre-censorship and other restrictions on the press. In August, 1942, Rama Rao saw the police raid of the office and press of the *Herald* and seizure of machinery which resulted in the closure of the paper. Rama Rao returned to his desk after the paper was revived in 1946 but left it shortly afterwards. He was a freelancer for some time and worked at Gandhi's headquarters. He took over as editor of *Searchlight* of Patna in 1948. His services were terminated in 1950. He saw service with some other newspapers and ended up as a legislator when he was nominated to the Rajya Sabha. His end was tragic when he was killed in a train accident in Uttar Pradesh.

Gandhi called him a "fighting editor". Nehru described him as "an outstanding figure in Indian journalism". For C. Rajagopalachari, he was a "dear dreadnought". The list of newspapers with which he was associated is pretty long and besides the papers we have already mentioned it includes *the Pioneer, Leader, Bombay Chronicle, Indian Daily Mail, Advocate of India* and *India News Chronicle.*

Rama Rao said: "Journalism is the destroyer of rust, a foe of pessimism and an amplifier of the areas of life and work", was a rebel who questioned many things accepted as gospel truth. When talking about the freedom of the press, he posed the question: "Freedom for whom? Freedom for the proprietor or freedom of expression in the public interest?" He said: "While the proprietor-editor has all the power and no responsibility and who reserves to himself the right to dictate policies with an eye to his several other interests, the editor *de facto* as distinguished from the editor *de jure* has all the responsibility and no power." Rama Rao recalled that journalism of the 1930s was of a very high standard. "Discussions were kept at a high level, if only because the traditional standards of this country demanded excellence in things pertaining to the spirit and the intellect, notwithstanding the vicissitudes of kingdoms and empires and the lapses and degradations of social life.

The newspaper was a lengthened shadow of its crusading owner-editor. Today, the Fourth Estate is, for good or evil, totally different in aim, purpose and content." He said: "From the point of effective service, moral values and social usefulness, the press in India can boast of a record as good as that of any other in the world. It has treated its work as a trust, sacred and vital. By and large, it has been loyal to the doctrine that facts are sacred but comment is free and it has been national in more senses than one."

> "What was the lure of journalism in the days when I started," Rama Rao asked and answered the question: "It was the nearest route of attack on an empire which we ail hated and wanted to overthrow and the best avenue of service in the cause of purposeful patriotism. We thought we could be Annie Besants or Hornimans, Tilaks or Motilal Ghoshs. It was the quickest way to fame which is certainly not the least nor the last infirmity of noble minds and is definitely an honourable ambition, an

> energising aspiration. I have enjoyed the thrills of the hourly chase, the sensations of the daily adventure. I have savoured the pleasures of success and suffered the pangs of defeat. The profession was a rough but challenging pathway to national service and incidentally to a good name."

Rama Rao believed that journalists should be trained and taught in schools of journalism. He said that a school of journalism could teach the beginner the essentials which could not be learnt by working in a newspaper for over five years. He himself trained many journalists who later came to occupy high positions in Indian journalism. He fought for the rights and protection of working journalists and helped in the formation of the Federation of Working Journalists in Delhi in 1950. He was a member of the Standing Committee of the All-India Newspapers Editors Conference for many years. He waged a relentless war against monopoly control of the press.

N. Raghunathan : Not many outside the world of journalism would have heard of N. Raghunathan, the celebrated senior assistant editor of *The Hindu* who virtually functioned as the *de facto* editor for over 20 years. He prided in his anonymity and allowed his writings which were marked by scholarly approach and erudition to speak for him. His mastery of the language was incredible and his arguments were irrefutable. His great weapon was a capacity to marshal facts and point to the unerring conclusions which destroyed the opponent's strenuously built up case.

Not for him the sword or aggressive language which attracted the spotlight and popular applause. He relied on cold logic and telling arguments helped by a prodigious memory, which was elephantine in character, which unearthed precedents and situations to demolish the points made by constitutional experts and politicians of the ruling race. He was a great constitutional foe of the colonial rulers from whom he commanded a measure of respect and also fear.

The leaders of the national movement found in him a stout champion and adviser in their fight against the alien rulers on the constitutional plane. He tore to pieces and ridiculed the futile arguments of British spokesmen, from the secretary of state downwards to the viceroy and his minions, to deny India freedom and dignity. He digested white papers and reports on constitutional reforms with relish and he was unsurpassed in his analysis and exposure of their weak points and unacceptable postures. It was nothing for him to dash off three two-column editorials in one day and once when his colleagues played a prank on him, he wrote all the editorials, sometimes extending four to five columns, for a week.

His friends and admirers thought Raghunathan would have been a fairly prosperous lawyer (he had a law degree), a fairly successful teacher or even a fairly good administrator. Raghunathan said he escaped being an administrator by "malice prepense". As for lawyering or teaching "I wonder whether I could have stood the hungry backchat of the bar room or the bland superciliousness of the common room for a day. Indeed, the more I think of it, the more I doubt whether I could have secured and kept any other respectable employment. By a strange quirk of fate I seem to have slid almost without knowing it into that odd shaped hole in a million which seemed to have been made for this oddly constructed individual.

That I have stuck there bespeaks therefore, no special virtue. I could not have got out had I tried.... I do not know whether the millions of words I have written ever influenced a single soul. It would be a relief to know that even if they did no good they did no evil. No man is good enough to tell another what to think. Aesop's fly on the wheel might have done far more harm if he could have put a spoke in it."

Raghunathan came to *The Hindu* in 1926 from a morning newspaper, the *Daily Express*, in Madras of which he had been editor for some years. He was a discovery of V.S. Srinivasa Shastri who was a close friend of Kasturi Srinivasan.

Raghunathan had rejected *The Hindu's* offer the previous year since he loved the freedom as editor, which he enjoyed. He, however, reluctantly accepted the offer when it was renewed the following year and thus began a historic and rewarding association with India's leading nationalist newspaper. He very soon established an intimate relationship with Kasturi Srinivasan and the two became inseparable associates in running the paper.

They had similar views on most subjects and the points of disagreement were far too few to break their intimacy. N.R., as he was popularly known, shaped the policy of the paper with Srinivasan in total agreement and together they made *The Hindu* the most powerful and influential paper in the country. So much was his confidence and trust in N.R. that when he wanted to retire in 1948, Srinivasan, who refused to let him go, said: "A memo from me will never go to N.R," N.R. did not retire till 1957 when Srinivasan reluctantly agreed.

N.R. was a master craftsman who sanctified everything that he handled. He was an outstanding sub-editor who could edit copy, especially *mofussil* copy (which had to be wholly rewritten) with an instinctive feel for mistakes in grammar, faulty style and expression. He wrote his editorials by hand with a sharpened pencil in bold letter which for all their hugeness in size were all the same mostly illegible and only the practised eye of the lino-type operator (what he wrote went straight to the press and was not typed) could decipher them. He wrote less than a dozen sentences on a sheet of paper and the matter was set up and the proof sent to him as fast as he wrote them.

During the 30 years he served *The Hindu*, his dedication to the paper was total and he had no other interest in life. He spurned invitations to go abroad and isolated himself from the outside world. Although he wrote about all the big leaders and personalities of India and the world, he never came in contact with any of them nor did he want to. He was not a crusader like a Horniman or a Rama Rao. His writing lacked passion and anger and the vibrant quality which roused the feelings of all those who read it. His strong point was argument and cold logic presented in a style which was majestic and powerful in its onslaught. He was an orthodox Hindu who fully believed in the tenets and rituals of his religion and in the wisdom of his ancestors. He was opposed to Gandhi's reform movement and asked to be excused from writing on it. A notable achievement of his was the *Literary Supplement* which he edited for *The Hindu* for over 25 years. It gained national and international reputation and it had a circulation independent of *The Hindu*.

It was not only as the *de facto* editor of *The Hindu* that N.R. was famous, but also as a columnist under the pseudonym, Vigneshwara. He was permitted by Srinivasan in 1946 to contribute a column to *Swatantra* and then to *Swarajya*, a weekly, edited by Khasa Subba Rao, which was titled *Sotto Voce*. Explaining his role as a columnist N.R. said: "I thought that it might be rewarding to examine current ideas and developments in the light of those basic purposes and abiding values that one who cares to look behind the superficialities of modern life may discern in the age-long culture and way of life of the Indian people.

As regards his pen name he said: "The adoption of a pen name was due partly to a self-imposed rule of anonymity which I observed all through my working life as a journalist and partly to a desire to prevent facile— and wrong—inferences being drawn as they might be if the writer of this column were known to be one who was closely associated with the political comment of a daily newspaper."

A staunch believer in the freedom of the press, N.R. advocated an independent press unattached to any party, ideology or group. "The press has a duty to expose and denounce force, fraud and chicanery by whomsoever employed. But it has no need to enter into a partnership with the state for this purpose. In fact, freedom from any commitments of any sort to anybody except its own conscience is a condition of its efficiency." To a press that knows its own mind, no man is a god, no power is infallible. It will refuse to be overawed by authority or smothered under the blanket of respectability. And it will avoid like the plague the bovine contentment of "forty head of cattle feeding like one."

N.R. was pessimistic about the future of the honest newspaperman. "The honest newspaperman," he wrote, "becomes less and less sure with the years of the rationale of the enterprise he is engaged in. He does not know for whom he writes and in serving up the day's news he engages in a process of selection and emphasis which is as irresponsibly hazardous as divination. He is exhorted to remember that he must give his unknown and unknowable reader what he wants. And he finds it a safe rule in the circumstances to give just what the paymaster, whom he knows only too well, thinks is good for that mythical being, the average reader. The one thing that seems to be fairly clear about the great public is that its understanding of the newspapers it consumes is in inverse ratio to its enjoyment."

N.R. thought aloud more on the "mythical average reader" "Your average man is a myth", he wrote. "The writer for the press who directs his daily fussilade of advice, remonstrance or exhortation at this phantom is really shooting his bolt in the dark. He has not the time, even if he had the capacity, for that candid self-questioning by which he may hope to understand something of our common human condition. Meanwhile, the 'people' are hot on his heels, gobbling up, like the ostrich, whatever they see in print.

The balance is not redressed by the handful of cynics who refuse to believe anything they see in print. The fusillades are so many, so furious and so contrary, the reader clings so desperately to his spar of private hopes and fears in a chopping sea of universal uncertainty and there is such an intermittent squall of irrelevant news blowing that the confused din of opinion seems to matter no more than the crackling of thorns. In the multitude of counsel there is an alibi for the muddled reader. But a newspaperless world is not necessarily a better world."

Noticing a lowering of standards in journalism, N.R. warned: "It was said of C.P. Scott that he made righteousness readable. The ambition may strike many of our smart newspapermen as amusingly old fashioned. But while by giving the public plenty of crime stories, spicy gossip and sports chatter, the journalistic cheap Jack may reap rich dividends, he is already steadily undermining in the safety of the realm. For he debases standards and renders the doped public incapable of rational judgement. No Government which works for the emergence of an instructed democracy can afford to look on unconcerned. If it actually helps in the demoralisation, though doubtless without intending it, where shall we look for succour? The influence of a newspaper is ultimately a matter of character.

The personality that an established newspaper has built up over long years is, like the coral reef, the work of innumerable hands. It is subdued to a design implicit in the social situation. The reader moulds his paper at least as much as the paper colours his thoughts. Such a paper evolves a style of its own, a way of doing things, which is the right way for it Bungling interference by authority which might have the effect of forcing its individuality into a strait-jacket would be a public misfortune."

N.R. was not happy with the radical policies of free India's government. "In their anxiety to make up for lost time, they shut their eyes to the realities of our national life. They resolved that radical changes involving wholesale adoption of the goals that the West had set itself as well as methods it had forged must be forced through. What they failed to see was that large-scale industrialisation and modem technology, though they had powerfully aided, were not solely or even primarily responsible for the Western nations having in varying degree opted for a secularist society and a planned socialism. These had evolved from certain specific and distinctive qualities of the European mind.

The character, temperament and outlook of the Indian people have been moulded by a different spiritual tradition. Gandhiji saw this clearly enough but not his successors who thought that on the old stock a new and in many ways alien tradition could be successfully grafted."

The born leader writer that he was N.R. noted with regret that the leading articles were on the way out in many countries. "The leading article was pronounced dead ages ago," he wrote, "and one or two papers have shown the world that they have the courage of conviction by actually dropping it. But others seem to be in no hurry to follow. On their broad pages, the fount of home-brewed wisdom has thinned to a trickle perhaps but has not dried up altogether. And in the place of one anonymous leader writer, there has sprung up a whole host of columnists and specialists whose names are household words in four continents."

In a tribute to N.R. as a columnist, K.R. Srinivasa Iyengar, the educationist, said: "The purveyor of serious political comment in a daily paper of national vogue became the miscellaneous columnist of an individualist weekly paper and the columnist presently revealed himself as the perfect humanist and the flawless literary craftsman. A lifetime of training in the exacting discipline of expression in a difficult foreign language now yielded results. Week after week the essay appeared— with somewhat quiet assurance and look of effortless ease—and as the weeks gathered into months and years, the *Sotto Voce* feature became almost the sole standard bearer of traditional values and robust sanity in world of rattle and glare and slogans and screams.

Raghunathan's is often the conservative, unpopular, diehard views; his assent in the tradition is apt to assume the tone of dissent with current notions of propriety and progress; and yet his views cannot be dismissed as of no consequence for these undertones of assent and dissent come with an accent of authority that compels attention if not acquiescence."

N.R. passed away in 1982 at a ripe old age, but for him there was no retirement. He produced two monumental works, translations of the *Bhagavatham* and the *Ramayana* besides minor literary works in the closing years of his life. They were masterpieces and perfect examples of his scholarship and mastery of both English and Sanskrit. He was the inimitable journalist till the last moment of his life.

M. Chalapati Rau : Among India's great editors M. Chalapati Rau stands out as the champion of the working journalist for whom he strove to secure basic rights as a worker and a decent wage, and as the uncompromising fighter for a free and independent press. He fought against pressures on the newspaper internally from the owner or externally from vested interests. He had a sharp wit and a keen sense of the absurd and ridiculous and used his powerful pen to deflate the egos of power crazy politicians and bureaucrats. The high point in his career was the close rapport he established with Jawaharlal Nehru and the vigour and clarity with which he expounded his ideals and philosophy. It was a "concordat of minds." It was a very special relationship between the man who founded the *National Herald* and the man who edited it during its great years.

Chalapati Rau or M.C. as he was known among his friends, joined the *National Herald* in 1938 as number 13 in the staff. Within two years he became number two. It was a phenomenal rise due to sheer merit. When the paper closed down in 1942, he spent some time working in the *Hindustan Times* and rejoined the *Herald* when it was revived in 1945. He was appointed editor in 1946 and held that post for 30 years which must be quite a record. His command of the language was the envy of his collegues in the profession and according to one of them there were not then a dozen in India who had that mastery.

In the words of one admirer: "He wrote in a heavy, granite-like style untouched by poetic feeling and imagery. He wrote with vigour and precision when putting forth his view or rebutting an opposite one. He could be delightfully allusive drawing liberally from the wells of literature and history. He owed this to wide and purposeful reading all through his life. He did occasionally dip his pen in vitriol to make sleeping statements and pass forth harsh judgments." He once wrote of Indian writers in English: "The Indo-Anglian writer is typical of our intellectual wastefulness."

> "Our Fleet Street is a street of ink", Chalapati Rau wrote, "a street of adventure but also a street of perils. Indian journalism has been one of many vigorous forms of the expressiveness of Indian nationalism. To Kristodas Pal, Motilal Ghosh, Subramania Aiyer, and Chintamani, Fleet Street was not their spiritual home, though the last one absorbed most of the traditions without being burdened by techniques. They were great journalists. They built up traditions which have made journalism what it is today or what it was till yesterday. Our society is still amorphous, weighed down by the millstone of an English-educated middle class and it seems difficult for journalism to recover its sociological functions. For one sad feature of our journalism is the lack of social vision which includes political vision."

"The editors of those days," according to one writer, "drawn from the learned professions, combined a fine public acumen, a flexibility of outlook that was well above the reproach of opportunism, a determination to keep the flag flying in the face of repression and press laws and find best way of doing well by themselves as much as by the country. There can be no questioning the quality of service they rendered to the country, their skill in that kind of tight-rope walking or skating on thin ice which was required to escape the attention of the new minister and at the same time adhere to the standards of courageous support of the national cause." Chalapati Rau must have had these editors in mind when he wrote about the Indian Fleet Street

M.C. was an expert in foreign politics. "His knowledge of foreign politics would suffice half a dozen chancelleries", says an admirer. His Sunday articles reviewing the progress of World War II were acclaimed as outstanding. He had that "inestimable virtue of a diplomat—he can be as silent and as enigmatic as the sphinx. Tickle him, he will not laugh; prick him, he will not bleed. His reserves are more intriguing than his revelations. He does not believe in going out to meet humanity at large; he is like a famous editor who said that humanity might as well meet him by appointment. He has a soft and warm heart which he hides effectively behind an austere and aloof pose." He spent almost his entire career as a journalist in one newspaper the *National Herald,* which although it did not have a big circulation, was a powerful voice of the national movement, the voice of its most enlightened section, under the stewardship of Chalapati Rau. His dedication to the paper was overwhelming.

Of the *National Herald's,* contribution he said: "In the process of Constitution-making, the integration of the country, in free India's contribution, to the fight for freedom in other parts of the world, in the shaping of India's plans and the ceaseless task of nation building, in the political, social and economic integration of the people—the *National Herald* has written stout-heartedly and freely as a critic and as a friend with the ideals of service for which it was started kept constantly in view. The *National Herald* wrote without fear but without malice."

The philosophy which guided him and to which he was deeply committed was the philosophy of Jawaharlal Nehru. "M.C. was the best and the most lucid exponent of Nehruism apart from Nehru himself," says a writes. "At the same time it was the freedom that Nehru always insisted that a journalist should be assured that enabled Chalapti Rau to rise to great heights as a distinguished editor whose views commanded wide respect.

The relationship between the two stands out indeed as a model of how a political leader and a journalist of integrity should interact in a democracy where the masses have to be informed so that they are equipped adequately to elect those who are to wield power. Not only did Chalapati Rau understand the significance of this relationship but this understanding became the basis of his monumental endeavour to popularise Jawaharlal Nehru as the architect of Indian democracy." Indira Gandhi once described Chalapati Rau "as the conscience keeper of my father."

It was said of him that reading his editorials in those days one felt that virtually every word in them had been tested and weighed against the quality of understanding and judgement that informed Jawaharlal Nehru's own approach to men and matters and policies. In the words of an admirer: "His finest hour, there is little doubt, coincided and was coterminous with Jawaharlal Nehru's stewardship of Indian affairs. He belonged to and represented what was the best in the Nehru phase to Indian journalism. He survived... to see another age begin... but he was not of it and it was hard at times altogether to avoid the impression that he was ill at ease in it and even seemed something of a forlorn, if distinguished alien in it."

Chalapati Rau had the remarkable capacity to absorb all that was happening around him and to react and convey his impressions of what they signified. There was no major event in his life-time on which he had not made weighty comments in his editorials. To the last he was uncompromising in his integrity and in his principles. An admirer wrote: "Himself living a life of an ascetic, he commanded a moral stature which acted as a living indictment of all those in the press who would for personal gains, make peace with inequity and injustice. He never forgave those in the journalist profession who would sacrifice their integrity for a comfortable life-style. Chalapati Rau could never suffer cant and hypocrisy in the community of pressmen as he stood for a cleaner public life."

He believed in a free press and for him it did not mean merely a press free from legal restrictions. The press must be free from both internal and external pressures, he said. "An independent press is not merely a press independent of the Government but independent of vested interests," he declared. "Internal pressures arise within the newspaper from the owner or from the manager on behalf of the owner. Editorial freedom and independence means not only the editor's freedom and independence but the freedom and independence which the editor's staff share with him.... Internal pressures are multiplied by the growth of what are known as chains, groups and multiple units.... There are pressures from advertisers also."

Working journalists will remember Chalapati Rau for the dedication with which he worked to gain them recognition and a decent wage. As a member of the first Press Commission he was greatly instrumental in focusing attention on the conditions of the working journalists and to suggest measures to bring cheer and hope into their lives. "He was no ivory tower editor," says a writer, "nor a fat salaried scribed insensitive to the lot of others in his profession. He was undoubtedly the builder of the working journalists' movement in the country.

Under his constant care and guidance, this movement has grown into a pivotal organisation in the world of the Indian press. Chalapati Rau looked upon the working journalists' movement not merely as a platform to protect the working conditions of the Indian journalists but as an organ to defend the freedom of the Indian press from pollution by proprietorial and other vested interests as also from executive pressures and blandishments." He founded the Federation of Working Journalists in 1950 and was its president for three terms. He commanded the respect and affection of his colleagues and peers in the profession.

"Journalism is not a matter of wages and benefits," he said, "It is a matter of craft and craftsmanship and journalists are expected to possess not only professional skill but professional pride. It is a free and equal profession. The competition is open. Anyone can rise by enterprise. There is a sense of fellowship between the editor and machine man, between the sub-editor and the proof-reader. The newspaper is one entity. Every member of the staff should stand or fall by it.

Chalapati Rau passed away in 1983. He was apparently killed in a road accident and his body was found on the road-side. In a tribute to him, one of his admirers wrote: "Chalapati Rau as a personality of outstanding calibre stood out in the national life of India. Behind this massive figure was a person of shy and gentle nature. With his abundance of wit and irrepressible humour, was not attracted by the glamour of social life; by temperament he was lonely—almost a lone wolf. But he was by no means unapproachable. Particularly to those younger to him, he had always something to impart out of his vast erudition and professional experience. He was a teacher *par excellence*--but only to those who could break through the outer crust of his strange aloofness. Even when he was irritated he bore no rancour. And he left this world as unobstrusively as he lived. All those who knew him could sense that a giant had departed, the like of whom is not to be found in the intellectual world of the India of today."

Prominent Papers

***Amrita Bazar Patrika* :** There are today in India five English dailies which have crossed the century mark. Three of them, the *Amrita Bazar Patrika, The Hindu* and the *Tribune,* are Indian owned and Indian edited and the other two, the *Times of India* and the *Statesman* were British-owned and British-edited and progressively changed into Indian hands after India became free. All these newspapers have played a major role in the evolution and growth of Indian journalism and the Indian-owned dailies made a striking contribution to creating and nurturing Indian nationalism and to the freedom struggle.

The *Amrita Bazar Patrika* is the oldest Indian-owned daily and in 1920, Lenin described it as "the best nationalist paper in India". It was born as a weekly in Bengali in February, 1868, in the village of Amrita Bazar in Jessore district (now in Bangladesh). It was started by four brothers to fight the cause of peasants who were being exploited by indigo planters. Sisir Kumar, the more famous among the brothers, was the editor and the story of *Patrika* was the story of Sisir Kumar's relentless fight against the alien rulers who were determined to suppress this mouthpiece of the poor and downtrodden Indians. The *Patrika* moved to Calcutta in 1871 and functioned as a bi-lingual weekly, publishing news and views in English along with Bengali.

Its anti-government views and its influence among the people provoked the Government of Lord Lytton to take action against the language press. But before the Vernacular Press Act of 1878 (said to be mainly directed towards the *Patrika)* When Tilak was promulgated, the *Patrika* overnight became an English weekly and so escaped the clutches of the law. With increased circulation and greater influence with the people, the *Patrika* continued to remain a thorn in the side of the administration. Every effort was made to buy the *Patrika* by temptations but Sisir Kumar refused to be tempted. The *Patrika* became a daily in February, 1891, and plunged into the nationalist movement which had received a fillip with the formation of the Indian National Congress in 1885. The *Patrika* created history during the term of Lord Landsdowne as viceroy when it published a confidential document of the Foreign Office concerning Kashmir.

It created a sensation among official circles and a law was passed to prevent disclosure of official documents and background material without prior permission. Sisir Kumar fought for the rights of Indians and demanded for them increased representation in the administration and in the professions. He launched vigorous campaigns against restrictions on civil liberties and economic exploitation. He pleaded for the establishment of representative institutions for Indians to have a say in the administration. He contributed much to arouse the political consciousness of the people and he founded the Indian League in 1875, which probably was the first political association in India.

Sisir Kumar and his brother Motilal Ghosh were deeply attached to Bal Gangadhar Tilak. When Tilak was prosecuted for sedition in 1897, they raised funds in Calcutta for his defence. When Tilak was again tried for sedition for articles in the *Kesari* and sentenced to six years' imprisonment by an Indian judge, Motilal Ghosh, who succeeded his brother as editor pointed out "the absurdity of a homeless Parsi judge (Justice Dawar) unfit to tie the shoelaces of Tilak, indulging in wanton insult to the distinguished accused and presuming to teach true patriotism to a proved and Unparalleled patriot."

The *Patrika* had many brushes with Lord Curzon, viceroy, who partitioned Bengal and roused the people to a paroxysm of fury. The partition saw the birth of the *Swadeshi* movement which spread like wildfire throughout the country. On one occasion, the overbearing and arrogant viceroy in an address to the Calcutta University said Indians were lacking in veracity. The *Patrika* replied to this sweeping denunciation with an equally scathing retort. It quoted passages from Curzon's book on the Far East which described the falsification of age and other particulars in his interview with the president of the Korean Foreign Office. It was unwise, it told the viceroy, for one who lived in a glass house to throw stones at others. When Curzon resigned in 1905, the *Patrika* wrote: "Young and a little foppish and without previous training but invested with unlimited powers, Lord Curzon, a superior' Curzon' rose like a rocket and fell like a stick."

The *Patrika* was one of the victims of the Press Act of 1910. When in 1913 a security of Rs.5,000 was demanded from it. Motilal Ghosh was charged with contempt of court in one case. He fought bravely in court and the case was dismissed. When Subhash Bose and other students were expelled from the Calcutta Presidency College for nationalist activities, the *Patrika* took up their case and succeeded in having them re-admitted. Motilal, who was an extremist in politics, often clashed with his Moderate counterpart, Surendranath Bannerjee, through the columns of their newspapers.

When for the first time an Indian member of the Imperial Legislative Council stood up to criticise the government's budget as Gokhale did in 1902, the *Patrika* wrote: "We had entertained the ambition of seeing some Indian member openly and fearlessly criticising the financial statement of the government. But this ambition was never satisfied. When members had ability they had not the requisite courage: when they had the requisite courage they had not the ability. For the first time in the annals of British rule in India, a native of India has not only succeeded in exposing the fallacies which underlie the Government statements but has ventured to do it in an uncompromising manner. Mr Gokhale has demonstrated that the members of the council have their duties towards their country and in performing them must not think of self."

A leading role was played by Motilal to bring about a compromise between Gokhale the Moderate leader, and Tilak, who were bitter political opponents. Motilal, who was a friend of both, advised them to end their feud and forge a united Congress. He wrote to Gokhale in November, 1914: "My heart weeps for the motherland.... I am anxious that you and Tilak should shake hands and embrace each other as brothers. I know you bear no malice or ill-will to him. I further know that even if you have any cause for offence, you are generous enough to forgive and forget, especially at the present critical moment. As you are in a more favourable position, it would be a graceful act for you to make an advance. If he rejects, the people will blame him and bless you. But I believe he will appreciate your motive. The so-called Bengali leaders are now fossils. It is a Mahratta intellect and patriotism which must save the country. If you and Tilak make up,, there is yet hope for India."

Motilal Ghosh has been described as a man "thin and erect with his mass of grey hair surmounting a face in which pathos, humour and subtlety were mingled." His occasional exuberant professions of loyalty to the British Crown could have shamed the most sentimental royalist in England. Writing in the *Patrika* in 1887, on the Madras Congress, he said it had drawn the hearts of the people towards the governor as their own real ruler. In short, the European community in general at Madras seemed to sympathise with the movement like true and genuine Britons. He added: "An institution like the National Congress implies, in fact, requires the permanent existence of British rule in India." His loyalty however, did not prevent him from directing the guns of the *Patrika* at the viceroy, the governor of Bengal, and other officials to the great delight of his readers and the great annoyance of his victims.

After the Surat Congress fiasco when the Moderates charged Tilak with being the villain of the piece, Motilal Ghosh persuaded Tilak to appease his opponents in writing what amounted to a letter of regret and waiving his opposition to the election of Rash Bihari Ghosh as president. He invoked he spirit of forgive and forget and offered his cooperation to preserve the unity of the Congress. Motilal himself took the letter to the Moderates but was, in his own words, "simply bowled out by the Moderate leaders headed by Pherozeshah Mehta."

When Motilal died in September, 1922, the *Statesman* wrote: "The death of Babu Motilal Ghosh removes perhaps the most remarkable personality in Bengal. For more than half a century he carried on through his paper what was neither more nor less than a journalistic vendetta against the British Government and against the English race. No incident was too trivial to be pressed into the service of his propaganda or to be twisted into some real or fancied grievance. Yet Motilal Ghosh had a warm corner in his heart for individual Britons even while he insisted on regarding the majority of their countrymen as vampires. He was in many ways a genial soul, which if it had not been warped by a fanatical hatred of everything British, might have done a great deal to promote a mutual understanding between the two races."

The *Patrika* contributed its share to the success of the freedom movement under the leadership of Gandhi and suffered for its views and actions at the hands of the British rulers. Its security of Rs. 5,000 deposited in 1913 was forfeited in 1919 and a hash security of Rs. 10,000 was demanded. The *Patrika* wrote: "We shall go on doing our duty as usual so long as life and freedom are preserved for us." The *Patrika* forfeited its security for a second time in 1932 during the Salt *Satyagraha* and it had to furnish a fresh security of Rs. 6,000. There years later its editor, Tushar Kanti Ghosh (son of Sisir Kumar) was hauled up in court on a defamation charge and sentenced to imprisonment.

The *Patrika* espoused the cause of communal harmony during the darkest periods of communal frenzy which disfigured Calcutta and other parts of the country. During the great Calcutta killing in 1946, the *Patrika* in anger and sorrow left its editorial columns blank for three days. When freedom dawned on August 15,1947, the *Patrika* wrote: "It is dawn, cloudy though it is. Presently, sunshine will break." In the words of an admirer of the *Patrika:* "In its 117th year, the *Patrika* continues to serve the public as a living example of responsible journalism, upholding the ideals of independence, democracy and secularism and holding its head high against all forms of communalism and parochialism."

The Hindu : Six young men, all in their twenties, founded *The Hindu* in Madras on September 20, 1878. Two of them. G.

Subramania Aiyer and M. Veeraraghavacharier, stayed on later to become joint proprietors of the paper which started as a weekly and became a daily in 1889. They all belonged to a society called the Triplicane Literary Society which was a forum for discussion of political and social topics and attracted the elite of Madras.

The immediate reason for starting the paper was the criticism by British-owned newspapers of the appointment of T. (later Sir T.) Muthuswami Aiyer as judge of the Madras High Court. In the words of Subramania Aiyer: "Unable to stand this unfairness, six of us joined together and started *The Hindu*. When we started the newspaper we had no idea of the responsibility which its publication would involve, of how to conduct it, of the expenditure to be incurred, etc. Since we had no money with us, we borrowed one rupee and three-quarters and printed and published 80 copies."

In its first editorial *The Hindu* wrote: "We are inclined to be conservative as much as it is consistent with the national progress of the natives. The principles that we proposed to be guided by are simply those of fairness and justice. It will always be our aim to promote harmony and union among our fellow countrymen and to interpret correctly the feelings of the natives and to create mutual confidence between the governed and the governors." At the time *The Hindu* appeared, public opinion in Madras Presidency was stagnant and there were very few recognised forums to voice the feelings and grievances of the Indian population.

It filled a vacuum and was instantly popular. Bipin Chandra Pal, who was at one time its Calcutta correspondent, said of *The Hindu* in 1881 "I found *The Hindu* had already become a great power and an influence for good in Madras Presidency." He said that the emphasis of English educated Indians was not on our respective provincialities, but almost exclusively on India's national unity. This helped *The Hindu* to be accepted from its very birth as an all-India paper even though it could not claim any large all-India circulation."

From its inception *The Hindu* clashed with officialdom and exposed its misdeeds and abuse of power. In line with the thinking of the nationalist leaders of the time it was a firm believer in British rule and its quarrel was with the bureaucracy, with the way it functioned in India. *The Hindu* and its editor, Subramania Aiyer, were from the beginning closely associated and the Congress and Subramania Aiyer had the distinction of moving the first resolution in the first Congress session in Bombay in 1885. This close association was to continue even after independence.

Subramania Aiyer, who started life as a college lecturer, was a great social reformer and he used the columns of *The Hindu* to propagate his views. He was much ahead of his time and his vigorous campaigns led to a fall in circulation and he had to part company with the paper in 1898. C.Y. Chintamani said of him: "He was the greatest journalist of his generation. He was not only great in Indian journalism but also a great social reformer whose revolutionary ideas were almost a century ahead of his times." *The Hindu* described him as the "maker of Indian journalism in Madras Presidency."

The Hindu changed hands in 1905 when S. Kasturiranga Iyengar, a lawyer, bought it and became its editor. He was a man of tremendous energy and capacity. Within a year he reorganised the paper, improved its get-up and news service and made it a commercial proposition. He had in his nephew, S. Rangaswami, a versatile writer, whose editorials were charged with power and emotion and were read with avidity. He hit hard at opponents and his main target was the Moderates whom he described as "lost leaders" who left their comrades for a "handful of gold or riband." His strong editorials on the Punjab atrocities in 1919 led to a demand from the government for a security of Rs. 2,000 under the Press Act.

The Hindu's entry was banned in Britain in 1918 even while its editor was in that country as a member of the editor's delegation which visited the war fronts, on the grounds that it carried news and views prejudicial to the conduct of the war. The Nizam of Hyderabad also had the distinction of banning *The Hindu* in 1923 because he did not like some articles on Hyderabad published in the paper.

A. Rangaswami Iyengar became the editor in 1928 and he performed the duties of both an editor and a Congressman. He was secretary of the Indian National Congress for many years and also a leading member of the party in the Central Legislative Assembly. *The Hindu* had many distinguished correspondents abroad, among them Subhas Bose in Vienna and V.K. Krishna Menon elsewhere in Europe. After the death of Rangaswami Iyengar, Kasturi Srinivasan, son of Kasturiranga Iyengar, took over as Managing editor of the paper in 1934 and remained in that post till his death in 1959.

Srinivasan's stewardship was the golden era of the paper when it forged ahead and established its reputation and fame not only in India but also abroad. Although Srinivasan did not actively participate in politics, he acted as a wise counsellor and guide to Congress leaders and sometimes as an intermediary for them with the government.

During the great confrontation between the Indian press and the alien government he was, as we have noted in an earlier chapter, the champion of the rights of the press and did not hesitate to non-cooperate with the government when it became necessary. He saw *The Hindu's* page one become a news page in 1958 when it abandoned its policy of over 80 years of carrying only advertisements on that page. His brother's sons, G. Narasimham and G. Kasturi took over after Srinivasan's death.

The Hindu has many firsts to its credit. It was the first Indian newspaper to have its own plane service for distribution of the paper to its far-flung readers. This was done in 1963, and in 1969, *The Hindu* achieved another first when it launched its facsimile editions in Coimbatore and later extended it to Bangalore, Hyderabad and Madurai. Again it was the first to introduce phototype setting for printing the paper. In 1978, *The Hindu* brought out a sports weekly, *Sportstar*. Its predecessor, *Sports and Pastime* which made its mark in sports journalism, had to be closed down in 1968 owing to labour trouble. In 1984 the *Frontline*, a fortnightly news magazine, made its appearance with news pictures as its strong point.

The Hindu has been praised as one of the world's best newspapers by the London, *Times* and western journalists and authors. It was the recipient of the World Press Achievement Award for 1968 from the American Newspaper Publishers' Association Foundation. When G. Narasimham passed away in 1977, the post of managing editor was abolished and G. Kasturi took over full control of the paper as editor, '*The Hindu* has had the good fortune to be served by a dedicated team of journalists during its long career who have made it an institution whose watchwords have been accuracy, reliability and credibility. Most notable among these men was N. Raghunathan, seniormost assistant editor, who retired in 1957 after 30 years of devoted service. We shall note his career in another chapter.

The Hindu in an editorial in 1967, wrote what can be termed as its testament: "We must make it clear", it said, "that we are an independent, non-party newspaper, wedded to the national interest as we see it. We are not the mouthpiece of any party. We have been more often critical of the ruling party perhaps than singing its praises. We have always made a distinction between programmes and measures on the one side and personalities and parties on the other. Our criticism have been primarily concerned with the non-wisdom or inappropriateness of certain policies or decisions and whatever governments may come to power we shall continue to judge them not by their professions but by their performance." *The Hindu* has postulated three basic principles to make freedom of the press real.

The first is that the press must keep its own house clean and exercise reasonable restraint on its functioning. Freedom should not be allowed to degenerate into licence which would open the door to government interference. The second is the response of authority to the smooth functioning of the press by removing physical restraints and to enable it to reach as wide a readership as it would wish.

The third and the most important is the attitude of society as a whole, which besides the public, includes politicians, trade unions, advertisers, etc. The press has been subjected to pressure from one or another of these sources and the less viable among the press have found it difficult to withstand it. "Press freedom can come to prevail only when all sections of the body politic resolve to make to prevail by removing all impediments in the way", *The Hindu* has said.

The Statesman : Jawaharlal Nehru, it is said, read the *Statesman* every morning during the days of the freedom struggle when he was out of prison and its was one of the newspapers supplied to him when he was in prison which happened frequently. In 1928, when the nationalists organised a boycott of the Simon commission which came to enquire into constitutional reforms, the *Statesman* applied to them to cooperate with the commission and this led to a campaign to boycott the paper and copies of the paper were burnt. But it did not deter a prominent nationalist-leader from reading the paper's editorials. Asked about it he said: "We may not agree with them but we must concede that they talk sense.

And look at the brilliant way they have put forward their arguments. What wonderful language, what style! No, no, we mustn't burn a paper like this." "The *Statesman* is singularly free from prejudice," *The Hindu* wrote in 1895, "and its sincere advocacy of the Indian cause is well and widely known. The pro-Indian attitude of our contemporary enhances the value of its opinion." Nirad C. Chaudhuri said that the Statesman had replaced Macaulay among the Bengalis in their worship of fine English. "If you want to write good English, read the *Statesman*, our elders and teachers admonished us."

Robert Knight, who founded the *Statesman* in 1875 (as we have noted in an earlier chapter) was one of the early British journalists, who like Silk Buckingham, encouraged critical review of the government's actions and policies which set him apart from other British-owned papers which while supporting the government steadfastly also indulged in denunciation of Indians and specially the nationalists. Knight welcomed the formation of the Indian National Congress in 1885. "The Congress needs no other justification than the truism that if the people of India are ever to enter upon a course of real progress, it can only be by their learning to govern themselves," he wrote. "No people can make any solid or enduring progress under any system of government which does not devolve upon them more or less completely the responsibility for their own advancement.

In India, we have, unwittingly and unfortunately, set up what is perhaps the very worst form of government that the civilised world has yet seen.,.. But the time for reform has come and while India will, we hope and believe, escape the sufferings and sacrifices by which the American colonists achieved their freedom, it is the primary duty of her educated sons—a duty to Englishmen as well as to themselves—that they should use every means in their power to awaken their rulers to the fact that no people can ever make solid or lasting progress under a system of government such as that exists in India.... It is not revolution that the Congress asks for but reforms that is as urgently needed in our own interests as theirs. Knight passed away in 1890."

The *Statesman,* which was described as the *Manchester Guardian* of the East, has had a long line of able and dedicated editors who have left their mark deep on it. There were many occasions when it got into trouble with the government. On one such occasion, Gokhale had to use his influence to rescue its editor, Samuel Ratcliffe, from government displeasure. This happened during the viceroyalty of Lord Minto. The paper had published a secret minute of Lord Curzon on the partition of Bengal and the Home Department withdrew from it government advertisements and other privileges as a punishment. Gokhale spoke to Dunlop Smith, private secretary to the viceroy, who helped to arrange an interview for Ratcliffe with the Home Member, Arundel. The *Statesman* published an apology and the government withdrew the ban.

During the turbulent days of 1930 and later when the freedom struggle was at its height, the *Statesman* came under fire from the nationalists. Describing the situation, James Cowley wrote: "An attempt on the life of the editor, Sir Alfred Watson, was made. They were turbulent times. The *Swadeshi* campaign was rapidly gathering momentum, bullets flew, and home-made bombs exploded, disturbingly often with lethal effect and the toll of heads broken by the ubiquitous iron-shod *lathi* was beyond count. The *Statesman* had incurred the activists' ire partly because of its allegedly unhelpful attitude to nationalist aspirations and partly because in those days that paper was British-owned which made its stance doubly offensive to many people."

The *Statesman* in the twenties represented what we now call the rightist point of view. It was both conservative and liberal; conservative in the sense that it wanted the country and people to conserve their best traditions and liberal in the sense that it reflected an attitude free from dogmas and prejudices. To the nationalists and fighters for freedom, however, it was the mouthpiece of British imperialism and of the British community in India. Even so, there were few nationalists and freedom fighters who did not read it daily. Its editorials were scrutinised and analysed by people holding diverse political views.

Malcolm Muggeridge came to India as an assistant editor of the *Statesman* during this period and he was not happy. "I should never have come," he wrote. "I am obsessed with the feeling that I am on the wrong side... and though I know what the Indian nationalist movement amounts to, it pricks my conscience sometimes to read Congress newspapers." He lived in a flat above the *Statesman* office with Wordsworth who was acting editor. Wordsworth, who claimed to be a descendant of the great poet and had gravitated from the Indian Educational Service to journalism, was a "short, plump, pasty man who had all the correct liberal views and attitudes of mind believing that it would be possible through constitutional changes to transform the British Raj peacefully into a Westminster style self-governing democracy,...His soft persistence in upholding such views led me to go out of my way to pour scorn and ridicule on them.,.." Muggeridge was convinced that there could be only one outcome in India—the British would have to go.

> "And yet they themselves, in their clubs and offices, on their polo grounds and tennis courts, were serenely convinced that with some adjustments here and there, the Raj, in one form or another, would go on for centuries yet. A favourite saying among them was that if the British left within six months, the Indians would be down on their knees begging them to come back." Muggeridge was posted to Simla as special correspondent and he was introduced to the Viceroy, Lord Willingdon, at one of his parties. The viceroy told Muggeridge: "People were inclined to think that India was difficult to govern, but I have found it almost ridiculously easy. You just have to be nice with these fellers and they respond. That, at least, had been my experience. 1 doubt if there is in all the world an easier country to govern than India."

This was Muggeridge's description of how correspondents functioned in Simla, headquarters of the Government of India: "Journalists follow authority as sharks do a liner hoping to feed off the waste it discharges with perhaps someone occasionally falling overboard to make a meal and once in a way the whole ship going down and providing a positive feast. There was a little band of us swimming along in the wake of the Government of India.... Public relations as we know it today, was in its infancy but already the Government of India had its spokesman whom we constantly pursued for handouts and leakages and to arrange interviews. Among other useful services, we made a point of mastering the first names of Indians who were going to be knighted.... I doubt if any government had ever existed so cut off from the governed as the Government of India nestling among the Himalayas in Simla."

Wordsworth under whom Muggeridge served was notorious for his absent mindedness. On one occasion the news editor was surprised by his enquiry whether he worked there. The news editor said he had been news editor for some years. I doubt it," Wordsworth said but did not say why. On another occasion, he summoned the news editor to his room and handed him a newspaper with his markings in red pencil and comments like "disgraceful", "criminal grammar", etc. The news editor told him that the newspaper which had provoked his comments was not the *Statesman* but a rival paper. "God bless my soul," Wordsworth said, "don't take any note of all that" Muggeridge's stay in India was very brief.

There were two great editors of the *Statesman,* Arthur Moore and Ian Stephens, who earned the admiration and gratitude of the Indian people by their sympathy and support for their political aspirations and for highlighting their legitimate grievances. We shall write about Moore Separately for he deserves a chapter to himself. Ian Stephens who succeeded Moore in 1942, was an unconventional editor. He cycled to his office in khaki shorts, singlet and chappals followed on another cycle by his bodyguard with a change of clothing.

Stephens' greatest achievement was to expose the horrors of the Bengal famine in 1946 through revealing pictures and gruesome stories day after day in the *Statesman* which made him unpopular in government circles in Simla. He did all a man could do to assuage human suffering on a massive scale and certainly brought the Government of India to its senses. The story is told that once when seeking an interview in the capital he wrote his name on the back of a particularly revolting famine picture and sent it in as his visiting card. In 1950, Stephens was in fear of assassination for some weeks and was guarded day and night by plainclothes police. "It was an occupational hazard for a *Statesman* editor," he said :

> For many years the *Statesman* published on the edit page an article by a Muslim contributor under the pseudonym Shahed. The identity of Shahed was kept a closely guarded secret Stephens did not know who he was even five years after he joined the paper and for several weeks after he became editor. "He was as much a mystery man to me as to the public," he said, "I then only discovered his identity by accident and thereafter had strong reason for secrecy." The mysterious contributor was Altaf Hussain, who was then in the service of the Government of India and who later became editor of the *Dawn*, the organ of the Muslim League. His articles in the *Statesman* provoked great controversy and were responsible for creating bitter feelings towards the paper among the nationalists.

On August 15, 1947, the *Statesman* wrote; "Now is the appointed day. Now is the day of salvation. If we start right, we can continue right. On everyone of us who live in India, be it in the Indian Union or Pakistan, there is a personal responsibility to start this day with our thoughts right.... It is the fitting climax of the intertwined story of Britain and India, the fulfilment of Britain's mission, a mission carried out under God's blessing with many failures to sense its greatness, with some inevitable personal yieldings to the lure of pomp and circumstance of pride and glory of the world and the love of money, but for all that a mission writ in the stars of the East and West and discharged from the British throne and the High Court of Parliament downwards with a large and steady faithfulness, through ever rarer good report and ever increasing ill-report.

Now the day has come and what was British India is resolved into two states. Let us waste no tears on that. The essential thing is to preserve and foster the unity of systems and of outlook that exists." Stephens, as we have noted already, resigned in 1951 as he disagreed with the Kashmir policy of the Government of India. The *Statesman* progressively changed into Indian hands and today it is a fully Indian-owned and Indian-edited newspaper.

When the *Statesman* celebrated its centenary in 1975, it wrote: "The *Statesman* has seen every development towards Indian independence, the Minto-Morley reforms, the Montagu-Chelmsford ones, the movements of Tilak, Gandhi, Subhas Bose and others. Its opinions have not always been popular though it was the first paper which Nehru used to read in the morning. But it has almost always been respected. Us technical standards have been high: for many years, for instance, either the Calcutta or the Delhi edition annually carried off the president's award for printing; several of its features, including the correspondence columns, have been rated by many competent judges as the finest in the country."

The *Statesman* was one of the papers which suffered during the Emergency for its anti-government postures. Today, it is a vigorous independent paper, fearlessly voicing its views on all questions affecting the common man and some of its investigative stories have achieved national prominence.

The Times of India : *The Times of India* is the oldest English daily in India and it is also a great newspaper which has played an important role in the development of journalism in this country. Before the advent of freedom and especially in the closing years of the last century and the beginning of this century, it had been a controversial newspapers which had stood as a bulwark of colonial rule and had nothing but contempt for Indians and their aspirations to freedom. It belonged to the class of British-owned newspapers which was described by one historian as those newspapers which were not "a model of sobriety and good manners. Their slighting and supercilious tone towards educated Indians wounded and alienated sensitive people." *The Hindu* wrote in 1900: "The *Englishman*, the *Pioneer* and the *Times of India* are three well-known organs of Anglo-Indian opinion which most violently oppose the advancement of the Indian people.

Much of the harsh treatment which of late we have received from our rulers is due to their incitement and in the future Indian reforms, we apprehend much trouble from these and other champions of the dominant class." It wrote again in 1909: "Most of the Anglo-Indian papers seem to consider themselves the watchdogs of the British Government in this country. They always take a high and mighty tone with the alleged delinquencies of Indians and think it their special mission to egg on the government to take this action or that."

In a vituperative attack on Indians in 1900, the *Times of India* wrote: "Mr Ranade's (Mahadev Govind Ranade, judge of the Bombay High Court) experience as a judge must have convinced him long ago that the people of this country set no value upon truth for its own sake. Indeed, the average Hindu lies by preference. Sentiments, however lofty and ennobling are thrown away upon people who are dead to the rudiments of virtue. Widow re-marriage, *sati*, polygamy, child marriage, all these are surface blemishes, symptoms and signs of the profoundly deep-seated canker at the heart, of Indian life—its hopeless want of honesty, its unexplained mendacity. The mass of the people are brought up in an atmosphere of lies. From the cradle to the grave, they are shadowed by the habits of lying and servility."

We have already seen in an earlier chapter how Robert Knight became editor of the *Bombay Times* and how by merging in it two other newspapers, renamed it *Times of India* in 1861. The first issue of the *Bombay Times*, a bi-weekly, appeared on November 3, 1838. Its editor was J.E, Brennan, a retired Irish doctor who was also secretary of the Bombay Chamber of Commerce. He wrote in the first issue on the need for education of the people of India "whose capacity for improvement is inferior to that of no one elsewhere", but who he thought were "spell-bound victims of ignorance and delusion." A later editor, George Buist, roused Indian sentiment by inciting other newspapers to demand reprisals against the Indians after the Mutiny in 1857.

The government did nothing to restrain him but when a Parsi shareholder, Nowroji Furdonji, objected, Buist was eventually dismissed. The *Bombay Times* had many Indian shareholders from 1850 to 1859 when Knight bought them. Under the editorship of Thomas J. Bennett, who later became the sole proprietor of the *Times of India*, the paper maintained close relations with Indians many of whom contributed to its columns. Bennett vastly improved the paper by bringing talented people from England among whom was a master printer, F.M. Coleman, who had wide experience of daily newspaper production.

With its high class printing and news service (it was the earliest newspaper in India to subscribe to Reuter's news service) the *Times of India* made rapid progress and in 1890 it printed daily 3000 copies. Indian subscribers were small in number because free public libraries served their needs. According to one writer, two circulating libraries between themselves took up one-third of the daily output of the paper at reduced rates. The copies were distributed to one class of subscribers at 6 a.m.: They were taken from them at 9 a.m. and passed on to a second group and then to a third group at noon. They were collected for a fourth time and "after ironing the well thumped copies were posted to upcountry places."

The *Times of India* in 1870 asked its readers to contribute items of interest and regular contributors were rewarded with a free copy of the paper. One observer of the period wrote: "The newspapers were never dull. When nothing outside deserved notice, editors started quarrelling among themselves which they pursued with rigour and diligence." Bennett and Coleman combined and formed a company called Bennett-Coleman Company which continues even today although it has changed into Indian hands. Bennett brought experienced journalists from England to edit the paper and they included Lovat Fraser and Sir Stanley Reed. Pat Lovett wrote in 1883, when he joined the paper, that it consisted of an editor, an assistant editor, a sub-editor, a chief reporter (all brought from England) and four reporters recruited locally, two of them Parsis.

In the wake of the partition of Bengal there was a spurt of violence and the British-owned press screamed for strong government action. It set itself to be a defender of the government and its technique was to snipe at Indians, both extremists and moderates. The government was in a mood to ignore their lapses from good taste and journalistic ethics. When the *Times of India* was hauled up for contempt of court during the trial of Tilak for sedition in 1897, it was let off with a warning.

Commenting on the articles in the British-owned press, Gokhale wrote: "The terms of race arrogance and contempt in which some of these newspapers constantly speak of Indians and specially of educated Indians cut into the mind more than the lash can into the flesh.... I would like to see the official who would dare to arrest and march to the police *thana* the editor of an Anglo-Indian newspaper. But so far as Indian editors are concerned, there are, I fear, officers in this country who would not be sorry to march whole battalions of them to the police *thana*".

The *Times of India* suffered serious loss of face in 1905 when an editorial writer or some imp of mischief played a dirty trick on it. A newspaper reprinted an article which it said had appeared in the *Times of India* and it was a condemnation of Lord Curzon, the viceroy. It began: "One might well wish that Lord Curzon had not returned to Indie for the second time for he could not have chosen a more effective way of wrecking his reputation than he has done." The article was reprinted by more and more newspapers and the *Times of India* which had always considered Curzon as its hero, was embarrassed.

It issued a contradiction but even then the article continued to be reprinted, both in India and England. At the Surat session of the Congress in 1907, which ended in confusion, a representative of the *Times of India,* Pears, who covered the proceedings for his paper, was manhandled and suffered injuries. When the president of the session, Rash Behari Ghosh was in physical danger, it was Pears who escorted him back to the pavilion.

The *Times of India* was favourite target in the early years of the century was Sir Pherozeshah Mehta, the Congress leader in Bombay. In 1901, during a debate on a land revenue bill in the Bombay Legislative Council Mehta, Gokhale and others staged a walk-out which caused surprise because it was considered strange for Moderates to indulge in that kind of protest. The *Times of India,* in an editorial written by Lovat Fraser (Mehua's bitter enemy) made fun of Mehta and his friends.

It wrote: "It is difficult to contemplate seriously the spectacle of Mehta striding towards the door in order to emphasise the novel theory that the duty of the true patriot is to run away while the gentlemen who rather sheepishly stole after him only excites feelings of compassionate amusement. Mr Meath does not often make tactical mistakes but he blundered rather badly in his pre-arranged exit from the council hall.

Meant to be dramatic, his performance was merely comic... He forgot too, that little scenes of this description should at least convey the idea of spontaneity; whereas a good many people knew beforehand what was going to happen. It is a risky experiment for public men to take to histrionics towards the end of their careers." In an earlier editorial, the paper complimented Mehta and his associates on their proficiency in the English language. Commenting on the speeches made at a meeting addressed by Mehta and others, it said at least two or three of the speakers "displayed knowledge of the English language in its more subtle aspects which is gratifying to those of us who believe that there is a great intellectual future before the leading Indian races. Indeed, three of the creators on the occasion, Messrs Telang, Badruddin and Mehta, showed themselves to possess as great a mastery of our somewhat difficult Cicero ever did as of the Greek, accomplishment on which the foremost Roman orator rather prided himself."

K. Rama Rao who served as a sub-editor of the *Times of India* in the 1920s wrote that "subject to the natural limitations of a European-owned institution, there was freedom from race prejudice, certainly on the editorial side." Once, he recalled, "a European official walked into the sub-editors' room with a communique announcing the release of Gandhi. He was so much surprised at the presence of so many Indians that the next day he confronted the editor in his club and in the presence of others called the *Times of India* a " Black man's show".

The editor complained to the governor and the official had to apologise. On another occasion, Sir Stanley Reed, editor, wrote that every Englishman in India was ashamed of the deeds of General Dyer at Amritsar (General Dyer was responsible for the Jallianwala Bagh massacre). A section of the Europeans in Bombay was offended and it was reported there was a plan to give a "sound thrashing to the impudent journalist who had let down his country." A timely hint enabled Reed to keep out of the club until tempers cooled down.

It was a complete paper, Rama Rao wrote, "carrying the highest prestige in particular for its sports and commercial coverage. It carried more Indian news than many Indian papers." The two basic principles which governed the *Times of India,* according to Rama Rao, were that the King's Government must be carried on and the political susceptibilities of the Indian people must be respected. Among the editors, S.T. Sheppard was one who was kind to the staff and stood up for their rights.

During the editorship of Sir Francis Low, which saw a climax in the battle for freedom and a confrontation between the press and the government, the *Times of India* touched heights it had not reached before and according to Rama Rao it outstripped other papers in point of circulation and volume of news printed. Frank Moraes became the first Indian editor when freedom came. The *Times of India* passed into Indian hands in 1946. Its sister journal, the *Illustrated Weekly of India,* started in 1888 is today one of the major weeklies and a host of other journals in Marathi, Hindi and English have been added to the group including the *Economic Times* (1916) which was the first daily dealing with financial and economic news to be published in India. The *Times of India* today occupies a premier position and it has the second largest circulation among English dailies, according *to Press in India,* 1984.

The Tribune : Gandhi said in 1932: "The *Tribune* is the best viewspaper......Its editor's readings and analysis of events are unsurpassed." He said of its great editor, Kalinath Ray: "Long live Kalinath Ray! His articles nowadays on the communal problem and on joint electorates for Harijans bear witness to his deep knowledge and wide experience." Kalinath Ray was to the *Tribune* what G. Subramania Aiyer and Kasturiranga Iyengar were to *The Hindu* and Motilal Ghosh to the *Amrita Bazar Patrika.* He was a Bengali who had worked on Surendranath Bannerjee's *Bengalee* Calcutta before he came to Lahore in 1917 to take over editorship of the *Tribune.* He was a fearless writer who bravely faced the risks involved in fighting the strongly entrenched alien government. His fierce attacks on the Punjab Government and on General Dyer, hero of

Jailianwaia Bagh in 1919 led to his being arrested and sentenced to two years' imprisonment.

On appeal, however, it was reduced to three months. Ray had his differences with Gandhi. He did not believe in non-violence and the methods adopted by Gandhi to achieve freedom but he was a good Congressman and took an active part in the freedom struggle. He told Mulk Raj Anand, the novelist: "We Bengalis do not agree with Gandhi that India can win freedom with non-violence. We can embarrass the government with non-cooperation. But they will not go with our *dharnas*.

Some of our young students have turned terrorists.... You know one of the men who threw the bomb at Lord Hardinge in 1911 was a Bengali called Rash Behari.... He escaped to Japan afterwards. And one of our writers, Sarat Chandra, has written a novel lauding the gospel of tit for tat." Mulk Raj Anand said he had heard that Rabindranath Tagore did not approve of Gandhi's non-violence. Ray said: "Yes, he says that the illiterate people in a non-violent *dharna* may not remain non-violent. The natural thing men do is to defend themselves. Only the Jains are supine and Gandhi is from Gujarat where Jainism is still practised." Ray added after some thought: "I wish I had the courage to do something more than write editorials."

Amolok Ram, a former editor, has said that Ray who edited the *Tribune* for 28 years was known for his uprightness, integrity, sobriety and independence. He did not allow his judgement to be influenced by personal or sectarian considerations. Nor did he brook any interference, internal or external in the conduct of the paper. "Intensely patriotic as he was, he wrote with passion and vehemence but his views were based on reason and fairness," Amolok Ram said.

"It was a treat to read his analytical editorials particularly at a time when the British bureaucracy was out to suppress all patriotic aspirations." Kali Babu, as he was affectionately called by his admirers, was generally disinclined to meet any

V.I .P. He rarely attended any social function. He had a deep insight into the affairs of state and the working of various political organisations. He differed from Gandhi on certain aspects of the non-cooperation programme and expressed his opinion candidly and freely.

But he had a high regard for those with whom he happened to differ. In spite of his differences, he gave unrelenting support to Gandhi in the long and arduous fight for freedom. Although the *Tribune* was an uncompromising critic of British rule, Ray commanded great respect even among the British bureaucrats of the day. He maintained the highest journalist standards. He did not indulge in character assassination, nor in hitting below the belt. J.N. Sahni who served under him says that Ray was the *Tribune*. He wrote the entire editorial page and sometimes his writing overflowed into another page.

"Whatever he wrote was logical, scintillating and convincing." A.C. Bali, special representative of the *Tribune,* told a story about Jawaharlal Nehru and Ray. Nehru had come to Lahore once in the course of a tour of the Punjab. He asked Bali why the *Tribune* took particular care to call him Mr. Nehru or Pandit Nehru. Why could it not call him just Jawaharlal Nehru as in the case of Stalin or Churchill? Ray's reply when he was told about this was that Nehru had not yet attained the heights which Stalin or Churchill had in the international sphere.

Ray emerged with chronic asthma from prison and never recovered. He passed away in 1943 and the *Tribune* passed through many ups and downs until the final calamity in 1947 when, on the eve of independence, two of its staff members were stabbed and the publication of the paper in Lahore was suspended.

The *Tribune* was started as a weekly in Lahore in 1881 by Sardar Dayal Singh Majithia who was a great admirer of Raja Ram Mohun Roy and the Brahmo Samaj. He was helped by Surendranath Bannerjee to buy a printing press and chose as its first editor, Sital Kanta Chatterjee of Dacca. The *Tribune,* which became a daily in 1906 had a number of Bengalis as its editors in its early career, including Kalinath Ray. Bipin Chandra Pal was its editor for some time in the early years. A great philanthropist and prominent nationalist of northern India, Sardar Dayal Singh established a trust for the *Tribune* which continues to function till today. In its first issue on February 2,1881, the *Tribune* said: 'The aim of the *Tribune* will be, as its name imparts, fairly and temperately to advance the cause of the mute masses.... We shall strive as much as lies in the compass of our humble abilities to create and educate such opinion."

The progress of the *Tribune* was intertwined with the country's political and social history and especially of the north-western region which at one time extended from Peshawar to Delhi and from Quetta to Karachi. It wielded great influence in the region comprising the North West Frontier Province, the pre-partition of Punjab, Sind and Delhi. From its inception, it succeeded in making itself a recognised organ of public opinion. It often clashed with the British rulers who were determined to suppress the freedom movement but it stood like a rock in the performance of its duty to educate the people and inculcate in them the spirit of patriotism and resistance to oppression and tyranny. It earned the reputation of being a fearless champion of the cause of the people and of freedom.

On the eve of independence when Punjab was partitioned, riots rocked Lahore and a mob attacked the office of the *Tribune.* Two members of the staff were killed, the printing machinery building and land were lost. The paper suspended publication. In a telegram to Vallabhbhai Patel, home minister, the manager of the paper, said: "*Tribune* Lahore has lost, property, cash, machinery, newsprint etc., worth Rs. 25 lakhs. Newsprint worth Rs. 2 lakhs removed under orders of the West Punjab Government to government printing press, Lahore. Our van and six typewriters have also been given over to *Pakistan Times*. Our press and office have been sealed by the government. I learn that our press and building are being given to *Pakistan Times"* Patel asked the Rehabilitation Minister, K.C, Neogy to give all facilities to the *Tribune* to resume publication from Indian soil.

The *Tribune* had opposed partition but when it became a *fait accompli,* its trustees decided to continue to publish it from Lahore and its editor wrote an editorial supporting Jinnah's views. Jinnah appreciated the *Tribune's* stand but the chaos and anarchy that followed partition left no option for the paper and it moved to Simla and later to Ambala in May, 1948. The paper's rehabilitation was unexpectedly rapid and the support it received from the people was phenomenal, said Amolok Ram, its editor.

The *Tribune* moved to its present home in Chandigarh in 1969. The paper, whose editor then was Madhavan Nair, got into trouble with the Government of India during the Emergence in 1975. It was one of the three papers blacklisted by the government and denied advertisements and other facilities. Two sister papers, one in Pubjabi and the other in Hindi *(Punjabi Tribune and Dainik Tribune)* were started in 1978 and were an instant success.

In the words of Sahni: "Apart from the high standard of integrity shown by its editors ever since the paper was founded, the *Tribune* has built up a rare tradition for fairplay, restraint and courageous pursuit of truth. This has been possible to a considerable extent also because of a succession of able managers (who resisted pressures from the advertisers' lobby) and the understanding shown by the trustees....The present Editor-in-Chief, Prem Bhatia, has not only preserved but also enhanced the reputation of the paper as a fearless exponent of public opinion and an understanding critic of the government."

5

National Movement

The impulse of national awakening generated by Rammohun Roy in Bengal soon spread to other parts of India. It resulted, by the mid-19th century, in the formation of British Indian Associations by educated Indians in the Presidency cities of Calcutta, Bombay and Madras as well as citizens' forums in some other large towns like Midnapore in Bengal and Poona in Maharashtra. These associations urged steps towards representative government and sent petitions to the British parliament for a less expensive and more responsive administration in India. Alongside the formation of political associations, Indian-owned newspapers sprang up in various parts of the country. Many of them advocated political and social reform.

Vital Contribution

The anti-British uprising of 1857, largely confined to upper India, did not spring from the forward-looking impulse generated by Rammohun Roy. The revolt was fuelled by a variety of grievances : the anger of the Indian sepoy (from the Hindi term sipahi) in the East India Company's forces at, the racial discrimination he suffered ("Though he might give, the signs of the military genius of a Haider, he knew he could never attain the pay of an English subaltern wrote a British officer, Lt. Col. J. Holmes); the anger of princes and princesses dispossessed by the British; and the resentment of the upper classes and castes at being treated on a par by the British, in law courts, with lower cast Indians-though Englishmen were not treated on a par with Indians.

The disaffection that found dramatic expression in 1857 was presaged by certain incidents. English officers of the Army, who had no understanding of the sepoy's psyche, introduced changes which the men resented. In 1806 in Madras, British officers of the local army of the East India Company decided to smarten up the appearance of the sepoys. They were ordered to discard their caste marks, trim their moustaches and to wear a leather cockade with the turban. Leather was a sensitive article. In the context of the widespread fear that the foreigners were out to make Indians lose cast : caste and convert to Christianity, Hindu sepoys feared that the cockade might be of cow's hide. Muslim sepoys suspected that it might be of pig's skin.

The Hindu veneration of the cow and prohibition of its killing had its origin as a safeguard for preserving this valuable species of animal, provider of milk as well as of draught animals, from being eaten up in times of famine and becoming extinct. The Muslim abhorrence of the pig was out of aversion to the filth which the animal wallowed in and consumed. There was a near-mutiny at Vellore on the issue of the leather cockade. The regulation requiring it was withdrawn — but only after severe punishment of the protestors.

Hindu sepoys shared the superstition that going out of the country, or crossing the sea, was sinful. In the war of 1824 with Burma, Hindu sepoys of the Bengal army feared that they might be asked to embark from Chittagong port. During the Afghan war they dreaded having to go beyond the boundary of the Indus river. These psychological anxieties had already heightened the state of tension when, in 1856, the East India Company dissolved the kingdom of Oudh and took over the territory. The soldiers from upper India in the Bengal Army felt outraged. It marked the onset of a rebellious mood in the Company's forces.

Against this background, the greased cartridge caused an emotional explosion. The Brown Bess fire-arm of the sepoy was being replaced by the Enfield rifle manufactured at Dum Dum near Calcutta. Word got round that objectionable animal fat had been used for greasing the cartridges, instead of wax and oil. Both Hindu and Muslim sepoys were enraged. That the sepoys suspicion was not groundless is clear from what the correspondent of the London Times wrote from India at the time: "The government ordered mutton fat for the purpose. Some contractors, to save a few shillings, gave pigs' and bullocks' fat instead."

Newspapers published in Indian languages reflected and strengthened popular sentiment. Jagdish Prasad Chaturvedi writes : "It was in 1857 itself that *Payam-e-Azadi* started publication in Hindi and Urdu, calling upon the people to fight against the British. The paper was soon confiscated and anyone found with a copy of the paper was prosecuted for sedition. Again, the first Hindi daily, *Samachar Sudhavarshan,* and two newspapers in Urdu and Persian respectively, *Doorbeen* and *Sultan-ul-Akhbar,* faced trial in 1857 for having published a fireman by Bahadur Shah Zafar urging the people to drive the British out of India." Rev. Long said in a report he prepared for the Government in 1859 : "The opinions of the native press may often be regarded as the safety valve which gives warning of danger. Thus, had the Delhi native newspapers of January 1857 been consulted by European functionaries, they would have seen in them how the natives were ripe for revolt, and were expecting aid from Persia and Russia."

An immediate consequence of the Uprising for the Indian Press was a Regulation which came to be known as the, Gagging Act. Promulgated by the Governor-General, Lord

Canning, on 13th. June 1857, it imposed in the whole of India the Adam regulations enforced in Bengal in 1823. The philosophy behind the 1857 Act was articulated candidly, by Lord Elphinstone, Governor of Bombay. He quoted approvingly the statement by Sir Thomas Monroe that "A free Press and the domination of strangers are things which are quite incompatible and which cannot long exist together." Elphinstone went on to say: "Our Government in this country can never be a popular government in any sense of the term.

It must be a despotism, tempered by wise and just laws impartially administered, tempered also by the education and feelings of its rulers, and by their responsibility to Parliament and to the British nation... No one who knows the country will be wild enough to assert that the people are fit for representative institutions-and self-government... If, then, a despotic form of government is, indeed, the only one suitable to the state of the country, it follows that if the unrestricted liberty of the Press is incompatible with this form of government, and with the continuance of our rule in this country, it must be curtailed."

The 1857 Uprising and its suppression made little difference to the process of national awakening that was initiated by Rammohun Roy. It continued, to spread all, over India and, resulted in the formation of citizens' associations comprising lawyers, teachers and other sections of the English educated intelligentsia and the emergence of nationalist newspapers. Illustrative of the link between, and the mutually reinforcing effect of, citizens' associations and the emerging nationalist Press is the fact that the Madras Mahajana Sabha was founded in 1884 in the premises of the Hindu, which had been established in 1878 as a weekly newspaper.

The term 'Hindu' at that time, and till the early part of the 20th century when the poet Mohammad Iqbal wrote his celebrated patriotic poem Sare jahan se achha Hindostan hamara, stood for Indian. It did not refer only to a particular religious community. Among the benefactors of the *Hindu* were Nawab Humayun Jah Bahadur, a descendant of Tippu Sultan, and a prominent Christian, William Pillai. G. Subramania Iyer, the first editor of the newspaper, was once asked how these non-Hindu friends approved its name. "Why,", he replied, "they all considered it the best name because it expressed the national sentiment best."

The interchangeability of 'Hindu' and 'Indian' must be borne in mind in connection also with the *Hindu* which was brought out in Sind in 1912 and had among its editors Jairamdas Daulatram and Dr. Choitram Gidwani till its closure at the time of partition. Earlier, the *Hindoo Patriot* was founded at Calcutta in 1853 by Girish Chandra Ghosh as a nationalist journal. Manmohan Ghosh, the poet, was associated with the newspaper and his campaign against the exploitation of peasants who were forced to cultivate indigo on uneconomic terms resulted in the formation of an Indigo Commission under the chairmanship of Seton-Karr, Secretary to the Government of Bengal.

The launching of the weekly *Sulabh Samachar* in 1870 as the organ of the Indian Reform Association of Bengal was a landmark in Indian journalism. Published by Keshub Chandra Sen, the Brahmo Samaj leader, at one piece -per issue it was the first attempt to reach those who were poor but literate. Its circulation rose to between three and four thousand, which was remarkable for the time.

There had been a lessening of government control over the Press following the Proclamation of 1st November 1858 by which Queen Victoria--meaning in effect the British government assumed direct responsibility for the governance of India; the Governor General now had the additional title of Viceroy. But the liberalisation did not last long. The promulgation of the Vernacular Press Act in 1878 marked a return to the punitive attitude that marked the greater part of the East India Company's rule. *Amrita Bazar Patrika,* which had been started as a Bengali weekly in March 1868 by Sishir

Kumar Ghosh and his brothers, changed into a Bengali-English bilingual journal in 1869 and was shifted to Calcutta in 1871. It thus remained out of the reach of the Vernacular Press Act.

This racially discriminatory law empowered the district authorities to demand and to confiscate security. It was opposed by Sir William Robinson, a member of the Madras Governor's Council: "Inconvenient though the extravagance and occasional want of loyalty evinced by the vernacular press may be, we possess in it a useful barometer of native feeling and sentimental barometer such as no manacled or sycophant press could possibly continue to be serious objections present themselves to my mind to the proposal to treat differentially the English and Vernacular press. The existing race-alienation, spreading and widening daily, is serious enough as it is; and I confess that I think that some of the low radical writing of England, e.g. of the Bradlaugh School, which is read with avidity in South India, is doing far more material harm than anything that the Vernacular press is diffusing.... The very existence of a press worthy of the name of a press such as we require in the country as an exponent of native feeling is at stake."

On the other hand, it was argued in defence of the measure by Sir Ashley Eden, Lt. Governor of Bengal, that the English language newspapers were brought out "by a class of writers, for a class of readers, whose education and interests would make them naturally intolerant of sedition", in contrast to the tone of many vernacular newspapers. The controversial law was eventually repealed in 1881 by Lord Ripon, the new Viceroy, after the Liberals under Gladstone, who had denounced the Vernacular Press Act, came to power in Britain.

But the relationship between the nationalist Press and the alien regime continued to be of tension and conflict. A notable instance was the sentencing of Surendranath Banerjee (a future president of the Indian National Congress) to two months' imprisonment on the ground of contempt of court, for a leaderette about the Calcutta High Court which appeared on

2nd April 1883 in the *Bengalee* of which Banerjee was the proprietor and editor. The editorial condemned justice Norris for ordering a Hindu idol to be brought into court for identification. "We have now amongst us a judge who, if he does not actually call to mind the days of Jeffreys and Scroggs, has certainly done enough, within the short time that he has filled the High Court Bench, to show how unworthy he is of the high office.... There have been very many cases both in the late Supreme Court and the present High Court of Calcutta regarding the custody of Hindu idols, but the presiding deity of a Hindu household had never before-this had the honour of being dragged into court. Our Calcutta Daniel looked at the idol and said it could not be a hundred years old. So Mr. Justice Norris is not only versed in law but is also a connoisseur of Hindu idols... It does seem to us that some public steps should be taken to put a quietus to the wild eccentricities of the young and raw dispenser of justice."

The comment was based on information which had appeared in the *Brahmo Public Opinion. As* there was no contradiction,, Surendranath Banerjee accepted the version as correct. *A* writ was served on him on 2nd May 1883. W.C. Bonnerjee (another future president of the Congress) undertook to defend him on condition that Banerjee should express regret for and withdraw the reflections he had made on justice Norris. Banerjee agreed because he felt that the comparison with Jeffreys and Scroggs was indefensible and written in a moment, of indignation. On 5th May the case was heard by a full bench consisting of five judges presided over by the Chief justice, Sir Richard Garth. The majority of the Judges, who were Europeans, were for sentencing Banerjee to imprisonment. Justice Romesh Chunder Mitter suggested fine only. The Chief justice talked to him to persuade him to agree with the majority but Mitter did not agree.

The sentence of the majority was pronounced, Mitter dissenting. Public reaction was swift and intense. Surendranath Banerjee wrote later in his autobiographical *Making of a Nation* about "the honour (for such I deem it) of being the first Indian of my generation who suffered imprisonment in the discharge of a public duty". He said: "I have never witnessed except in connection with the agitation for modification of the, partition of Bengal, an upheaval of feeling so genuine and so widespread as that which swept Bengal in 1883.

Public meetings of sympathy for me and of protest against the judgment of the High Court were held in almost every considerable town. So strong was the feeling that in some cases even Government servants took part in -them and suffered for it. These demonstrations left an enduring impress on the public life of the province."

Surendranath Banerjee also took a leading part in the campaign in support of the Illbert Bill of 1883 which sought to remove racial discrimination in the administration of justice. The Criminal Procedure Code had, till then, limited the jurisdiction over European British subjects to judicial officer who were themselves European British subjects. The Bill, which came to be named after Sir Courtney Illbert who moved it, sought to remove this distinction.

The European community, official and non-official, launched a virulent agitation against the Bill. They even insulted the Governor General, Lord Ripon, at the gate of Government House when he returned from Simla to Calcutta in 1883. A compromise was eventually reached under which district magistrates (who included Indians) would be empowered to try European British subjects but by a jury of which at least half the number was to be European.. As European jurors were not easy to find in the districts, most cases would have to be transferred to the High Court with its European majority.

The outburst of Anglo-Indian anger at the Illbert Bill was a recrudescence of the white racialist feeling which was expressed in the British-owned Press following the events of 1857. On the reaction to the 1857 Uprising, Sir George Trevelyan had remarked "The tone of the Press was horrible. Never did the cry for blood swell so loud as among those Christians and Englishmen in the middle of the nineteenth century. The pages of the brutal and grotesque journals published by Herbert and Marat, during the agony of the French Revolution, contained nothing that was not matched and surpassed in the files of some Calcutta papers... What could be more audacious than to assert that Providence has granted us a right to destroy a nation in our wrath?"

On the other hand, it must be acknowledged to the credit of a minority of liberal-minded Englishmen in India that they supported the Indian advocates of reform on democratic lines, and of a free Press. Even as James Silk Buckingham had stood by Rammohun Roy in the early part of the 19th century, Robert Knight of the British-owned *Statesman* of Calcutta was on the side of Indian nationalists vis *a vis* the Vernacular Press Act and the Illbert Bill. On the Press legislation, the *Statesmant* wrote: "Sir Ashley Eden's discreditable measure was brought suddenly before the Council, and passed through all its stages at a single sitting." Robert Knight also joined Surendranath Banerjee in condemning the opposition to the Illbert Bill. Interestingly, among the opponents of the Bill was Justice Norris.

Primary Political Strength

To Surendranath Banerjee (1848-1925) belongs the credit it, at least as much as to Allan Octavian Hume, for the formation of the Indian National Congress in 1885 Banerjee sought to bring together on a national forum the numerous citizens' associations that had been formed in the capitals of the three Presidencies and in other towns. The kind of issues that were taken up by these regional political associations, and the close link between nascent patriotism and the nationalist Press, are illustrated by the following extract from the biography of the *Hindu* of Madras published on the occasion of its centenary:

> "At the time the *Hindu* appeared on the scene, public opinion in Madras was stagnant and there

were very few recongnised forums to voice the feelings and grievances of the Indian population. The earliest popular association to be formed was the Madras Native Association which came into being in July 1852 through the efforts of a group of English-educated Indians. Its object was to investigate and ventilate public grievances and to submit petitions and memorials to the powers that be to redress them. Its first president was Gazulu Lakghminarasu Chettiar. Almost the first thing the Association took up was a campaign against proselytisation, which had assumed serious proportions; attempts were being made to introduce the Bible as a textbook in government schools.

The Association was aided in its work by a journal *Crescent* founded in 1844 by Laksminarasu Chettiar for the amelioration of the Hindus'. The association became the focal point for an agitation against torture for collecting government dues. As a result of its campaign, a torture commission was appointed which found most of the allegations well founded and suggested steps for, their removal. With the death of Lakshminarasu Chettiar in 1868 the association and the paper which he founded languished and died.

"Soon after, another journal, the *Native Public Opinion,* was launched owing to the efforts of Sir T. Madhava Rao and Dewan Bahadur Raghunatha Rao. Some time later, A. Ramachandra Aiyer brought forth the *Madrasee,* and with it was amalgamated the *Native Public Opinion.* The amalgamated journal fell into the hands of men who were opposed to the general current of educated Indian opinion... When the *Hindu* made its appearance it became the sole representative of Indian opinion. With its arrival, political activity was also revived, with the Madras Native Association coming back to life under the presidentship of V. Bashyam Iyengar.

A number of government officials were members of the association, as there was no ban on their participation in public associations. But the position changed when Sir Mountstuart Grant Duff became Governor of Madras in November 1881. Though no ban as such was imposed, the activities of officials in the association were looked upon with suspicion and many of them left the association, which came to an abrupt end. There was no political association to ventilate the people's grievances till the Madras Mahajana Sabha was formed in the premises of the *Hindu* in 1884.

Famed for his eloquence, Surendranath Banerjee was the first nationalist to achieve all-India influence. He undertook a speaking tour of India during 1877-78 to protest against the reduction of the age limit for competing in the Indian Civil Service examination. He convened in December 18.83 at Calcutta a national conference of the politically conscious among the intelligentsia. Attended by more than a hundred delegates from various parts of the country, it was something like a national parliament and thus a precursor of the Congress sessions of subsequent years.

Around the same time the formation of an all-India forum of educated Indians was canvassed by an Englishman, Allan Octavian Hume (1829-1912). He had come to India in 1849 as a member of the civil service and spent the greater part of his career in district administration. Having served during the 1857 Uprising in the North West Provinces, where much of the fighting took place, Hume felt the need for a channel of communication between the rulers and the ruled. He proposed, on his retirement from government service in 1882, the formation of an association which would, in his own words, serve as "a safety valve for the escape of great and growing forces".

The British rulers at that time had contacts with members of the 'princely order, but not with educated Indians of the middle class. Hume put it to the Viceroy, Lord Dufferin, that it would be advantageous to the government to have a responsible body through which 'the best Indian opinion' could be gathered. Dufferin did not demur, though he was shortly to form an adverse impression both of Hume and of the Congress.

Thus came to be formed towards the close of 1884 an Indian National Union- which, in consultation with the Bombay Presidency Association, the Sarvajanik Sabha and others arranged to hold an all-India conference in December 1885. The aim was to "effect cooperation between the leaders of thought in various parts of the country and decide upon a plan of political campaign."

The all-India conference was to have met at Poona, with the Sarvajanik Sabha forming the reception committee. But an outbreak of cholera led to the shifting of the venue to Bombay where the trustees of the Gokuldas Tejpal Sanskrit College and Boarding House at Gowalia Tank placed the spacious building at the disposal of the organisers. On 28th December 1885, '72 good men and true', representing a cross-section of the most advanced political opinion, assembled at the Congress--as the gathering was appropriately named.

It is noteworthy that there was a sizeable contingent of journalists along with other categories such as lawyers, representatives of regional political associations, members of municipalities and local boards, and doctors. The 14 journalists were, in the alphabetical order of the cities they came from:

> Agra : 1. Babu Jamnadas, Pleader, municipal commissioner and editor, Nassim; Allahabad: 2. J. Ghosal, editor, Indian Union; Ambala : 3. Babu Murlidhar, pleader, representing the Tribune; Bombay : 4. Behramji M. Malabari, proprietor and editor, Indian Spectator; 5. N. G. Chandavarkar, editor, Indu Prakash; Calcutta : 6. G.B. Mookerji, editor, Nababibhakar; 7. Norendranath Sen, proprietor and editor, Indian Mirror; Coimbatore : 8. S.P. Narasimhulu Naidu, editor, Crescent and

member of the Local Board; Lucknow : 9. Munshi Gangaprasad Varma, proprietor of Hindusthani; Madras : 10. G. Subramania Aiyar, editor of the Hindu; 11. M. Viraraghava Chariar, sub-editor, the Hindu, and secretary, Madras Mahajana Sabha; Poona : 12. Ramchandra Moreshwar Sane, Marathi editor, Dnyan Prakash; 13. Sitaram Hari Chiplonkar, honorary secretary and editor of the quarterly journal of Poona Sarvajanik Sabha; and 14. Gopal Ganesh Agarkar, Professor, Fergusson College, and editor, Mahratta and Kesari.

Conspicuous by his absence at the founding session of the, Indian National Congress was Surendranath Banerjee, who organised a similar gathering at Calcutta a few days earlier. It is possible that he deliberately kept himself away lest the new organization should be suspect in the eyes of the British authorities through association with a forthright nationalist.

The Press in the Maharashtra region of western India grew at an impressive rate. It reflected the trends, sometimes conflicting, of social reform and of single-minded patriotism.

Mahadev Govind Ranade (1842-1901), a leading social reformer, started the *Indu Prakash* in 1862, editing the English side of the bilingual paper while J.S. Gadgil was his associate as the Marathi editor. In 1898, Ranade put down the following survey of the Marathi Press : "As regards newspapers, at present we have a large number, about 100. Three of them are dailies and the rest are mostly weeklies. Every zila town, and in some districts every taluka town, has one or more newspapers. Compared with the state of things thirty years ago, no department of literary activity has made more sensible progress than the newspapers.

The best newspapers, some 16 in all, count their subscribers by thousands, whereas thirty years ago it was difficult to secure as many hundreds. On the staff of the best newspapers literary talent of a very high order is engaged, and in some cases the editors are well paid for their labour. Still it must be remarked that most of these mofussil newspapers are enterprises carried on for finding work for the press hands which cannot be fully engaged otherwise in their own proper work, and the so-called editors are insufficiently educated and poorly paid."

Another early social reformer was Gopal Ganesh Agarkar (1856-95) On graduation from the Deccan College Poona, he decided to lead a frugal life and apply himself to social service. Along with Vishnu Krishna Chiplonkar and Bal Gangadhar Tilak (1856-1920), Agarkar founded the nationalist weekly *Kesari* in Marathi. The *Mahratta* was its English counterpart *Kesari* said in the first issue in January 1881 : "A continuous flow of writing in the newspapers from various places have the same value as the street lights and the regular police patrol in the night have. The honesty of government officers is maintained so long as their functioning is brought before the eyes of the people from time to time.... One can well imagine how much benefit will accrue by discussing in newspapers matters like which old practices are worth giving up, and which new ones worth taking up."

Agarkar relinquished the editorship of *Kesari* when he found that Tilak's views were at variance with his own on subjects like child marriage. Tilak was a radical in his nationalist fervour but a conservative in social matters. On one occasion he performed penance after taking tea in a Christian missionary school. On 24th March 1918 he attended and spoke at an all India Depressed Classes Conference under the presidentship of the progressive Maharaja of Baroda, but could not bring himself to sign a personal pledge against observing untouchability in day-to-day life.

Tilak wanted to concentrate attention on the struggle for political freedom. When the Indian National Congress met in 1895 in Tilak's home town of Poona, those opposed to Congress involvement in social reform threatened to bum down the *pandal* if the National Social Conference founded by Ranade in 1887 (which had for years met annually as an adjunct of the Congress) was allowed its use.

In the words of Aurobindo Ghosh, the patriot who turned his back on the Indian Civil Service after passing the examination with high distinction, and was later to become the sage of Pondicherry: "Tilak has felt strongly that political emancipation is the one pressing need for the people of India and that all else not directly, connected with it must take a second place... A subject nation does not prepare itself by gradual progress for liberty; it opens by liberty its way to rapid progress." On leaving *Kesari,* Agarkar started own bilingual journal *Sudharak* (Reformer). The English columns were contributed by Gopal Krishna Gokhale (1866-1915), who founded in 1905 the Servants of India Society and was acknowledged by Gandhiji as his mentor.

In the south there was a similar parting of two distinguished journalist colleagues on the issue of social reform: G. Subramania Iyer and M. Veeraraghava Chariar. They were among the founders of the *Hindu* as a weekly in September 1878 and were its joint owners when it became a daily in April 1889. G. Subramania Iyer (1855-1916), the editor, was devoted as passionately to social reform as to political advance. Veeraraghava Chariar felt perturbed by the adverse effect of the *Hindu's* advocacy of radical reform (ending untouchability, boycott of child marriage, remarriage of child widows, and women's education) on a section of the newspaper's clientele; he also feared that it might affect the expansion of the *Hindu's* circulation. This prompted the establishment of a journal, the *Indian Social Reformer* by K. Natarajan who, was on the staff of the *Hindu.* (Natarajan later moved to Bombay from where he continued to publish the journal.)

G. Subramania Iyer moved at the founding session of the Indian National Congress at Bombay the first resolution that called for the appointment of a Royal Commission, with adequate, Indian representation thereon, to enquire into the working of the Indian administration. A social reformer who practised what he preached, Subramania Iyer conducted, while at Bombay, the remarriage of his daughter Supriya, who had become a widow at the age of thirteen, with a young man of his choice who was working in that city. The marriage took place in the house of Raghunathdass, well-known champion of widow remarriage in western India, and was attended among others by Dewan Bahadur Raghunatha Roy, a pioneer of social reform in the south.

Subramania Iyer's devotion to the improvement of the status of Indian women was so strong that he dissented from Annie Besant's high praise of Hinduism coupled with condemnation of western civilisation in the course of a speech she delivered at Madras in 1893. He wrote : "If nothing else, western civilisation is superior to that of the East in being able to produce women of the culture and capacity and courage of conviction which have made Mrs. Besant and many others of her sex a power for good in their land and in other lands... Until it (Hinduism) does produce such a one, we for our part cannot appropriate for Hinduism the praises which Mrs. Besant so generously lavished on our ancestors." The differences between him and his partner reached breaking point in October 1898, when Subramania Iyer left the *Hindu.* He applied his full attention to the *Swadesamitran,* which he had started as a Tamil weekly even while he was editor of the *Hindu,* and which he converted into a daily.

In Punjab, a prominent leader both of social reform and of political awakening was Lala Lajpat Rai (1865-1928). He belonged to the Arya Samaj, founded by Dayanand Saraswati who denounced the belief in short cuts to salvation through fasts and pilgrimages or through listening to medieval Puranic texts. Taking his stand on the very Vedas that were invoked by orthodox Hindus, Dayanand campaigned in the mid-19th century against idol worship, untouchability,- child marriage and the relegation of women to an inferior status; he advocated women's education, free choice of husband, and the right of everyone to study the Vedas. Lajpat Rai started a newspaper called *Bande Mataram*, the rallying cry of the movement against Bengal's partition in 1905.

Following the failure of the 1857 uprising which aimed at rescuing the Mughal emperor from usurpation by the British, Indian Muslims withdrew into the shell of religious orthodoxy. They kept away from the new educational institutions which taught modern knowledge through the English language. Since the national movement spearheaded by the Congress was led mainly by English-educated Hindus, the British rulers of India found it expedient to patronise the leaders of the Muslim community : the surviving aristocracy of Nawabs, and the conservative religious leaders. Even-an advocate of social reform and modernisation like Sir, Syed Ahmad Khan (1817-98) was, unlike many of his Hindu counterparts, a loyalist who urged his co-religionists to seek advancement through allegiance to the alien rulers.

The partition of Bengal, mooted by Lord Curzon as Viceroy in 1903 and implemented in 1905, were designed ostensibly to improve the administration by breaking up an unwieldy province, but it was meant in fact to weaken the nationalist movement by striking at its base. Of the 18 annual sessions of the Congress held from 1885 to 1902, four (the maximum at any one centre) had been hosted by Calcutta. Bengali leaders had presided over six of the fourteen sessions held outside Calcutta. Curzon made no secret of his intention of encouraging Muslim separatism.

Addressing a gathering at Dacca in Muslim majority East Bengal, he said: "When a proposal is put forward which would... invest the Mohammedans in Eastern Bengal with a unity which they have not enjoyed since the days of the Mussalman viceroys and kings, which must develop local interest and trade to a degree that is impossible so long as you remain the appendage of another administration-can it be that the people of these districts are to be advised by their leaders to sacrifice all these great advantages from fear ? Do you mean to be so blind to your future as to repudiate the offer ?"

Implementation of the partition decision set off a vigorous movement of mass protest in the province, with sympathetic reaction in other parts of the country the like of which had not been witnessed before. The common people, including women, were for the first time galvanised into political action. During the anti-partition agitation were forged the weapons of Swadeshi (buying only Indian-made goods) and its counterpart Boycott (of foreign, specially British-made goods which were being dumped in the captive Indian market). Little could Charles S. Boycott, the agent for Lord Erne's estate in Ireland who refused rent reductions during the land struggle of 1880 and was subjected by the Irish tenants to the withholding of all services and social contacts, have imagined that his name would enter history. The technique employed against him came to be known as boycott, and was adopted in far lands.

The harsh measures adopted by the alien rulers to suppress the anti-partition, movement led to acts of violence directed against British officials, and to revolutionary journalism. The revolutionary course had been advocated even earlier by pioneering radicals like Shyamji Krishna Varma and Bhikhaji Rustom Cama. Repression served to confirm and strengthen the revolutionary viewpoint.

Shyamji Krishna Varma (1857-1930), who mastered both Sanskrit and English, was attracted by Dayanand Saraswati's advocacy of cultural nationalism based on India's Vedic heritage. Returning to India after studying at Balliol College, Shyamji served as administrator in Ratlam and some other princely States, regarding them as old citadels of the country's freedom in contrast to 'British India' which was directly under the foreign heel. When the alien authorities made it impossible for Shyamji to function in, India, he left for England where the climate for freedom of expression was relatively more favourable. In 1899 when Britain declared war on Transvaal, wanting to annex this territory in southern Africa where gold and diamond fields had been discovered, Shyamji supported the Dutch descended Boers in their fight against aggression. (This was in contrast to the attitude of young Mohandas Karamchand Gandhi who, as a barrister in South Africa, assisted the British during the Boer war).

In relation to India and every country, Shyamji believed in the dictum of Herbert Spencer, the British thinker whom he greatly admired, that "Resistance to aggression is not simply justified but imperative. "These words served as the motto for *The Indian Sociologist*, a political monthly which Shyamji started in London in 1904. He also instituted a scheme of scholarships in memory of Shivaji and of the heroes of the 1857 Uprising, for Indian students who wished to pursue higher studies in England. A condition attached to these scholarships was that the recipient would not, after his return to India, accept any paid post or honorary office under the British (whereas the aspiration of most educated young Indians of the middle class in those days was to enter the Indian Civil Service or at least a provincial civil service).

Shyamji established an India House at Highgate (much before the present building of that name in Aldwych which houses the Indian High Commission), to provide board and lodging for Indian students. He founded in February 1905 a Home Rule for India Society (anticipating the Home Rule League of Annie Besant and Bal Gangadhar Tilak) with the objective of obtaining for India what was its indefeasible right-a government of the people, by the people and for the people."

While London was hospitable in those days to refugees from the rival imperialist countries of Europe, there were definite limits to the British government's tolerance of critics of its own colonialism. Shyamji had to shift his headquarters and his journal *Indian Sociologist* to Paris (which did not grudge protection to rebels against its British rival). He left India House in the care of a younger revolutionary, the redoubtable Vinayak Damodar Savarkar (1883-1966). Savarkar had come to London in 1906 on a Shyamji scholarship named after Shivaji, for which he had been commended by Bal Gangadhar Tilak.

Bhikhaiji Cama (1861-1936), from an affluent Parsi family of Bombay, was one of the earliest to take to the revolutionary path. She lived abroad from 1902 and was associated in London and Europe with the revolutionary leaders Shyamji Krishnavarma, Virendranath Chattopadhyaya (a brother of Sarojini Naidu), Savarkar and Lala Har Dayal. She began in 1909 the publication from Paris of a journal under the title *Bande Mataram.* Madame Cama explained in a message to the people of India, published in her journal, why she had taken to the path of violent revolution : "Some of you say that as a woman I should object to violence. Well, I had that feeling at one time.

It was repugnant to me even to talk of violence... (But) why should we deplore the use of violence when our enemies drive us to it? How is it that the Russian, Sophy Perovoskai and her comrades are heroines and heroes in the sight of Englishmen and Englishwomen while our countrymen are considered criminals for doing exactly the same thing for the same cause ?" Madame Cama was imprisoned for three years during the First World War and was allowed to return to India only in 1935.

Virendranath Chattopadhyaya brought out another revolutionary journal, *Talwar* Sword from Paris in November 1909. In the course of an article contributed to the opening issue of this journal, V.D. Savarkar justified the recourse to violent methods in these words : "We feel no special love for secret organisations or surprise and secret warfare... It would be a crime to talk of revolution when there is a constitution that allows the fullest and freest development of a nation. Only because you deny us light, we gather in darkness to compass means to knock out the fetters that hold our mother down. You rule by bayonets.

It is a mockery to talk of constitutional agitation when no constitution exists." Savarkar was of the view that Gandhiji's method of passive resistance was bound to fail "because it presupposes all men to be selfless and (that they) will not cooperate with the aggressor"; further, it "blindly presumes that the aggressor has a high sense of morality." Across the Atlantic, Har Dayal, another emigre revolutionary, published *Ghadar* as the organ of the party that he founded under the same name, consisting of Indian settlers in the U.S.A.

In India, Barindra Kumar Ghose, younger brother of Aurobindo Ghose, founded *Yugantar* in 1906 as the journal of the revolutionaries. About the writings in *Yugantar* a sessions judge remarked: "They exhibit a burning hatred of the British race; they breathe revolution in every line; they point out how revolution is to be effected." The articles recalled the history of revolutions in France and other countries and commended the winning over of soldiers to the cause along with their arms, pointing out that the revolutionists in India had the additional advantage that the rulers were foreigners.

Aurobindo Ghose himself attracted the adverse notice of the authorities for his writings in *Bande Mataram,* run by Bipin Chandra Pal from August 1906. Aurobindo wrote a series of articles propounding the doctrine of passive resistance as an instrument of political action : "In a peaceful way we act against the law or the executive; but we passively accept the legal consequences." Aurobindo was prosecuted for seditious writing. During the trial Bipin Chandra Pal, when questioned as a witness about Aurobindo's editorship, refused to testify and was sentenced to six months' imprisonment. The magistrate .acknowledged that "the general tone of the *Bande Mataram is* not seditious", but sentenced the printer to a few months' imprisonment.

Aurobindo was again among those arrested and charged for conspiracy in connection with a bomb incident on 20th April 1908 at Muzaffarpur in Bihar. The attack was aimed at D.H. Kingsford who had earlier, during his posting as chief presidency magistrate at Calcutta, ordered the severe flogging of several nationalist young men.

The Government responded to the revolutionary situation by promulgating in June 1908 the Newspaper (Incitement to Offences) Act. Tilak was tried for writing articles containing alleged incitement to rebellion. When a jury of seven Europeans and two Parsis held, by a majority, that Tilak was guilty, he was awarded the harsh sentence of six years' transportation and was imprisoned at Mandalay in Burma.

The 1908 Act was followed by a more comprehensive measure, the Indian Press Act of 1910. It empowered district magistrates to levy and to forfeit security deposits from publishers of newspapers and keepers of presses; to authorise searches and to declare printing presses and newspaper copies forfeited to the Government; and for prohibition of the transmission by post of copies of newspapers deemed to contain objectionable matter.

During the agitation against the partition of Bengal, the British authorities tried to make it appear that disaffection was confined to Hindus. Bengali Muslims, it was claimed, were opposed to the campaign of Boycott and Swadeshi.

The *Manchester Guardian* sent out its own correspondent, Henry W. Nevinson, to find out the truth and report it. This is what he said in a despatch carried by *M.G.* of 3rd January 1908: "Late the other night, as I sat on the river steamer after a long day of listening to leaders of Hindu opinion, leaders of Mohammedan opinion, and English officials, five or six dark forms gathered round me with gestures of secrecy. They were merchants who had large dealings in Manchester cotton and in consequence were generally shunned. Barbers would not shave them, milkmen would not sell them milk, friends would not go to their daughters' marriage. It was distressing and inconvenient. Would I please set everything as it was before?

> "I have no doubt all they said was entirely true, except perhaps their assertion that the Mohammedans insisted on having Manchester

> goods. The Mohammedans in this province have most to gain by the Swadeshi movement, for they form the great majority of the handloom weavers, and owing to Swadeshi that industry, for which Dacca was long famous over the world, has in the last two years not only revived but redoubled,."

The fair coverage of the anti-partition agitation by *Manchester Guardian* was all the more remarkable because Manchester cloth, brought into India at a negligible or nil import duty, was the principal target of the Boycott campaign. This objectivity was characteristic of the newspaper which, under the editorship of Charles Prestwich Scott since 1872, had become 'an engine of liberalism'. Forty years after Nevinson's despatches from Dacca, the great regard in which Indian nationalists held *Manchester Guardian* found expression when talks took place in London, on a partnership arrangement, between Reuters and a delegation representing Indian newspapers. J.R. Scott, second son of C.P. Scott and manager of the *Manchester Guardian,* was a member of the Reuters team, but he was ill and could attend only the first few meetings.

After the negotiations had failed to yield a final agreement, Swaminath Sadanand—the one who was most out of sympathy with Reuters among the five members of the Indian team-wrote to J.R. Scott on 23rd June 1948 : "It was a great privilege to me, as to my other colleagues, to make your acquaintance. The *Manchester Guardian is so* woven into the fabric of the Indian freedom movement that we look upon it as much our institution as yours. That knowledge, I trust, will be of great satisfaction to you. The way to one world and world citizenship lies through the ways of the *Manchester Guardian.* We all wish you a speedy recovery."

Force from Opposite Side

A natural sequel to the creation of a Muslim-majority province by dividing Bengal was encouragement by the British rulers of the formation of an all-India Muslim political organisation that would be loyal to them and would counter the Indian National Congress.

Two decades prior to the emergence in 1906 of this prop to British rule, a Muslim journal had argued against the introduction in India of representative institutions on the Western democratic model. *The Mohammedan Observer* wrote in January 1887, justifying the policy of abstention from the Congress pursued by the Central National Mohammedan Association: "English education has not made such progress among Muslims as among Hindus. To insist upon open competition as the only mode of selection for state employment means the absolute exclusion of the Mohammedans from the public services. To ask for representative institutions, without sufficient guarantees for the representatives of the minority, means swamping of the minority by the majority.

There is more hope of a fair equilibrium being maintained from the political wisdom of a neutral government than from the generous instincts of a majority looking primarily but naturally to the interests of its own bulk. The minority have a right to see their interests safeguarded. And we say advisedly that until our people have come abreast of the Hindus in education and political intelligence, political concessions to the majority, without sufficient guarantees for the protection of the minority, would be destructive to the latter."

The approach commended by this journal was articulated by a Muslim delegation headed by the Aga Khan that waited on Lord Minto, Curzon's successor, at Simla on 1st October 1906. That the delegation was sponsored by the British authorities is clear from an entry of the same date in the diary of Lady Minto : "This evening I have received the following latter from an official: 'I must send Your Excellency a line to say that a very, very big, thing has happened today. A work of statesmanship that will affect India and Indian history for many a long year. It is nothing less than the pulling back of sixty-two millions of people from joining the ranks of the seditious opposition."

What was His momentous event ? It was the Viceroy's acceptance of the principle, urged by the Muslim delegation, of separate communal electorates of Muslims instead of the territorial electorates that send representatives to democratic assemblies.

The delegation told Lord Minto that representative institutions of the European type should be "adapted to the social, religious and political conditions obtaining in India." The delegation wanted that Muslims, who formed between one-fifth and one-fourth of the total population of India, should be given a more than proportionate share both in the legislatures and in public employment—"The position accorded to the Mohammedan community in any kind of representation, direct or indirect, and in all other ways affecting their status and influence should be commensurate not merely with their numerical strength but also with their political importance and the position which they occupied in India a little more than a hundred years ago, and of which the traditions have naturally not faded from their minds." In other words, Muslims as the former ruling class were to be treated as more than equal to other Indians.

The Viceroy's reaction was predictably sympathetic. He agreed that "any electoral representation in India would be doomed to mischievous failure which aimed at granting a personal enfranchisement regardless of the beliefs and traditions of the communities composing the population of this continent."

Within three months, Nawab Salimullah of Dacca proposed the formation of a central Muslim organisation to the leaders of the community who had gathered there for the Mohammedan Educational Conference. Accordingly, on 30th December 1906, a political association called the All India Muslim League was formed. Its objects were to promote feelings of loyalty towards the British government and to protect and advance the interests of the Muslims of India.

Separate electorates for Muslims or the election of Muslim members of legislatures by Muslims only were provided for in the Indian Councils Act of 1909. This meant that candidates would seek votes through competitive espousal of Islam and thus strengthen the sense of a separate Muslim identity. Based on the reforms formulated by the Viceroy, Lord Minto, and the Secretary of State, Lord Morley, the Act provided for the appointment for the first time of an Indian member on the Viceroy's Executive Council, and the appointment of Indian members in the provincial executive councils.

The central legislative council was to have a majority of official members. The elected members were to be chosen on a narrow franchise based on property and education qualifications, with lower qualifications in the case of Muslims. There was weightage for Muslims through reservation of seats in excess of their share in the population.

Ramsay MacDonald of the Labour Party, who later became Prime Minister of Britain, observed that "the Mohammedan leaders are inspired by certain Anglo-Indian officials, and these officials have pulled wires at Simla and in London, and of malice aforethought sowed discord between Hindu and Mohammedan communities by showing the Muslims special favour."

The representation granted to Muslims was so disproportionate that *Empire,* an Anglo-Indian newspaper of Calcutta, wrote: "When the Councils meet, there seems every probability of the Government finding themselves in a position analogous to that of the Light Brigade in the famous verse, slightly adapted:

'Moslems to right of them
Moslems to left of them
Moslems behind them
Volleyed and thundered!

> "Probably the Government never imagined that they would have so many Mohammedans to deal with, but there the fact remains."

Lord Hardinge, who replaced Minto as Viceroy towards the close of 1910, realised that there could be no peace till the partition of Bengal was ended. Its annulment was announced on the occasion of the visit of the British king and queen, George V and Mary, for the Delhi Durbar in December 1911. Simultaneously, it was announced that the capital would be shifted from Calcutta to Delhi.

Though the annulment of Bengal's partition was widely welcomed, it came after the British had injected the poison of Muslim separatism into India's body politic. This was to lead to a second partition of Bengal in 1947 as part of the break-up of the sub-continent into Pakistan and a diminished India.

Pivotal Players

The beginning of the 20th century was marked by fierce repression by the alien rulers and persecution of the Indian press, especially the language press, in the wake of the anti-partition agitation and the *Swadeshi* movement which spread to all parts of the country. The centre of activity shifted to Maharashtra where a new revolutionary leader was born. His countrymen called him "Lion of Maharashtra" but the rulers in the words of Valentine Chirol, viewed him as the "father of Indian unrest". He was Lokmanya Bal Gangadhar Tilak who dominated the Indian political scene and journalists for two decades.

Chirol described him as "one of the most dangerous pioneers of disaffection". "He was the triumphant champion of Hindu orthodoxy", he wrote, "the high priest of Ganesh, the inspired prophet of a new nationalism which in the name of Shivaji would cast out the hated *Melachas* and restore the glories of Mahratta history. The government feared him. His activity was unceasing. He disdained none of the arts which make for popularity.... In private and public, through his speeches and through his newspapers, he worked upon the prejudices and passion of both the educated and the uneducated and especially upon the crude enthusiasm of the young.... He had been one of the first champions of *Swadeshi* as an economic weapon in the struggle against British rule and he saw in the adoption of the boycott with all the lawlessness it involved, an unprecedented opportunity of stimulating the active forces of disaffection."

Chirol said that Tilak relied on the enthusiastic support of men like Bipin Chandra Pal and Aurobindo Ghose, who were his political disciples though their religious and social views greatly differed from his. Chirol noted that not even Gokhale with all his moral and intellectual force could stem the flowing tide of Tilak's popularity in Maharashtra. Barristers, teachers and, in fact, the large majority of the educated class worshipped him and his propaganda filtered down even to the labourers in the cities and the riots in the villages. "His house was a place of pilgrimage for the disaffected from all parts of India" Chirol said. "His reputation for profound learning... his trenchant style, his indefatigable activity, the glamour of his philanthropy, his accessibility to high and low, his many acts of genuine kindness, the personal magnetism which, without any great physical advantage he exerted upon most of those who came in contact with him and especially upon the young, combined to equip him more fully than any other Indian politician for the leadership of the revolutionary movement."

Tilak was the first Indian to understand the political importance of mass communication. He was also the first to exploit conservative religious sentiment for political work. Tilak's methods as a journalist were not those of the Bengali journalists. In his own words, "the Bengali journalists sought to teach people how to criticise the bureaucracy and at the same time keep oneself safe, bodily at least, if not pecuniarily," but this was foreign to Tilak's nature.

Fresh Approach : An Indian historian has noted that the most paradoxical aspect of the Indian ferment was that "new ideas and aspirations were being thrust upon a traditional society the bulk of which was still far from education and modernism. The unrest wanted to be comprehensive enough to appeal to the Old and the young, the illiterate and the educated, the reactionary and the nihilist alike." Alfred Lyall was surprised at the strange spectacle in certain parts of India "of a party capable of resort to methods at once reactionary and revolutionary; of men who offer prayers and sacrifices to ferocious divinities and denounce the government by seditious journalism, preaching primitive superstition in the modern form of leading articles."

> "The rise of radical nationalism in India", says an Indian writer, "which became marked after 1904 was at once a conservative and a revolutionary phenomenon. It drew its inspiration on the one hand from the reaction towards Indian religion and Indian way of life of which the chief exponents had been Dayanand Saraswati and Swami Vivekananda in the last quarter of the 19th century. On the other hand, it tries to apply to the Indian situation methods of mass agitation and even terrorism borrowed from the west."

Tilak disguised his political movement behind a religious revival by organising the Ganesh festival. He gave it a secular garb by bringing in Shivaji the founder of the Mahratta empire and reviving in the minds of the people memories of the glorious past. He denied it was an anti-Muslim gesture and said: "Our political aspirations need all the strength which the worship of a *Swadeshi* (native) here is likely to inspire in our minds. For this purpose, what greater hero than Shivaji could be found in Indian history?"

Taste of Success : Tilak's achievement was to give for the first time to the nationalist movement a much broader basis, than neo-western liberalism could ever supply. A Western observer wrote that it was in the press rather than on the platform that Indian politicians, whether "extreme" or merely "advanced" were apt to let themselves go. "They write down to the level of their larger audiences." Lord Morley said about articles in the language press: "It is said these incendiary articles are mere froth. Yes, they are froth but froth stained with bloodshed."

The writer we have quoted continued; "Even when they contain no definite incitement to murder, no direct exhortation to revolt, they will show how systematically, how persistently the wells of Indian public opinion have been poisoned for years past by those who claim to represent the intelligence and enlightenment of modern India. Only too graphically also do they illustrate one of the most unpleasant characteristic features of the literature of Indian unrest—namely the insidious appeals to the Hindu scriptures and the Hindu deities and its deliberate vilification of everything English. Calumny and abuse combined with a wealth of sacred imagery supply the place of any serious process of reasoning."

In 1906, the Viceroy, Lord Minto, was worried over the close connection between the Congress and the language press. In a letter to the Governor of Madras, Sir Arthur Lawley, he said: "One cannot disguise from oneself the danger ahead—the close connection of Congress with the vernacular press, generally disloyal... while at home political agitators from India, in close cooperation with members of Parliament are, I am afraid, bringing influence to bear on H.M.'s Government which may make things very difficult here."

Lovet Fraser, editor of the *Times of India,* accused the government at home of having instigated men like D.O. Donnell to write to Indian leaders like Surendranath Bannerjee with the intention of keeping the anti-partition agitation alive and affording the liberal ministers an opportunity to reopen the issue of partition. D. O. Donnell had written to Bannerjee in March, 1906: "Keep on agitating and do so effectively. Large mass meetings are the most useful... you have the justest of causes and I hope you will make your voice heard. Everything depends on you in India and remember a Whig does nothing unless pressed."

Minto saw for the first time in December, 1906, "a direct attempt to sow disaffection or rather revolt in the native army" in the extracts from the Indian press including one from the Bombay language paper, *Vihari,* placed before him. The viceroy thought: "If tampering with the Indian Army were to increase and if there were any signs of its gaining a foothold, it would be impossible to shut one's eyes to the danger one is face to face with risks here which it is impossible to express to people at home without being looked upon as an alarmist." Minto believed that the inflammatory articles in the Indian press "hurled contempt and hatred at the administration. If this journalism was merely an expression of impossible ideas it would not have mattered much but a good deal of it was direct instigation to get rid of the British."

In June, 1907, Lord Kitchner, commander-in-chief, in a secret minute mentioned the "harmful influence which the native press is having on the native army". "I have had occasion", he said, "to notice the extent of this evil before now, but within the last few months so much additional evidence has been brought to my notice that I have no hesitation in saying that from a military point of view I am convinced that the time has now come when it is absolutely necessary that we should take steps to put an end to or at least to modify the very mischievous effect which the native press is now unfortunately having on the Indian Army."

Minto began to take action against the Indian press in 1906. He launched many prosecutions which brought him into conflict with the Secretary of State, Lord Morley. In June, 1906, *Punjabee,* a Lahore newspaper was prosecuted and its editor was sentenced to six months' imprisonment. In the same year, the editor of *Hindu Swarajya* a Bombay newspaper, was sentenced to one year's rigorous imprisonment. Morley was not quite happy with the campaign against the press and he wrote to Minto: "Press prosecutions and editorial imprisonments are delicate things with a strongly Liberal House of Commons in front of one. I think it is only too likely that we shall before long be in for some measures of the repressive sort. But before entering on that policy, we must have consultation and discussion."

There were protest demonstrations and unrest in Punjab following the conviction of the editor of the *Punjabee.* Minto wrote to a worried Morley: "The *Punjabee* is really owned by Lajpat Rai, one of the most advanced Congress leaders and I have no doubt the action of the paper was deliberately prompted. It may be open to doubt if the Punjab Government should have prosecuted or whether it should have been left to the police officer concerned... to prosecute the paper off his own bat for libel. I am inclined to think the Punjab Government was right." The Government of India wished to support the Punjab Government strongly because sedition was spreading rapidly in the province, Minto said.

Any lukewarm support of the local Government was fraught with danger. Elsewhere, the utterances of newspapers were growing outrageous, he said. The Government could not ignore them. To punish them lightly would only make matters worse because it would give the newspaper the publicity a seditious editor sought. Severe treatment was the only remedy. "It is a question whether we can count on inflammatory writing falling flat or whether we consider it so dangerous that we must, by some means or other, put a stop to it", the viceroy told the secretary of state. Morley said so long as press offences were dealt with by courts of law, justice might be done but prosecutions without the process of law were grave matters. He advised the viceroy not to forget the susceptibilities of the people at home "to the virtues of an unfettered press.... So I do hope you will keep a sharp hand over the local Governments and bid them to seek orders from you in matters of this delicacy."

The Government of India admitted that some press prosecutions "were foolish" and to ensure legality, it asked the Home Department to draw up regulations for press control. The viceroy realised that the Anglo-Indian press was equally responsible in fomenting discontent but in a different way. He referred to a letter in an Anglo-Indian newspaper written by a "Britisher" and said: "One could not have read anything much more worse—the bitterness of the writer's demand for immediate punishment of native political organisations and his eagerness to be selected to administer that punishment himself. Nothing could be worse than the native press, but the low standard Britisher can do much to increase the evil."

However, little was done to check the Anglo-Indian press which carried on a tirade against Indians, while restrictions on the Indian press were tightened. In June, 1907, the Government of India published a resolution "warning all newspapers against publishing seditious matter and authorising local Governments to institute prosecutions for sedition.

The resolution said: "The Government of India have recently had under their consideration the unbridled licence of certain publications of the press throughout India. They have also considered the deleterious moral effect which such publications are having throughout the country. The governor-general in council is convinced that such a state of things cannot be allowed to continue and it is, therefore, resolved that in all cases where matter tending to create sedition, ill-will towards government, of ill-feeling between the various races inhabiting India has been published in any newspaper or other publication, local Governments and administrations shall be empowered to proceed against those responsible for all such publications under the existing powers of the law."

The viceroy said in justification of the resolution, that the country required the "preservation of the *izzat* of the local authorities which was in the eyes of many people much more important than the rectification of grievances." He added that the press had begun to influence the army and this was "too grave a menace to ignore.,"

The year 1907 saw a series of arrests and prosecutions of editors and journalists and confiscation of presses. The editor of *Hindustan,* Dina Nath was arrested in June, 1907, for complicity in the charges brought against the editor of *India* in Gujranwala (Punjab). In July, the editor of *Yugantar* of Calcutta was prosecuted for sedition and sentenced to a year's imprisonment. The magistrate ordered the confiscation of the press where the paper was printed. In the same month, the editor of *Sonar Bangla* also of Calcutta was arrested. Later in the month, the police raided the office of *Bande Mataram* and the editor, Aurobindo Ghose, was arrested for sedition. The editors of *Hindustan* and *India* were sentenced to five years' rigorous imprisonment each.

But apparently these convictions did not produce results, for the governor of Bengal pointed out: "We can put the wretched editor into jail but until we can also stop a paper upon conviction for sedition, I do not think that we can achieve any result worth the cost." The governor said some "miserable and unworthy person" achieved martyrdom and the paper "goes on all the same, stirring up greater bitterness." Press Prosecutions, prescriptions and confiscations became the order of the day in 1907 and 1908.

Tilak, himself, was sent to prison for articles in his paper *Mahrana* and Aurobindo Ghose, editor of *Bande Mataram,* sought asylum in the French territory of Pondicherry. Police raids, house searches and espionage became everyday affairs in the lives of Indian journalists. In January, 1910, the viceroy told the newly enlarged Legislative Council that the government would no longer tolerate the freedom of a revolutionary press which led to outbreaks of violence. He had said earlier in another speech that he did not think India was ripe for freedom of the press.

On February 8, 1910, the Indian Press Act which imposed fresh restrictions on the press was passed. Between 1910 and 1914, several demands for security were made on the press. Two papers in Bombay which were asked to furnish a security of Rs. 5,000 each, closed down. There were cases of papers in other provinces closing down being unable to pay security. A statement by the Press Association of India, formed in 1915 to protect the interests of the press, said that up to 1917, 22 newspapers had been asked to furnish security and 18 had shut down.

Between 1917 and 1919, 963 newspapers and printing presses which had existed before the Press Act of 1910 had been proceeded against under the Act. The statement mentioned that 173 new printing presses and 129 newspapers were killed at birth through demands for security. The government collected about Rs. 5 lakhs during the first year of the Press Act through securities and forfeitures. Over 500 publications were prescribed under the Act.

As the gulf between the rulers and the people widened still further with the wave of repression and action against the press, political leadership passed from Bengal to Maharashtra where Tilak held sway through his journals and on the platform. Tilak was the soul of Indian politics in western India. His audacity and adventurous spirit his geniality and easy accessibility made him an ideal leader of a popular movement. It was said of him: "There are abler politicians in India as also men gifted with better constructive statesmanship but no politician or publicist comes up to him in point of tenacity of purpose, courage and bulldog determination."

Tilak began his journalism career when he and his associates started the *Kesari* (Marathi) and *Mahratta* (English) in January, 1881. It was announced that the *Kesari* would deal with political and economic developments in the country and also world events. It would write objectively and impartially and truth would be its watchword. "The evils of flunkeyism and flattery", the sponsors said, "have been growing since the beginning of the imperial rule and surely every honest man will admit that it is harmful to the true interests of the country." In its first editorial, the *Kesari* compared newspapers to night watchmen and said their responsibility was to keep executive officers in wholesome fear of public opinion. It declared its intention of improving social conditions by frankly telling the people what was bad and harmful.

The *Mahratta* aimed at the educated section of the community "who required to be provided with material for thinking intelligently on the important topics of the day." While the *Kesari* sought to educate the public and promote popular agitation, the *Mahratta* set out as the authoritative spokesman of educated public opinion in Maharashtra. In addition to discussing at length every political question, it presented to its readers a selection of views from foreign and Indian journals.

The two journals became an immediate success. The *Kesari* became by the end of 1882 the largest circulated language paper in the country and the Mahratta was acknowledged as the leading mouthpiece of Indian political thinking in western India. "The two papers" one writer remarked, "owed their success to virile, impassioned writing, animated at all times by lofty patriotism and the courage of conviction".

6

Academic Elements

Tilak firmly believed in the benefits of English education and strove hard to promote it. He used to say that English education like Tiger's milk was a strong diet. If Indian youth had an English education, the country's freedom would not be far away, he said. "Tilak was a great writer in every sense of the term", an admirer has written. "Yet, oddly enough, he was a writer who disliked writing. Most of his journalistic writings were dictated by him and they read like speeches. This, however, served to increase their effectiveness for when his views on healed issues were read to groups in villages—this was the usual way of spreading the message of his newspapers—people accepted them as if Tilak were speaking to them in person. His style was always direct and his sentences short and crisp. His writings were crystal clear and went straight to the heart of his readers.

They were full of quotations from the ancient Sanskrit works, popular sayings, historic parallels, apt metaphors and, above all, pregnant with forceful and original ideas. Tilak was an editor-philosopher who had a message to give to his readers and he gave it with fire and imagination.... Week after week, he poured out his soul on day-to-day problems, economic questions, philosophical ideas, historical researches, literature and art. Whatever subject he touched, he gave it a new lustre and lucidity."

The editor of *Subhodha Patrika,* an influential reformist weekly, said that Tilak's writings had a "bullet-like piercing quality—the shot told because it was meant to tell.... Behind the *Kesari* was an editor who knew his facts thoroughly, who knew the art of selecting the right thing at the right moment and whose powerful pen was wielded with a single pointed aim to make his political gospel a living sentiment among his people—and, above all, who was absolutely indifferent to dangers in furthering the cause of his country's independence which was the supreme aim of his life".

In an interview Tilak said: "When I started the *Kesari,* people asked me why I was going to publish it in Marathi. They said, 'None will read it'. But I was determined to publish it in Marathi and I said my decision was final. They then asked me to reserve at least two columms for English material. Again I replied categorically that it was impossible. *Kesari* was for the people and the people were sure to give it a rousing reception. Today, the *Mahratta* (English weekly) has to be financed from the funds of *Kesari.* When we started *Kesari* we had to make almost a new language.

In the old Marathi there was plenty of writing on devotion and philosophy; also the ballad writers had introduced an element of heroics into it. But to discuss serious matters of politics, to attack and rebut opponents, to crush them with satire and ridicule, for all this, the old Marathi was of very little use. And so we were forced to develop a new terminology to make our writings effective. A man who feels intensely, who is burning with new ideas finds words to express them. He becomes, indeed, capable of creating a new language."

Tilak believed that lack of political freedom was at the root of all evils in the body politic of India. He was not an opponent of social reform but said it should wait till the achievement of political freedom when it could be carried out without difficulty. The Anglo-Indian papers, especially the *Times of India* and *Pioneer*, called Tilak a bigoted Hindu leader dreaming of a *Mahratta* empire. Their campaign against him descended to absurd and indecent levels.

Tilak first clashed with the government when they decided the ultimate course of Tilak's career. From then on we see him not only as a leader in the fight for national independence but also as the special champion of the peasants whose emancipation became the purpose and passion of his life."

During the plague which ravaged Pune and the countryside, Tilak appealed to the Government to seek the cooperation of the people and direct the officials to show a little more common sense and consideration. He led a citizens deputation to the Special Officer, W.C. Rand, to protest against the harsh and oppressive measures taken by him to deal with plague. *Kesari* wrote that popular resentment had reached to breaking point and it asked: "What people on earth, however docile, will continue to submit to this sort of mad terrors?" Tilak was not opposed to anti-plague measures; he only pleaded with the officials to treat the Indians with decency and humanity when they went to their houses for disinfection measures and to aggregate plague victims.

Opposition to Special Officer Rand culminated in his murder along with that of another official. The government thought there had been a conspiracy to murder Rand and that Tilak was the moving spirit behind it. When people had complained of British soldiers, 'misbehaviour' Tilak advised them to use "force in self-defence which is legal". Tilak condemned the repressive measures which followed Rand's murder in two articles in *Kesari* headed: "Has the government lost its head?" and "To rule is not to wreak vengeance". Friends warned him that his language was harsh and might get him into trouble. Tilak replied: "I write strong language, I admit.

But my heart is full of indignation at the injustice which is being perpetrated by the officials and the words which come out are the natural outburst of the feelings inside me. I am convinced that I am within the limits of the law in criticising the government's measures, however strong the language I use."

Four weeks later, Tilak was arrested on a charge of writing seditious articles. The Bombay governor's action was a sequel to the attack on Tilak by the Anglo-Indian press led by the *Times of India* Tilak hit back at them in a series of articles in *Kesari.* He wrote "English editors have begun to rave in a fit of anger.... The Anglo-Indian community is at present exceedingly prejudiced and is in a fit of frenzy. It is not in a mood to listen to reason.... In our view, Indian newspapermen have done their duty admirably in this crisis and if anybody is to be blamed it is the government itself because it turned a deaf ear to the genuine complaints of the public. All this talk of branding Indian newspapermen as seditious is nothing but an attempt to evade responsibility and to put the blame on others."

Tilak said. "To create or lead peaceful opposition to foreign rule and to rouse a spirit of resistance is not sedition. True sedition is to incite people to armed rebellion in order to secure independence or the redress of a wrong. If anybody follows the line of direct incitement to violence, then it is sedition and it is the duty of government to punish such people. But to inflict punishment indiscriminately on the guilty and innocent alike is certainly atrocious. If the government abides by the law and keeps its head, then the people will also remain peaceful.

The responsibility of avoiding an armed revolution is on the leaders of the public; so also is it on the government officials, but if the latter do not do their duty and the people take to violence, it is sheer injustice to hold the leaders responsible for the violence because they preach patriotism, devotion to religion and resistance to injustice which is not incitement. To work against the British is included among the crimes listed in the category of sedition. This means that any article which is likely to lead to a revolution or a rebellion can come under the sedition section (of the I.P.C). At the same time, the explanation which is appended to this section states that to point out the mistakes and injustices of the administration is not sedition and, therefore, we see no reason to desist from strongly criticising any government action.,"

The Anglo-Indian papers tore the words in these articles out of context and twisted them to suggest they were seditious and preached murder. The *Times of India,* which published extracts from the articles, said: "The atmosphere which such teaching must have created is precisely the atmosphere in which violence to individuals, hatred of government and widespread contempt for authority and law would necessarily grow...."

Popular Case

Tilak's trial began on September 8,1897, and lasted six days. In his summing up, the Judge, Strachey, defined "disaffection" as simply "want of affection" which he further explained as "ill-will, dislike and enmity." Tilak was sentenced to 18 months rigorous imprisonment. Tilak told an official who talked to him after the verdict: "The Anglo-Indian newspapers have branded me anti-British, but they forget that I pay the highest tribute to the British and their character by following their example in opposing what I consider evil in the administration. Then again, as there is no Parliamentary system in India somebody has to perform the duties of the opposition. I have constituted myself and my two newspapers as the permanent opposition of H.M.'s Government of India."

Attempts were made prior to the verdict by Tilak's friends to persuade him to apologise to the government and save himself from prosecution and imprisonment. Among them was Motilal Ghosh, editor of *Amrita Bazar Patrika* of Calcutta, who was anxious that Tilak should not challenge the government at that stage. Tilak replied to them "My position among the people depends entirely upon my character and if I am cowed down by the prosecution—in my heart of hearts I know the case for the prosecution is the weakest that was ever placed before a jury—I think living in Maharashtra is as good as living in the Andamans.... Their object is to humiliate the Poona leaders and I think they will not find in me a *kutcha* reed as they did in some others. As an honest and honourable man, how can I plead guilty to the charge of entertaining ideas of sedition when I had none? If I am convicted, the sympathy of my countrymen will support me in my trouble."

Indian newspapers without exception condemned the verdict and Justice Strachey's definition of "disaffection". *The Hindu* wrote: "The news (conviction of Tilak) has been received everywhere with intense grief and with a sense of humiliation. It is not law and justice that have been vindicated, but that the policy of reaction, which for some time the enemies of the Indian people have been urging, has triumphed.

It has been the great object of these unscrupulous men whose one aim is to keep the people of India in a condition of slavery, to strike a crushing blow at the party of progress and they now have succeeded in their object. They have succeeded in producing depression and despair everywhere." The *Indian Mirror* of Calcutta said: "It seemed the judge and the advocate-general had changed places.... What with the tendencies of the times, the present temper of the European community in India and the prejudice excited against the *Mahrattas* of Poona since the murder of Rand and Lt. Ayerest, the verdict was practically a foregone conclusion."

Tilak resumed the editorship of the *Kesari* in July, 1899, with these words. "Despite the new situation now created (by the novel definition of sedition), we are determined to continue to work for the attainment of our objective *(Swaraj)*. We need not be afraid of anybody so long as our hearts are pure and unsullied by hatred."

In the thick of the agitation against the rigours of the anti-plague measures in Pune, Gokhale figured in a controversy which brought him publicity in the Indian press. Gokhale, who was in London, in an interview to the Manchester Guardian accused British soldiers in Pune of rape among other charges while carrying out anti-plague measures in Indian homes. Subsequently, he withdrew the charges and wrote a letter of apology to the governor of Bombay. While the *Dnyanaprakash* and the *Indian Spectator* of Bombay praised him for acting like a gentleman, many other papers were critical. The *Kaiser-i-Hind* wrote: "This much is certain that he has much compromised his reputation." Tilak's papers were far from sympathetic. The *Mahratta* could not appreciate why the "humiliated professor had withdrawn all the charges when he was unable to substantiate one (rape) of them." In a letter to Motilal Ghosh, Tilak wrote: "I think in me they (government) will not find a *kutcha* reed as they did in Prof. Gokhale."

The cult of violence had taken root in the Indian soil and the use of the bomb for political ends became frequent in the early years of this century. Tilak was accused of fomenting violence by the Anglo-Indian press and he had to pay the price for it. In 1908, in a bomb outrage in Muzaffarpur in Bihar the wife and daughter of a European barrister were killed. The bomb had been intended for D.H. Kingsford, district magistrate, who had achieved notoriety with his savage sentences in political cases. The Anglo-Indian press clamoured for tightening of screws on the Indian press and drastic action against the nationalists. The *Pioneer* wrote: "The wholesale arrest of the acknowledged terrorists in a city or district, coupled with an intimation that on any repetition of the offence, ten of them would be shot for every life sacrificed would soon put down the practice...."

An anonymous correspondent wrote to the *Englishman:* "I submit that powers should be given to the authorities to suppress agitators by the most ready and simple methods; and were a few of these worthy agitators flogged in public by the town sweepers and their press confiscated, much of the glamour of the righteousness of their agitation for the people would be destroyed and their dupes would see them as they are and not in the kaleidoscopic light which they endeavour to attract to themselves." The *Times of India* charged the Indian press and well-known speakers with the responsibility for "working ferments in the yeasty brains."

The *Statesman* wrote: "The new school (of Tilak) not only preached a doctrine of unreasoning hatred of England but hinted at the necessity of deeds which were only possible if those who did them were willing to die for they country. Those apostles of violence scoffed at the mendicant policy as they called constitutional agitation and advocated a vague and undefined but obviously mischievous gospel of self-help. There can be little doubt that their teaching has had the effect of turning the heads of a number of enthusiasts." The *Englishman* went to the extent of suggesting that Europeans should organise for self-defence.

Tilak replied to these attacks saying that the fundamental cause of the bomb outrage was not the political agitation of the extremists but the repressive policy of the government which was trying to throttle public opinion by gagging the Indian press and prohibiting public meetings. Goaded by the Anglo-Indian press, the government took the offensive measures against the Indian press. The Bengal Government put on the black list many papers that were carrying on the anti-partition agitation and a campaign of prosecutions was started. One of these prosecuted was Upadhyay, editor of *Sandhya* who told the courts: "I do not want to take part in the trial because I do not believe that in carrying out my humble share of the God-appointed mission of *Swaraj* I am in any way accountable to the alien people who happen to rule over us and whose interest is, and must necessarily be, in the way of our true national development."

Tilak himself became the victim of the panic of the rulers. He was prosecuted for two articles appearing in *Kesari* and sentenced to six years rigorous imprisonment on July 22,1908, by an Indian judge. The action had been taken under the Indian Newspapers (incitement to offences) Act which was passed in that year and which gave wide powers to the government to proceed against seditious writings. Surendranath Bannerjee, Tilak's political opponent, wrote in the *Bengalee;* "With all respect for the judge, we regard the sentence as monstrous—as utterly out of proportion to the offence alleged to have been committed and as one which will be universally condemned by our countrymen and all right thinking men." *The Amrita Bazar Patrika* wrote: "If Mr. Tilak were tried in England and two jurors were in his favour, the presiding judge would not have accepted the verdict of the majority but would have ordered a re-trial and the accused would not have been convicted till the jury were unanimous. What then could have led Mr. Justice Devar to follow a procedure which no judge in England would venture to follow?"

When the anti-partition agitation was in full swing in Bengal, Tilak realised the potential of the ferment in Bengal for the cause of Indian nationalism and he joined hands with Bipin Chandra Pal and Aurobindo Ghose and other Extremists in Bengal to forge an alliance, which caused deep concern not only to the government but also to the Congress leadership. Tilak told a Calcutta audience in 1906: "If you forget your grievances by hearing words of sympathy then the cause is gone. You must make a permanent cause of grievance. Store up grievances till they are removed. Partition grievances will be the edifice for the regeneration of India. The grievance is not only against an unpopular act of an alien regime but against the alien regime itself".

The widening cleavage between the Moderates and the Extremists surfaced on the eve of the Calcutta session of the Congress in 1906. The Moderates were under fire from Pal and the young radicals, products of the anti-partition agitation. No love was lost between Pal and Surendranath Bannerjee or between Bannerjee and Motilal Ghosh. There was continual sniping between the *A.B. Patrika* and the *Bengalee*. The Anglo-Indian papers added to the confusion by playing off one Congress faction against the other and Muslims against the Hindus. Tilak wrote in the *Kesari:* "Dadabhai (Naoroji who presided over the Calcutta Congress and proclaimed India's right to *Swaraj),* the venerable priest of patriotism has joined in holy wedlock the National Congress and India's right to *Swaraj*. This marriage is not entirely approved by some of those who claim paternity of the Congress but now that the marriage is effected, no one has the power to dissolve it or hinder its final consummation—the attainment of Swaraj."

On the opening day in the Congress session, *Bande Mataram* published an article titled: "The man of the present and the man of the future," comparing Dadabhai Naoroji and Tilak. It described Naoroji as "worn and aged, bowed down with the burden of half a century of labour... a man of the past, reminding us of a generation that is passing away, ideals that have lost their charm, methods that have been found to be futile, and energy, and hope, once buoyant and full of life which now live on only in wearied and decrepit old age, phantom-like still babbling exploded generalities and dead formulas." A similar sentiment was expressed by another writer: "The Moderates... made on occasions fiery and eloquent speeches but their British listeners well knew that their fire did not burn; they flourished swords but they had no edge on them. How could the rulers take the Moderates seriously when they were convinced that the spiritual basis of their politics was a full-some adoration of the British way of life and, above all, a sincere belief that the British ruled India by divine dispensation?"

What did Gokhale think of Tilak? This is what he said of him: "Mr. Tilak has a matchless capacity for intrigue and he is not burdened with an exacting conscience. As a result he is often about to play for his own hand when to all appearances he is fighting for a principle only. His great talents, his simple habits, his sturdy and dauntless spirit and above all the cruel persecution which he has had to bear at the hands of the government have won for him the hearts of millions in all parts of the country. And the general affection and admiration make it comparatively easy for him to play his game."

Secretary of State Morley was not happy with the prosecution of Tilak for sedition and his conviction. He wrote to Mintor: "I confess (after reading one of the offending editorials in *Kesari)* that at the first glance, I feel as if it might have been passed over.... Bad enough to warrant a persecution if you wanted one on general political grounds, but not at all so bad as to make a prosecution inevitable... of course. Clarke (Sir George Clarke, governor of Bombay) might easily have convinced me that the proceedings were wise if he had shown that the state of his Presidency made a severe lesson and stern example necessary. But I gather from his letters that he thinks nothing so ill of his people and he plainly has not weighed all the ulterior consequences of every sort. If his people are in an inflammable state, the trial will inflame them still further. If they are not, he could afford to let Tilak's shuffling stuff with all its vicious innuendoes and mischievous possibilities go by."

Morley, who felt that the prosecution was a "grievous error" added: "The conviction of Tilak fills me with anything but exultation." "If you had done me the honour to seek my advice as well as that of your lawyers," Morley had written to Clarke a week earlier, "I am clear that I shall have been for leaving him alone. And I find no reason to believe that any mischief that Tilak could have done would have been as dangerous as the mischief that will be done by his sentence. We must keep order but excess of severity is not the path of order, on the contrary it is the path to the bomb."

Writing to Morley about his impressions of Tilak, Clarke said; "I can't help thinking that long ago he might have been taken in hand but a high caste Brahmin—I am told—never forgives imprisonment." Six months earlier the governor had played host to Tilak and 70 other local editors of the language press. When the party was over, the governor later said, "To my astonishment Tilak got up and thanked me very nicely in the name of the assembly. I shook hands with them all, including Tilak, and we parted with great cordiality, they cheering me most heartily."

Replying to Clarke, Morley said: "I like this high caste Brahmin of a man never forgiving the stain of imprisonment, as you say, quite a man worth trying to get hold of and I dare say you are right in thinking it might have been possible at an earlier stage. Alas!" Minto, however, assured King Edward VII that Tilak's conviction and other prosecutions and punishments "had the most marked effect in reassuring the local population as to the determination of the Government of India to maintain order and put down the preaching of anarchy and murder."

Leader of Immense Greatness

The Anglo-Indian press spread a scare on the eve of the 50th anniversary of the 1857 Mutiny that the nationalists were planning a revolt in Punjab under the leadership of Lajpat Rai. These papers published wild stories about Lajpat Rai having collected 1,00,000 men to attack the Lahore fort on May 10, 1907. Detachments of the British cavalry and artillery paraded the streets of Lahore. The press in Britain carried sensational reports about the Punjab. The *Daily Mail* reported that an attempted revolt whose object was to proclaim Lajpat Rai Maharaja of Punjab had been crushed. The Evening Standard reported a riot in Delhi and said that the statue of Queen Victoria had been mutilated and European women insulted by their *ayahs.* The Anglo-Indian press cried for action against the Indian press.

Lajpat Rai was arrested on May 8,1907 in Lahore and deported to Burma. In a letter to the *Times of India,* Gokhale said that although Lajpat Rai's language was at times a "trifle strong" his aims and methods had always been "strictly constitutional". Gokhale said the Punjab police had been misled by the police and secret service. "The government has misjudged the volume and character of the unrest prevalent in the Punjab," he said. "People in this country believe and will continue to believe that there never was any real chance of a second mutiny and that Lajpat Rai has been sacrificed to the nervous apprehension that suddenly seized the authorities."

The viceroy wanted to enact a law to curb the press but the secretary of state opposed it despite a warning from the king that the "freedom of the press although an undoubted boon to a free people under self-government is apt to be abused by a people under the autocratic government of another race." A press law was, however, passed in 1908.

Writing to Dunlop Smith, Private secretary to Minto, Lovat Fraser, editor of the *Times of India* said in July 1909: "I lunched with the Aga Khan.... I am sure you realise as keenly as he appears to do, that probably our greatest danger in India is the likelihood of an entente so much desired by many of the younger and abler Mohammadans, between Hindus and Musalmans. Men like the Aga Khan feel that in pressing for large separate treatment for Mohammadans, they are fighting our battle much more than their own. We have far more to lose than the Muslims by an entente between Islam and Hinduism."

The foundation for the special treatment to Muslims was laid by Minto in 1906 when he received a Muslim deputation led by the Aga Khan and conceded their demand for separate voting rights. This was in line with the open partisanship of the Anglo-Indian press with the Muslims and they gloated over the success of the deputation. The *Amrita Bazar Patrika* described the deputation as a "got-up affair fully engineered by interested officials" to whitewash their designs.

The authorities wanted a few simple minded men of position to give them a certificate of good conduct. They knew the Hindus would not do it, so they began operation among the older classes of Musalmans." The full implications of the concession made by Minto were not immediately realised by nationalists and the Indian press. The *Advocate* of Lucknow "refused to believe that any British *statesman* will give countenance such a pro-Muslim movement." Even Tilak's colleague N.C. Kelkar, editor of *Mahratta,* expressed his satisfaction that the isolation of the Muslim community was breaking and said that even political aspiration in the Mohammadans was a national asset for all India. "We for one can find it in us", he said, "to rejoice, if as a reward for not joining in the Congress, the Mohammadans are appointed to the membership of the Supreme Executive Council. A Mohammadan governor of a province would be still more welcome."

The *Hindu* spoke of "the intelligent awakening on the part of some of the members of the Muslim community to an apprehension of some of the factors which keep their material position in an unsatisfactory state. This is the first important impulse which leads to the amelioration in the condition of any community. The striving after a more elevated position in society than they now occupy is a worthy ambition, as the viceroy said, on the part of the descendants of a ruling race." The *Hindu Patriot* of Calcutta, a Congress paper, praised the viceroy for his performance. The *Indian Mirror* also of Calcutta, wrote: "We are in entire sympathy with the aims and aspirations of our Mohammadan brethren. Hindus and Mohammadans are after all children of the same soil. Their interests are the same and their hopes and yearnings must be the same."

When World War I broke out in 1914, Tilak was among the very first Indian nationalists to declare his support to the war effort. In a letter to the press he declared: "I have no hesitation in saying that the act of violence which have been committed in different parts of India are not only repugnant to me but have only, in my opinion, unfortunately retarded to a great extent the pace of our political progress. Whether looked at from an individual or from a public point of view, they deserves. I have said before, to be equally condemned." He referred to the war and said; "It is the duty of every Indian, be he great or small, rich or poor, to support and assist H.M.'s Government to the best of his ability."

This change of attitude in Tilak was warmly welcomed by the *Advocate of India* of Bombay, an Anglo-Indian paper which called Tilak "one of our loyalist and truest friends" and asked his detractors to "admit their mistake and make at the earliest possible moment the amends honourable." Tilak wrote many articles in *Kesari* urging Indian youth to enlist in the army and fight in the war. At a conference of leaders in Bombay called by the Government, Lord Willingdon, to promote the war efforts Tilak said the enthusiasm of the people could be roused better if the appeal was coupled with a promise of Home Rule. The governor did not like this reference to Home Rule and ordered Tilak to sit down.

Tilak walked out in protest followed by others including Gandhi and N.C. Kelkar, editor of Mahratta. Tilak later started a Home Rule movement which had similar aims as the one similarly named and started by Annie Besant in 1916. When political reforms were announced in 1919, he favoured their acceptance while Gandhi opposed them. He argued in favour of what he called "Responsive Cooperation" with the rulers and broke away with Gandhi along with his one time extremist colleague, Bipin Chandra Pal, the non-cooperation movement was launched in 1919.

The *Mahratta* wrote on October 4, 1914: "Indian hearts will be thrilled to know that Indian troops have landed in France." The award of the first Victoria Cross to an Indian made banner headlines in the Indian press. In the Imperial Legislative Council, Surendranath Bannerjee suggested that the cost of the Indian Expeditionary Force should be borne, contrary to precedents, by the Indian Exchequer.

Annie Besant, who launched her Home Rule League in September 1916, started two newspapers, a weekly and a daily, to support cause. She expressed her goal in these words: "In political reform we aim should be at the building up of complete self-government from village councils... to a national parliament equal in its powers to the legislative bodies of the self-governing colonies."

Bipin Chandra Pal said of Besant: "There is no other person to whom the heart of awakened India goes with greater reverence and deeper affection than it does to the strange woman from beyond the seas. She was the first to point out that educated India had lost faith not only in their ancient and medieval doctrines but also in their own powers and possibilities". K. Rama Rao said that to Annie Besant Journalism was a handmaid to nationalism. "Brought up in freedom she displayed a fine contempt for the repressive laws of British India. She was a born controversialist, hitting hard, giving no quarter and asking for none."

Besant had figured in a controversy earlier when she protested against racial discrimination that was rampant in India. During the time Lord Minto was viceroy she issued an appeal to the viceroy and European community to check and abstain from insult to Indians. She said: "Your excellency, your Indian and English children are brusing each other's hearts to the death and wrecking the future.... Oh! raise your powerful voice to check the hatred that divides heart, from heart community from community. Speak strongly, as you alone can do to these lower English who are destroying your work and undermining the Empire. Bid your officials everywhere to guard your Indian children and to shield them from outrage and from wrong."

The appeal shocked Europeans who accused her of deliberately attempting to encourage racial antipathy. She was condemned by the governor of United Provinces who threatened to persuade the princes who were patrons of her college in Benares (Hindu Central College) to dissociate themselves from her. The Maharaja of Benares wrote to her a letter of protest. Lord Minto was angry with her. Besant told him: "I would not have issued the appeal had I thought for a moment that you would have disapproved. I am very sorry." The Indians rallied round her while the Europeans continued to suspect her.

Besant wrote this of Gandhi in *New India* in 1915 after she met him in Madras: "I was for the first time brought face to face with this great man known in this life as Mohandas Karamchand Gandhi. He was short of stature, not too robust in health but looked beautiful in his homespun dress of a Kathiawar fanner, simple but attractive. I looked in his eyes and saw through his eyes Jesus of Nazareth of old who stooped down in order to lift others. About him it was said he tried to save others but could not save himself. May it not be repealed of this great man."

Unfulfilled Dreams : Besant's *New India* was the old *Indian Standard* which she purchased and renamed in 1913. The *Madras Standard* started in 1877 as a tri-weekly by an Englishman, passed in 1892 into the hands of G. Parameswaran Pillai who converted it into a daily. Parameswaran Pillai who was 21 when he took over the *Standard* was a very influential public figure in Madras and his political views were considered radical. He was described as a "powerful speaker and a fearless fighter". He was of great help to Gandhi when he visited Madras in 1896 to gather support for the cause of Indians in South Africa.

New India became a powerful vehicle for Home Rule movement which dominated the political scene until the Besant's national leadership passed over to Gandhi. She wrote vigorous articles day after day championing the cause of Indian freedom and she came into conflict with the law more than once. Action was taken against her paper on a number of occasions under the Press Law of 1910 and the securities which she deposited were forfeited and fresh ones were demanded. However Besant wrote fearlessly and in vehement language but without infringing the law and this caused a good deal of embarrassment to the government. Says a writer: "Many an eminent lawyer admitted that although Besant was not a lawyer she wrote in a manner which would baffle the best among lawyers who tried to discern in her remarkable articles a branch of the Press Act."

New India gave a much needed new tone to the entire press in India, said B.G. Horniman. "Before Besant entered journalism", he said, "the most valiant of editors, including myself, found it difficult to give free and fearless expression to their thoughts." When a security of Rs. 2,000 was demanded from *New India* in 1916 under the Press Act, *The Hindu* called it an "arbitrary step" taken "to undermine the influence of Mrs. Annie Besant, an Englishwoman of striking personality and generous instincts who has done splendid service in the cause of India and who has recently given a powerful stimulus to the movement for self-government for India.

The zeal and earnestness with which she is advocating the cause of Indian political development on the platform and in her paper, New *India*, have rightly earned for her the gratitude of the people of this country whose resentment and grief at this official action will be keen and poignant." Within four months the government forfeited the security and demanded a fresh one which Besant paid. In June, 1917, Besant and two of her associates were interned by the Madras Government under the Defence of India Rules but they were released in September. The *Madras Mail* criticised her release and said it would affect the prestige and authority of the local government.

It appealed to the European community and conservative Indian opinion to rally round it and force the secretary of state to change the mind of the Government of India. The paper sent a cable to the secretary of state airing its views and threatened to launch a passive resistance campaign if its efforts to halt political reforms did not succeed. It secured the support of the leader to the non-Brahmin movement, Sir P. Thyagaraya Chetti who cabled to the secretary of state, supporting the *Madras Mail.* Earle Welby was the editor of the paper at that time and he later told Secretary of State Montague during his visit to Madras that the Besant incident had made him determined to resist all reform. He said that his was a daily newspaper and he did not think much of what he wrote; that if he had been editing a weekly he might have watered down his language. After retirement Welby worked as the literary correspondent of the *Hindu* in London.

There was a wave of press prosecutions and forfeitures of security all over the country following material law incidents in Punjab and the Jallianwala Bagh massacre in 1919. Even the most respectable nationalist papers were not exempt from the repressive policy. There was a blackout of news from the Punjab and correspondents who managed to smuggle out reports were arrested and punished under a special law made for the purpose. Newspapers which strongly criticised the government were gagged and heavy security was demanded from them.

One of the victims of the government's wrath was the *Bombay Chronicle,* which under the editorship of B.G. Horniman, published detailed reports of the Punjab horrors. Pre-censorship was imposed on the paper and for many days it came out with its editorial columns blank, Homiman himself was arrested and deported. In Punjab itself Kalinath Roy, editor of *Tribune,* was arrested and sentenced to two years' imprisonment for an editorial, "Blazing indiscretion", which had criticised the governor.

The *Bombay Chronicle* was forced to close down and was allowed to resume publication after it paid a security of Rs. 10,000 and under strict censorship. The *Amrita Bazar Patrika's* security of Rs. 5,000 was forfeited and it was asked to furnish another (Rs. 10,000). *The Hindu* and the *Swadeshamitran* in Madras were also asked to furnish securities for articles published on the Punjab incidents. When Gen. Dyer, the hero of the Jallianwala Bagh massacre, returned to England he was interviewed on board the ship at Southampton by a *Daily Mail* reporter. Dyer said: "It was my duty, my horrible, dirty duty. I had to shoot. I had 30 seconds to make up my mind what action to take.

Every Englishman I have met in India has approved my act, horrible as it was....'The *Times of India,* however contradicted him and said: "wherever the tragedy is discussed, there is heard nothing but loathing of the horrible circumstances which linked the slaughter at Jallianwala Bagh with the name of an Englishman." The *Pioneer,* however, took an entirely opposite view and it published a number of letters which supported a proposal to set up a fund to present Sir Michael O'Dwyer, governor of Punjab, and Gen. Dyer with swords of honour "for their services in saving India from the horrors of another 1857."

When the *Morning Post* of London opened a fund for the "man who saved India", money poured in from Anglo-Indian papers and Englishmen in India. The *Pioneer* and *Englishman* (Calcutta) sent Rs. 10,000 each. The Calcutta correspondent of the *Morning Post* collected Rs. 5,000 each from the *Madras Mail* the *Civil* and *Military Gazette* and many other newspapers.

We have mentioned the *Bombay Chronicle* as one of the victims of the repressive policy followed by the government after the Punjab incidents. The paper was founded in 1913 by Sir Phirozeshah Mehta, veteran Congress leader of Bombay to fill a vacuum in that city where there were only Anglo-Indian newspapers and no nationalist English daily. Mehta easily raised the money required to start the paper and he appointed B.G. Homiman, an Englishman, as the editor. For three years, While he was alive, he kept tight control over its editorial policy. The *Chronicle* soon established itself as the foremost Indian English daily championing the nationalist cause. After Mehta's death,Chimanlal Setalvad took over as chairman of the Board of Directors which consisted mostly of Moderates.

The paper faced many crises in its career and moved over as an ardent supporter of Gandhi and the non-cooperation movement with S.A. Brelvi as its editor.

Pandit Madan Mohan Malaviya launched the *Leader,* later to become a great newspaper voicing moderate opinion under the editorship of C.Y. Chintamani, in Allahabad in 1909. With the exception of *The Hindu,* which adopted a professionalism which gave it an advantage over the British-owned *Madras Mail* most Indian papers neglected the business side of their venture, and functioning under various official restrictions, they lived a hand to mouth existence, forced to live in the present rather than to build for the future.

The *Independent* of Lucknow was started by Pandit Motilal Nehru in 1919 and its first editor was Syed Hussain. The paper, however, did not prosper and had to close down in 1923.

In Bombay, *Young India* was started as a weekly by the Home Rule party in 1918, which later was taken over by Mahatma Gandhi.

The Justice Party in Madras organised by the non-Brahmin movement started its own paper, *Justice,* in 1918 and it was edited by the leader of the Party Dr. T.M. Nair who wielded his pen and tongue with equal force and fluency. Later, A. Ramaswami Mudaliar took over the editorship. The *Justice* ceased publication when the Justice Party lost power in the 1930s.

The influence of the language press was steadily growing during this period and it reached its peak after Gandhi took over the leadership of the nationalist movement. Speaking about its influence, Gokhale said in a speech in England that "although the educated classes in India numbered only a million in a population of 30 million, they constituted the 'brain, of the community. They did the thinking not only for themselves but also for their ignorant brethren. They controlled the Indian language press which shaped the thoughts and swayed the feelings not only of the 15 million literates in vernaculars whom it reached directly but also of many more who were indirectly under its influence."

In August, 1909, Lord Minto wrote to the princes of India on the prevailing unrest in the country and sought their opinion "with a view to mutual cooperation against a common danger." The rulers of native states, according to Chirol, with one voice condemned disaffection "with the exception of the Gaekwar of Baroda whose reply without striking any note of substantial dissent is marked by a certain coolness that has won for him the applause of the nationalist press, they respond heartily to the Viceroy's request for suggestions as to the most effective measures to cope with the evil.

Most of them put in the very forefront of their recommendations the necessity of checking the licence of the Indian press to which they attribute the main responsibility for the widening of the gulf between the rulers and the ruled. And it should be remembered that the opinions were expressed some months before the Government of India decided to introduce the new Press Act (of 1910).

The Nizam (of Hyderabad) holds that newspapers publishing false allegations or exaggerated reports should be officially called upon 'to print formal contradiction or correction as directed.' For in his opinion "it is no longer safe or desirable to treat with silent contempt any perverse statement which is publicly made because the spread of education on the one hand has created a general interest in the news of the country, and a section of the press, on the other hand, deliberately disseminates news calculated to promote enmity between Europeans and Indians or to excite hatred of government and its officers in ignorant and credulous minds."

Main Contributors

Oldest of the modern media of mass communication, the Press has by and large served India better than the others, both before and after independence. Films, too, played a socially purposeful role in the pre-independence period and the early years of freedom.

In contrast to the scope afforded to the socially conscious communicator by newspapers and films, both of which are in the private sector, monopoly control of radio by the Government since before independence, and of television since its advent in the 1960s, has proved statisfying.

Two Aspects : It is the middle class that contributes most of the personnel of all the mass media. But since the Press, besides being free of government control, is relatively less market-driven than films with their large budgets and generally short life, many newspapers have from time to time exemplified the idealism that marks the more attractive of the two faces of the middle class.

Jawaharlal Nehru said of the Janus—like middle class in the course of his presidential address at the Lucknow session of the Congress on 12th April, 1936 : "Being too much tied up with property and the goods of the world, it is fearful of losing them, and it is easy to bring pressure on it and to exhaust its stamina. And yet, paradoxically, it is only from the middle class intellectuals that revolutionary leadership comes, and we in India know that our bravest leaders and our stoutest comrades have come from the ranks of the middle class."

The beginnings of the Press in India revealed both the faces: newspapers as commerce and as social mission. The first printed periodical, the *Bengal Gazette,* which appeared in Calcutta on 29th January, 1780 was a commercial venture and it illustrated the nexus that often exists between newspapers and politicians. Though published on Indian soil the weekly was meant for English-speaking foreigners residing in India, not for Indians. James Augustus Hicky, the publisher and editor, openly sided with the Governor-General, Warren Hastings, in the in-fighting between two factions in the Governor-General's Council.

The opposition to Warren Hastings was led by Philip Francis, whose ambition was to become Governor-General himself. The journal would lampoon Elijah Impey, Chief Justice of the Supreme Court and a friend of Warren Hastings, as 'Poolbundy' (pul in Hindustani means bridge) in an obvious reference to a contract for maintaining bridges which the Chief Justice had secured for a relative. Warren Hastings and his wife were also boldly satirised. The types of Hicky's press were seized and his journal was suppressed in 1782 after Philip Francis decided to leave India. Warren Hastings for his part patronised a rival weekly, the *India Gazette.* which was given postal facilities not available to Hicky.

We have been witness, two centuries later, to a similar struggle between some journals affiliated with rival barons of industry who, in turn, enjoy the support of rival princes of the State. A conspicuous example is the campaign carried on in recent years against each other by the Ambanis of Reliance Industries who own the *Observer* group of publications and Nuslia Wadia, of Bombay Dyeing, who is a director of the *Indian Express.*

A half-way house in the emergence of a truly Indian Press was marked by the journals brought out, early in the 19th century, by Christian missionaries in Bengal. Though published by foreigners, these journals were addressed to Indians, and some of them were in Indian languages. They promoted the dual objectives of promoting the Christian religion and the British empire.

It was in order to counter the attacks on Indian religions which these missionary journals carried, and to assert national self-respect that the first Indian newspapers, properly so called, were established by Raja Rammohun Roy (1772-1833), the initiator of India's renaissance in the modern period. Born in a well-to-do family, he represented the finer of the two faces of the middle class.

Rammohun Roy advocated, through the journals launched

by him in the 1820s—the weeklies *Sambad Kaumidi* in Bengali and *Mirat ul Akhbar* in Persian and irregular in publication, the *Brahmunical Magazine,* a brief-lived magazine in English—many social reforms that were to become part of the plank of the nationalist movement. These included abolition of Sati or the custom, already on the wane in most parts of the country, of Sati or the burning of the widow on the funeral pyre of her husband, equality before the law, and modern education through the English medium. He did not press for representative government, it being too soon for that—with an entrenched imperial power and a people steeped in illiteracy and superstition and with little sense of a national identity; the affiliation of caste was, at that time, all that mattered for self-identity.

But Rammohun Roy's readiness to assert national self-respect is evident from his courageous criticism of the brash methods of the foreign missionaries who reviled the religious beliefs and practices of Indians, both Hindus and Muslims.

The role of the Press acquired a new dimension with the advent of daily newspapers in the 19th century. Several of them were moderate or conservative, both with regard to political and social issues; some were moderate in their politics but radical in their attitude to social reform or *vice versa;* and some others were radical both in politics and on social issues without necessarily subscribing to the tactics of law-breaking in the name of Satyagraha.

The complexity of the scenario is illustrated by the instance of Annie Besant (1847-1933) and her daily newspaper *New India.* Having fought and suffered in England for many causes—as a free-thinker, trade unionist and proponent of planned parenthood—she became a theosophist, found in India her spiritual home, and settled at Adyar, in Madras, in 1907. Through *New India* which she ran from 1914, Annie Besant advocated a political line that was bold in comparison with the petitionary politics of the then Congress leadership. In 1916 the British authorities demanded a security from Annie

Besant for "the better conduct of her publications". It was to protest against this action that young Jawaharlal Nehru, then practising law at Allahabad, made his first public speech in June 1916.

Annie Besant was chosen, while under internment as punishment for her advocacy of self-government for India, as president of the 1917 Congress session at Calcutta, becoming the first woman to be so honoured. But her popularity declined when she refused to endorse Gandhi's movement in 1919 against the Rowlatt Bills, his advocacy of Non-Cooperation, and support to Khilafat. She held that there was nothing in the two Bills to which an honest citizen could take exception, and that, instead of non-cooperation, the best men and women should enter the legislative councils and press for the transfer of greater power to the people's representatives. Civil disobedience, she warned, was "rearing huge obstacles in the way of the first Home Rule government."

The over-simplification and consequent misrepresentation in branding a person as a 'moderate' or a 'radical' is illustrated also by the case of Bal Gangadhar Tilak. He was a conservative in his attitude to social reform, while being a radical in politics; he coined the pledge 'Swaraj is my birthright, and I shall have it.' Though Tilak suffered imprisonment and deportation, he was for a constructive response to any move that the British were prepared to make in the direction of self-government, such as the Montagu Reforms Act of 1919.

Gandhiji was an exemplar of educative journalism. His first journalistic venture was 'Indian Opinion', a weekly brought out in 1904 in South Africa. It was published in four languages—English, Gujarati, Hindi and Tamil—in order to reach all the major elements of the Indian population in natal and the Transvaal. It is characteristic of Gandhiji that while, on the one hand, he utilised the journal to ventilate the grievances of Indians who were grossly discriminated against by the regime of the white colonists, he also exhorted his countrymen to give up insanitary habits, to overcome feelings of difference based on caste or religion, and to observe truthfulness in their business dealings.

After returning finally to India in 1915, Gandhiji conducted three weekly journals: 'Navajivan' (1919-31) in Gujarati; 'Young India' in English (1919-32); and 'Harijan' in English from 1933 till his martyrdom in 1948. So widespread was the interest in Mahatma Gandhi's views that what he wrote in these journals was news.

> "I have taken up journalism", he wrote in 1919, "not for its sake but merely as an aid to what I have conceived to be my mission in life. My mission is to teach by example the matchless weapon of Satyagraha which is a direct corollary of non-violence. To be true to my faith, I may not write merely to excite passion. The reader can have no idea of the restraint I have to exercise from week to week in the choice of topics and my vocabulary. It is a training for me." And in his autobiography : "One of the objects of a newspaper is to understand the popular feeling and give expression to it; another is to arouse among the people certain desirable sentiments ; and the third is fearlessly to expose popular defects."

A major consequence of Gandhiji for Indian journalism was the emergence of new dailies as radical alternatives to the nationalist but somewhat staid Indian-owned newspapers of long standing. These emerged as a third alternative to the loyalist newspapers, many of them British-owned, and to the newspapers which were once described by Nehru as 'immoderately moderate'.

The first, and towering, personality who roused nationalist consciousness among the Indian Muslim community was Maulana Abul Kalam Azad (1888-1958). After the British suppressed the 1857 Uprising which aimed at restoring power and dignity to the last Mughal emperor, Bahadur Shah Zafar, who had been reduced to a figurehead by the East India Company, Muslims were in a demoralised state and withdrew into the shell of orthodoxy. Sir Syed Ahmad Khan (1817-98) advised his co-religionists to reform their social practices and take to modem education through English, but to seek their advancement through loyalty to the British rulers. He founded in 1875 the Mohammedan Anglo-Oriental College at Aligarh, later raised (in 1920) to the status of a university.

The alumni of Aligarh remained by and large adherents of the founder's philosophy of a separate Muslim identity even though the great majority of Muslims in the Indian sub-continent including present-day Pakistan and Bangladesh—are descendants of converted Hindus. Maulana Azad poured scorn and ridicule on the Aligarh School through his writings, as in the following passage from the daily *Al Hilal* founded by him in 1912:

> "The future historian will write that, ultimately, what had to happen, happened. In the 20th century no country could remain in bondage, and none remained. The British government was a constitutional entity. It was not the autocratic rule of Chengiz Khan. Therefore it did what was expected of it, and India became free. But the world will remember that this turn of events owned nothing to the Muslims; whatever happened rebounded to the credit of every other community except the Muslims. History will record about seven crore people of India that there was an unfortunate and ill-fated community which always hindered the country's progress, and proved an everlasting impediment to its advancement. They were an obstacle in the path of freedom, a toy in the hands of covetous rulers, a puppet for the aliens, and a deep wound on India's brow."

Among other prominent nationalist Muslim publicists were M. Asaf Ali of Delhi, Syed Hosain, Syed Abdullah Brelvi and Shoebullah Khan of Hyderabad. The case of Asaf Ali—as of Maulana Azad and Dr. M. A. Ansari—illustrated how the pan-Islamic and anti-British sentiment generated among Indian Muslims by the attack on Turkey during World War I matured into territorial nationalism and sympathy for all—and not only Muslim—victims of western domination. Asaf Ali, who had served the British administration till 1914, writes in his memoirs : "I was more pro-Turkey than I knew. The entire early training and home influence of sentimental attachment to the Turks sprang into the saddle of my reason and, driven by impulse, my decision was irrevocably taken. My resignation was cabled out (from London). Simla must know how war on Turkey was likely to react on Muslims, if I could chuck away what was the promise of a high career."

On returning to India in January 1915, Asaf Ali threw himself into the work of organising the Home Rule League and the Congress in Delhi. A creative writer in Urdu, he also wrote for two nationalist English newspapers, the 'Bombay Chronicle' and the 'Independent' launched by Motilal Nehru in Allahabad. A Swarajist, he advocated the entry of nationalists into the legislative councils rather than their boycott since, otherwise, loyalist elements would parade as representatives of the people. When Asaf Ali was adopted as the Congress candidate for the Central Legislative Assembly from Delhi in 1934 he received a telegram from Gandhiji published by the 'Hindustan Times' on 13th November, 1934 : "I hope every Delhi vote will be cast in your favour." On Asaf Ali winning by a large margin, Gandhiji wrote to him : "How I wish your success will lead to heart unity between the two brothers—Hindu and Mussalman."

The Mahatma's wish was not to be fulfilled. The Muslim League grew from strength to strength, thanks to Congress ambivalence towards separate electorates by which the League swore, and the negative policies pursued by the Congress during World War II beginning with the resignation of popularly elected provincial Ministries in October 1939 which left the field clear for the League to bask in the sunshine of British patronage.

However, there were brave spirits among Muslims who held to the ideal of national unity as against the League's advocacy of partition in order to create Pakistan. Among such was Shoebullah Khan.

Born in 1919 he entered journalism after graduating from Osmania University. He first worked on the weekly 'Taj'. The journal was banned for carrying an article of his criticising the Nizam's complicity in the activities of the Ittehad-ul-Muslimeen and the Razakars under Qasim Razvi's leadership. Shoebullah Khan joined the 'Rayyat', but that newspaper too was forced to stop publication because it was critical of the Nizam's administration. Shoebullah then started his own daily, 'Imroze'. His advocacy of Hyderabad's accession to India invited the anger of the Razakars.

Their threats did not cow him down. On the night of 21st August, 1948, while he was returning home from office, he was pounced upon by Razakar miscreants who shot him and cut his hands. He dragged himself towards his house and collapsed when he was a few yards away. Khasa Subba Rau said in the course of the first Shoebullah Khan Memorial Lecture in 1952 : "We journalists deal in words of varying power to put our stories and ideas across to the public. But Shoebullah delivered his message in letters written with blood."

Taste of Freedom : Kasturi Srinivasan, of the 'Hindu', said at a meeting of the All India Newspaper Editors' Conference, of which he was president, in October 1942 that the Press could be fully free only after the country became free. But it soon turned out that, in certain respects, each State is like every other—whether it be alien and autocratic or native and democratic, capitalist or socialist. None of them will tolerate attempts at subversion through sedition and violence, or the disclosure of State secrets.

The 'Free Press Journal' of Sadanand learnt this to its cost. This Bombay newspaper disclosed in September 1947 that Indian naval and land forces were being moved towards Jurtagadh, a Hindu-majority State on the Gujarat coast whose Muslim ruler acceded to Pakistan and was seeking armed help from outside, sparking off vigorous popular protest. The Central Home Minister, Sardar Patel, was furious. Sadanand, who had made arrangements for starting an Indian international news agency after visiting Cairo, London and Mew York during 1945-46 and making arrangements with foreign news agencies and individual journalists, was denied the lease of teleprinter lines though he had placed a large order for teleprinters. This was the beginning of his financial decline and serious ill-health. He died in 1953, a heroic and tragic figure in the history of Indian journalism.

Not many newspaper editors and publishers showed thereafter the courage to publish and be damned which characterised the nationalist Press prior to independence and which Sadanand displayed in the early years of independence. One reason was the creeping commercialisation of the Press, which became more and more a business for the publisher and a profession for the journalist and less and less a mission for either.

Partly because of the desire on the part of publishers to play safe, and partly because Prime Minister Nehru was Prince Charming who bewitched not only young men and women but most of the intelligentsia including journalists, the Press was by and large uncritical in its appraisal of government policies. It is only with the benefit of hindsight that Nehru has begun to be criticised for making acceptance of the accession of Jammu and Kashmir to India conditional on—and liable to be rejected through—a plebiscite under international auspices. It was a tiny section of the Press that criticised the Indian

Government's muted disapproval of Soviet colonialism in Eastern Europe in contrast to its loud denunciation of the surviving vestiges of Western colonialism in some parts of the world.

In the long years of the verbal border dispute with China, hardly any Indian newspaper questioned the propriety of the authorities of free India making their own the delineation of the border with Tibet as laid down by imperial Britain, and treating as sacred Indian territory areas in Ladakh and in the North East Frontier Agency (now Arunachal Pradesh) about whose terrian New Delhi had only a hazy notion and over which its authority was next to nil. It is, again, in retrospect that Nehru is being blamed—and only by a few—for his off-the-cuff declaration in September 1962, on a halt in India during his international peregrinations (he had returned from a visit to London and was taking off for Colombo) that the Indian Army had been instructed to clear NEFA of the Chinese. India is still to recover from the ignominy of the bloody nose administered by Communist China in retaliation.

In contrast, the Press was bolder and more critical in its appraisal of the Government's domestic policies, specially in the economic sphere. Even here, however, the country might have suffered less from the horrors of insurrection and terrorism if Indira Gandhi's handling of political problems in Assam and Punjab had been subjected to investigative and candid analysis; likewise with Rajiv Gandhi's misadventure in relation to Sri Lanka.

Such deficiencies notwithstanding, the performance of the Indian Press after independence has been creditable enough to merit praise by the Second Press Commission which reported in 1982. Though the Commission was split seven-to-four on issues of newspaper ownership and of governmental regulation of newspaper economics (the majority favouring State intervention and the liberal minority dissenting), the eleven members of the Commission were unanimous in expressing their appreciation of the role played by the Press in India's public life. They said : "It is to the credit of the Indian Press that, despite its predominantly urban and middle class moorings, it has evinced interest in the problems of farmers, agricultural workers, artisans, tribal groups and other sections of the rural population.

Though, judged by readership or by ownership, it is not necessary for most of our newspapers to highlight the issues of poverty, the Press has made a major contribution by reminding readers of those who live below the poverty line, and giving the ruling middle and upper classes a feeling of guilt. Many newspapers have, from time to time, drawn attention to such matters concerning the weakest sections of society as non-enforcement of minimum wages and the failure to revise them to keep pace with the fall in the purchasing power of the rupee; the persistence of bonded labour despite its abolition by law, or its emergence in a new guise as contract labour; the generation of black money and its use, frequently entailing the involvement of corrupt officials and politicians, etc. Such creditable instances deserve wide emulation."

The Press could play this role because it is much closer and open to the people than are All India Radio and Doordarshan, the proximity of whose personnel is to bureaucrats and to politicians in power. The rapport between the Press and the people—at least the literate—is illustrated by the rapid strides made by newspapers brought out in Indian languages.

The first Press Commission made an attempt to ascertain the circulation of dailies published in India. This figure, taking all languages together, came to 25 lakhs (2.5 million) in 1952, when there were an estimated 330 dailies. The data furnished annually to the Press Registrar, an institution established in terms of the first Press Commission's recommendations, show that the circulation of the reporting newspapers has gone up.

Whereas the growth rate of all dailies taken together was upwards of nine times over the 1952-1990 period, the growth rate in the case of Hindi dailies was more than 21 times. This is in contrast of the growth rate of only five times in respect of English-language dailies. Other Indian languages which have recorded an impressive growth rate include Gujarati, Malayalam, Marathi, Tamil and Urdu.

An indicator of the strides made by the Indian language Press is the number of newspapers with a circulation of one lakh and above. There were only two such in any language in 1960, and both were in English. In 1979, Indian languages accounted for 20 out of the 30 dailies in this circulation category. In 1990, the number of newspapers selling more than a lakh of copies rose to 46, and out of these only 10 were in English and 36 were in Indian languages.

While noting with gratification the growth of the Indian language Press in absolute terms, the Second Press Commission drew attention to the need for assessing the state of development of the Press in an Indian language in relation to the number of persons speaking that language. "Though Hindi has the largest share in the total circulation of dailies", it said, "the circulation of Hindi dailies per 1,000 of the linguistic population is very low. It stood at 12 copies in 1979 (though it is a big increase over the figure of 2.8 copies in 1952), in contrast to the circulation of 47.9 copies of Malayalam dailies per 1,000 linguistic population.

The introduction of adult franchise after independence, the formation of linguistic provinces, the emergence of regional political parties and increasing literacy are among factors that have contributed to a considerable broadening of the readership base, and changes in the contents as well as the style of expression, in the Indian language Press. A landmark was the publication of a handbook by S. B. Adityan, editor of the highly successful 'Thanthi' chain of daily newspapers in Tamil. It provided guidance on how to write in simple language, for readers with a modicum of education. How Indian language journalism has both reflected and stimulated changes in popular usage was the theme of a Seminar on Modernisation of Indian Languages in Mews Media organised at Hyderabad in February 1978 by the Department of Linguistics of Osmania University.

Another major factor in the development of the Indian language Press in recent years has been the introduction of computerised typesetting technology. This has liberated the Indian language scripts from thraldom to metal typesetting which could not handle with elegance complex characters involving compound consonants and the like. It has become possible, thanks to the new technology, to combine speed in production with preservation of the identity and aesthetic appeal of the alphabets of Indian languages.

On the negative side, a disturbing trend in the Indian Press after independence has been a creeping commercialisation which has eroded the concern for public interest, conceived in the broadest sense. This trend has gained momentum over the last decade, diminishing somewhat the validity of the tribute paid by the Second Press Commission, quoted earlier, to the role played newspapers. Advertisers, and the advertising agencies employed by them, are interested not only in the size of circulation of a newspaper but in the purchasing power of its readers.

Many newspapers have tended to increase their appeal to the middle and upper classes by pandering to their Western-oriented interests and tastes, specially among the younger generation many of whom ape every changing Western fashion in hairdo, dress, eating habits and in the high-decibel noise that passes for music. Illustrative of this trend is the hiring of time in All India Radio's metro FM Channel by Bennett Coleman, publishers of the 'Times of India', to purvey pop and rap Western music to anglicised and Americanised youth.

Other instances of newspapers competing with Doordarshan in providing titillating fare are recent news reports such as 'Race on to find Europe's biggest bust' and

'Russian women complain they do not get enough sex' newspapers regularly carry pictures of exiguously clad beauty contestants, Indian and foreign, and of fashion shows featuring bizarre dresses. Such are the lengths to which even newspapers with a reputation to lose are prepared to go for maximising readership among the affluent, who have money to spend on the luxury goods and services advertised in the Press.

During the Indira Gandhi years, when the Government kept threatening the Press with enforcement of a news-to-advertisement ratio in newspaper space, even those among the radical intelligentsia who looked with disdain on conspicuous spending and consumerist advertising came to realise the importance of revenue from advertising for the survival of a free Press.

Thus, an article in the 'Business Standard' supplement of 27th September, 1982, by G. N. S. Raghavan, who had just concluded his assignment as secretary of the Second Press Commission, said : "Before I had occasion to study the economics of newspaper publishing, I used to be upset by much of the advertising in our Press : the textile brand that will win the heart of the young woman or man of the reader's dreams; the portraits and eulogy of unknown founders of family-owned enterprises; the delights of bar, bed, board and swimming pool in five-star hotels (many of them in the public sector in our socialist democracy), and the matrimonial ads which seek to unite middle or upper class boy with middle or upper class girl.

> "I know now that financial viability which requires substantial revenue from advertising, is essential for sustaining the freedom, and improving the quality, of a newspaper. Instead of feeling upset, I feel reassured by the profusion of ads in the best of our newspapers. Whether it is a daily or a journal of less frequent periodicity, the newspaper is the only commodity which is marketed at a price lower

> than the cost of production. Revenue from circulation has to be supplemented by advertising, to cover the balance of the cost and yield a surplus for growth and for qualitative improvement."

It is useful to recall what the three Royal Commissions on the Press in Britain have had to say on advertising revenue and advertising space. The first, known as the Ross Commission after the chairman's name, said in its report of 1949 : 'As long as newspapers are sold to the public for less than they cost to produce, they will need a supplementary source of income. Of the various possible sources of income, the sale of their space to advertisers seems to us to be one of the least harmful. The income to be feared is that which comes from a concealed source and can be earned only by the sale of the editorial columns.

It has been proposed that a limit should be set either to the amount of advertising a newspaper of a given size may carry, or to the amount of advertising revenue it may earn. We do not think that these proposals would necessarily achieve their ostensible object; in normal circumstances, their effect might merely be to drive advertisers to use other media than the Press.'

The Shawcross Commission (1961-62) said : 'A diminution of Press advertising would mean that newspapers generally would economise by carrying fewer pages of editorial text.'

"The McGregor Commission (1974-77) said : 'Advertising is much the most important source of revenue for all classes of publication except for national popular newspapers and 'consumer' periodicals...Some advertising, especially classified, is as interesting to readers as editorial.'

Finally, in the circumstances of media ownership in India, it may fairly be asked why the Press should be singled out for restrictions on advertisement revenue when State-owned radio and television have been making more and more money from commercial advertising.

While standing by all that has been stated above, the writer of the article now feels disturbed deeply by the thought that if the argument for maximising revenue is carried too far, matters might end up by the Press, too, deadening the social conscience, as Doordarshan is doing, by presenting the life style and interests of the well-to-do as the sole Indian reality.

A measure of the dualism in Indian society as reflected in the Press is the success in terms of circulation and revenue enjoyed by such periodicals meant for the leisured and affluent class as 'Femina' and 'Debonair', 'Women's Era' and 'Savvy, and 'Sports World' and 'Sports Star'. Even in daily newspapers, the emphasis is on the sensational and the transient rather than the basic problems of India such as mass poverty and mass illiteracy, and the pollution of the country's rivers and urban environment.

A newspaper reader summed up the situation in a letter published in a letter to the editor published in the 'Indian Express', Delhi, of 4th August, 1995 : "Tonnes of precious newsprint are wasted daily by the Press to deify criminals, both killers and white-collar cheats like Harshad Mehta, Charles Sobhraj, Phoolan Devi, Rajan Pillai, Veerappan, Haji Mastan, Dawood Ibrahim and their ilk. But it is quick to forget Bofors or scams like the securities scandal. It only shows that the Press is in the business of entertainment, not setting the nation's agenda.

> "V. P. Singh became Prime Minister on the Bofors plank, promising the nation not only to disclose the names of recipients of the kickbacks but also to recover for the national exchequer the entire bribe paid to secure the Howitzer deal. But the Press seems to have forgotten all about it."
>
> "P. V. Narasimha Rao had promised to punish the guilty, however high and mighty, in the securities scam. But the matter has been given a burial after the Prime Minister managed to secure a couple of

> contrived resignations, not only are the scamsters going unpunished and the end users of the colossal slush funds remain unidentified, but even the allegedly guilty foreign banks have been let off the hook. And the Press in not bothered. What could be more glaring examples of doublethink and doublespeak ?"

At the individual level, among journalists, economism is the counterpart of the commercialism that has overtaken the bulk of newspaper publishers. The two trends have, between them, diminished the role of the Press in spreading knowledge and awakening the social conscience.

In the early, missionary phase of nationalist journalism, the wages and working conditions of journalists and other newspaper employees were, at best, modest. They depended on the fortunes of the patriotic publisher who was also often editor. By the 1930s, some nationalist newspapers began to do quite well: the 'Hindustan Times' for instance. Pothan Joseph as editor pressed for improvement of the emoluments of journalists, arguing that the publisher should share the newspaper's prosperity with those who made it possible. The management offered an increase in salary to the editor. Joseph, insisting that the entire journalist staff should be given a rise, walked out, accompanied by Edatata Narayanan, assistant editor.

Syed Abdullah Brelvi took the initiative to form the first association of journalists to secure improvement in wages and working conditions. The situation has changed beyond recognition after the Government sponsored the Working Journalists (Conditions of Service) Bill, which was supported by every political party on its introduction in Parliament in 1955 and was passed the same year.

The change is brought out vividly in a paper prepared for the Second Press Commission by Balraj Mehta, economic journalist. He said : "Once security of service has been assured and pay scales etc. have been made somewhat rewarding, the working journalists' movement and individual working journalists seem to have lost interest in improvement in professional work and standards in journalism. The Indian Federation of Working Journalists was essentially a trade union formation which was soon infected by the trend towards economism in the trade union movement in general.

> "As part of the general trend towards divisions and splits in the trade union movement, and trade union rivalry precipitated largely by narrow political party affiliations, there emerged a rival working journalists' organisation, the National Union of Journalists (India) which, too, has been functioning in the style of the IFWJ. Working journalists now tended to operate as a lobby and not as a profession with its own standards, code of conduct and ethics. They began to hanker after privileges comparable to those of higher echelons of the bureaucracy."

This observation is even more apposite today than when it was made more than a decade ago. When, in April 1986, the Wage Board headed by Justice (Retd.) Bachawat recommended interim relief at the rate of 7.5% of basic wages, subject to a minimum of Rs. 45 per month, the Government in response to pressure from unions of journalists and others, doubled the quantum of interim relief to 15% and the minimum to Rs. 90 per month.

The clamour of journalists' unions became so loud that on 22nd October, 1991, speaking at the Madras Press Club, the then Information and Broadcasting Minister, Ajit Kumar Panja, felt constrained to advise newspapermen to evolve their own methods to get wage board awards implemented. This was in response to suggestions from journalists' organisations that Government should withhold its advertisements and newsprint quotas to force the hands of newspaper managements.

Any such attempt, the Minister said, could be interpreted as muzzling the Press.

On the part of journalists of the top level, namely editors, economism manifests itself in a fortune-hunting movement from well-paid to better-paid position, with the policy if any of the new employer being of little consequence. For promoting the publisher's interest in maximising circulation, some editors resort to sensationalism. One of its consequences is the blurring of the distinction between news and views. This imposes on the reader the task of gleaning the news from the comment. For example, the opening paragraph of the lead story in the Delhi edition of a newspaper chain on 28th March 1993 read: "The Surajkund A.I.C.C. session saw the Congress sliding back on Saturday to its days of decadent loyalism as dissent was stifled, and the nomination culture reintroduced by all the Prime Minister's men who were determined to have everything their way down the line.

They put all their might together to hijack the dissidents' resolution on the one-man-one-post issue and replace it with a harebrained motion leaving it all to Mr. Narasimha Rao." Two days later :

> "New Delhi—The Congress leadership, increasingly faced with allegations of wrong-doing, did a neat trick at the just concluded Surajkund meeting of the All India Congress Committee by rejecting an amendment seeking a declaration from all Ministers and Judges of their assets. The amendment to the political resolution, moved by Congress M.P. Inderjit on corruption, was rejected by Mr. Sharad Pawar, who had moved the political resolution, on the specious ground that the amendment was more appropriate to the economic resolution."

The search for enlarged circulation takes the form also of peddling soft pornography and of other forms of appealing to the lowest common denominator of popular interest such as astrological predictions, and imported cartoon strips even if they are racist like the Tarzan series, or if the words in the balloons, translated into an Indian language, sound incongruous.

These manifestations of commercialism on the part of newspaper publishers and of economism on the part of journalists have evoked anguished comment from journalists of integrity and public men concerned about the moral health of the Press as an important limb of a democratic polity. Several of them referred to the disclosure of large payments made from public funds to some journalists, and to institutions floated by them, by Mulayam Singh Yadav of the Bahujan Samaj Party during his tenure as Chief Minister of Uttar Pradesh.

In the course of the D.R. Mankekar Memorial Lecture delivered on 5th August, 1995 in New Delhi, N.A. Palkhivala, eminent jurist, expressed regret at the fact that the main aim of most journals and newspapers today is to increase circulation, which has resulted in the lowering of standards.

A columnist wrote in the *'Indian Express'*, Delhi, of 13th August 1995 : "Journalists have been getting their free lunches and free safari suits for the last couple of decades at least. The first signs of the changing nature of corruption in Indian journalism came with the rise of new industrial houses trying to make it to the top in the licence-permit raj. They needed to control both the politicians and the media...What ought to be happening in the legislatures— critically examining the government's policies? exposing its wrong doings and holding it accountable, taking it to task for the corruption of its ministers and bureaucrats—is today expected to be done by newspapers.

Hence the yearning of the public for investigative reports. The Arun Shouri phenomenon is partly explained by this displacement of the political opposition."

A journalist who interviewed the new Chairman of the Press Council, Justice (Retd.) P.B. Sawant, quoted him as saying that unfortunately there have been occasions when the Press has blacked out vital information. Deploring the edging out of everything else by politics, he said : 'We should look forward to the day when politics will be relegated to the second and the third position."

Mahendra V. Desai, veteran journalist who is Oxford-educated but belongs to the Gandhian school, said in the course of an article in the *'Indian Express' of* 18th August, 1995 : "Thanks to the gifts of cash and real estate by Mr. Mulayam Singh Yadav, the names of some journalists and editors in Lucknow and Delhi are mud. They have been found only too willing to be bribed...News manipulation is a legacy of the British, was resurrected during Mrs. Gandhi's Emergency, and has now been upgraded to a fine art. As a result, never has the credibility and accountability of journalists sunk so low....So it remains to be seen what the professional journalist is prepared to do to make Justice F.B. Sawant's tenure (as chairman of the Press Council) a success rather than a sinecure."

The diversification of the business of some major newspaper houses into television is a recent development which calls for attention both as to the causes and the possible consequences of cross-media ownership. The facts relating to the share of newspapers in total advertising expenditure in the country reveal a decline (even if advertising revenue of the Press has gone up in absolute terms). This clearly points to the desire to secure a bigger slice of the advertising cake as the motivation for diversification.

In its report (1985) the Bachawat Wage Board for journalist and non-journalist newspaper employees said in para 42 of Chapter III : "With all-round growth, classified advertisements and public notices including statutory ones are bound to go up in number and volume. The apprehension about future growth of advertisement revenue in the context of competition from TV and radio are not well-founded. Experience of the West shows that, while initially print media lost some market share to TV, in recent years electronic and print media are developing together without any devastating competition. In fact, advertising market share growth of the electronic media has to some extent stagnated, and the value of newspaper as advertisement carrier is more appreciated.

In India too, the share of ads of durables and industrial goods on TV has found some decline in 1987-88 over 1986-87. Furthermore, the fact remains that advertisement on TV being a costly affair is more or less a monopoly of certain leading advertisers. Others have necessarily to depend upon the print media. Superiority of print media also lies in its portability, durability and convenience. Finally, the increasing share of advertisement revenue in total revenue, as represented by rise in proportion of advertisement revenue to non-advertisement revenue, from 130.47 in 1983-84 to 143.61% in 1987-88 further testifies to the future growth potential of advertisement revenue."

This prognosis has proved to be somewhat over-optimistic. The scenario is complex. The Indian experience has been an exception to the tendency in recent years in many parts of the world for newspaper circulations to fall, parallel with the growth of television. Though the expansion of television in India has been spectacular (from 3.6 million sets in 1984, when the system of annual licensing of television sets was abolished, to 30.8 million in 1991 and nearly 50 million by mid 1995), the circulation of daily newspapers has also gone up steadily, from 22.64 million in 1990 to 29.49 million in 1993 (the latest year for which data of the Registrar of Newspapers are available).

However, the growth of the advertisement revenue of Doordarshan has been faster than that of the Press. From 15.9 crores in 1982 it shot up to Rs. 136.3 crores in 1987; 300.6 crores in 1992; 360.2 crores in 1993; and, Rs. 398 crores in 1994. In contrast, though the absolute figure of advertisement revenue of the Press has been higher than that of Doordarshan in each of these years, the relative share of the Press in total advertising outlay in the country has been going down while the relative share of Doordarshan has gone up. Total advertising outlay in the country was estimated to have been about Rs. 1,000 crores in 1987-88; and in 1993-94, Rs. 2,500 crores.

There are two points to be kept in mind while appraising the above figures. First, newspapers recover only a part of the direct cost of production from their revenue through sale of copies, and advertisement revenue is what they rely on to pay their way. Doordarshan, in contrast (like All India Radio), has its hand in the taxpayers' pocket. The extent of support from public funds for Indian television will be evident from the fact that Doordarshan's budget for 1994-95 was Rs. 957.32 crores, as against the commercial earnings of only Rs. 398 crores.

Secondly, Doordarshan's earning from advertisements is not to be equated with what Indian advertisers spend in order to reach Indian audiences through the television medium. They spent nearly Rs. 150 crores on advertisements in programmes made by private producers in India and telecast by Doordarshan. This figure, however, is only a rough estimate since private producers allow discounts on the amounts shown in their rate cards. Also, Indian-owned Zee Television, uplinked abroad but addressed mainly to India via satellite channel, is estimated to have earned Rs. 130 crores during 1994-95 from Indian advertisers. It may be assumed therefore that total spending by Indian advertisers through the television medium is now of the order of at least Rs. 650 crores.

It is the pulling power of television as an advertisement medium, with its capacity for lively demonstration of the virtues of a product or service, which accounts for the edge that this medium has over the static print medium. But the newspaper has its own plus points. The discerning citizen likes to have more than one Sanjaya reporting and interpreting to him the Mahabharata war that is being fought in various spheres of life, from politics and economics to sports and the battle for gender equality. The viewer who has watched the live telecast of a cricket match, and heard the expert commentators on television or radio, still likes to read the story of the contest as narrated in the next morning's newspaper, even as students of current affairs find it useful and necessary to read more than one newspaper.

Moreover, in the Indian context the Press has enjoyed the great advantage of credibility which Doordarshan, as a monopoly run by the Central Government, has sadly lacked in its news and current affairs programmes. But things can change in the not remote future. The Supreme Court directed in its judgment of 9th February, 1995 that an independent public authority should be established to regulate broadcasting in the public interest, as distinct from the interest of the government of the day. If and when this is done (the apex court set no time limit), the news and current affairs programmes of a truly autonomous Doordarshan (or Prasar Bharati if it is so rechristened) can become a real rival to newspapers.

The threat of competition from television to newspapers is likely to be even stronger if there emerge private television channels, specially at regional level. In order to pick up a share of the advertising revenue that has got diverted from the Press to Doordarshan, some leading newspaper establishments have already entered the television field : e.g. Bennett Coleman which runs the 'Times of India'; 'Hindustan Times'; and 'India Today'. These television ventures of newspaper groups have served a good purpose. They have brought a whiff of fresh air and the professional touch to Doordarshan's programmes, which are made by men and women who may not lack talent but who have to work under the watchful eyes of bureaucrats and politicians.

But there is also a danger in a closer nexus between the Press and television media. It is the danger of a condominium being established over public opinion by the print and electronic wings of communication barons.

A scenario is of the 'Eenadu' group of newspapers in Andhra Pradesh opening a television channel in Telugu, offering both entertainment and news, or only news and current affairs programmes. As a television channel not dependent on government funding, and with proven professional competence, an Eenadu television channel is likely to prove quite a success in competition with the Telugu wing of a public television service. Is such a development desirable, considering that 85% of newspaper readers in Andhra Pradesh are already Eenadu readers ? This is not to say that the print and electronic wings of the Eenadu group will necessarily play favourites, or show bias, but to point to the danger inherent in such a situation. Similar scenarios can be visualised in respect of other linguistic regions.

The challenge is to find ways of ensuring that competent communication professionals can find entry into, and prove their worth in, the media whether print or electronic. This will be possible only if there are a number of competing organisations that are potential employers of men and women of talent with dedication to the public good.

There should be no monopoly, whether in the public sector or the private. A situation of near-monopoly in influencing public opinion, through cross-media ownership in the private sector, will be as bad as the government monopoly in radio and television that has prevailed so far.

Like some other things in our country, the media scene has been changing fast, particularly in the past few years, and the Press is naturally affected. Until 1984, the urban middle class had the option of seeing Doordarshan programmes or beguiling themselves with listening to the radio, reading newspapers and magazines or books, or calling on one another and socialising in the traditional manner. In that year, enterprising cable TV operators in Bombay city and some parts of Gujarat brought the latest as well as old feature films to the viewers in the afternoon hours when Doordarshan would be availing of a long siesta. By 1990, the cable operations had spread to other parts of the country, and in the following year satellite TV made its appearance. This was through the courtesy of the cable people who, by installing a dish antenna, could get more subscribers for their services by disseminating the satellite channels; and the latter were happy that they got viewers through the cable.

The options now available to viewers made more and more people go in for a TV set even if they had to make other sacrifices in their family budget, and the TV antenna became a familiar sight in the cities and towns as well as many villages. Of the 45.68 million sets in the country by the end of 1994, urban people had 29.71 million and the rural people accounted for 15.71 million. In terms of percentage of the population, the rural areas were lagging much behind their urban counterparts, with less TV sets in villages though they hold a higher proportion of the Indian population. But the nation's half-a-million villages were trying not to be left far behind in the race.

Both DD and the satellite channels have increased their output of programmes and there is a rivalry, often assuming unhealthy proportions, between the national network and the Indian or foreign satellite channels and their cable collaborators. We are concerned here not with the ethics and other problems of this rivalry, often called a cultural invasion of India, but with the impact TV has been having on the print medium.

Newspapers have registered substantial growth in terms both of circulation and the number of publications coming out (although quite a few are also closing down.) But the growth of television is definitely faster. Will TV swamp newspapers and lead to the closure of many of them, as has happened in several Western countries ? The Indian newspaper Society (INS) said in its 1993-94 report :

> The liberalisation policies of the government have opened many avenues for the electronic media

> which has resulted in the commissioning of multiple channels on Doordarshan and also that of foreign TV networks in the country. This, along with video and cable TV, is a major challenge for press advertising as a good part of advertising which otherwise would have gone to the print media is being diverted to the electronic medium." The report goes on to say that the Society has launched a campaign to stress the benefits of press advertising.

Foreign print media have been kept out of India, for the time being at least, but foreign satellite TV channels are having a field day. Although the national network has taken a series of measures to meet their competition, in the process it has made quite a few compromises too. Advertising revenue, which sustains the Press as well as TV, goes out of the country through ads released on the foreign channels by Indian advertisers, including Indian brands of liquor addressed to viewers in India watching the foreign channels. The impact of the entertainment-oriented TV medium on the Press can also be measured in terms of the reach of the two media. According to a survey, this reach is higher for TV in almost all areas of the country except Kerala where the Press has a greater reach, and radio even greater than either TV or the Press.

The easier-to-watch TV medium has also other advantages like demonstrability of the consumer durables or fast-moving consumer goods advertised on TV. You cannot show, or make a show of, the effectiveness of a brand of detergent or toothpaste as well as you can do it on the TV. So, what is the remedy and, as we asked earlier, what is the future for the print medium ?

Some stalwarts of the print medium have in a way found their own solution. For some time now, recognising the power of the visual medium, they have begun diversifying their media business and sought to get for themselves a slice of the growing TV cake. The 'Times of India' group, a front-runner in the print media, is trying hard to make a niche for itself in the television sphere too. Its Times TV has several programmes to its credit and, what is more, it has shed its adversary attitude to Doordarshan, a government organ.

It marketed the live telecast of the World Cup of Football for Doordarshan in 1994 and also the three-nation one-day cricket matches among India, West Indies and New Zealand as welt as the India-West Indies Series in the same year. The 'Hindustan Times', its arch rival, has also acquired a TV image with its Eye Witness programme, featured regularly on DD-2, after the video magazine experiment failed. It has other serials to its name. 'India Today also gave up the video news-magazine experiment and chose DD-2 for a weekly display of its News-track' programme.

The list is quite impressive although the large majority of newspapers, particularly the Indian language papers, have been untouched by the sudden spurt of TV. While most newspapers, for reasons not difficult to fathom, have not ventured into the TV arena, the more ambitious and business-minded have been casting about for collaboration with foreign channels, or owning a channel.

In many countries newspapers have entered the TV area. Rupert Murdoch, one of the big operators who owns Star TV and 49.5% of Zee, branched out into TV via newspapers. India is thus not a solitary example of this phenomenon of the print media giants, or even small ones, pushing themselves into the TV business. In some of the advanced countries the growth of TV has wiped out many a flourishing newspaper because the ad revenue was not enough to sustain both the local TV station and a modern-day newspaper. In India the share of the Press in the total budget of Indian advertisers has declined—in eight years from 1985 to 1993—by nine percentage points (from 75% to 66%), while the share of TV (taking Doordarshan and satellite/video together) has increased over the same period from 12% to 21%. Radio has lost much of its share and now has only 2% as against 4% eight years ago, while outdoor publicity has gone up from 6% to 11%, with a wide range of messages coming to you on the streets from hoardings, banners, kiosks, busboards and even from balloons up in the sky.

The Press's total advertising revenue has indeed been going up, but what should have gone to it, if the TV were not there as a rival and potentially more attractive proposition, has gone to the new medium. Over the years, if this trend continues, what will happen to newspapers ? Interestingly, the big papers have not been affected and, in fact, never had it so good. Their ad revenues have been rising substantially, so much so that in Delhi at least the big ones—'Hindustan Times', 'Times of India' and 'Indian Express'—slashed their subscription rates to just Rs. 1.50 per copy except on one day of the week. Retaining and increasing the circulation is vital, because that helps the papers to hike the ad rates again and again and thus offset decline in circulation revenue.

The spurt in the ad revenues, specially of the big papers, owes not only to the fact that the rates are higher but because they are the chosen medium for classified advertisements, company notices including announcement of new capital issues, appointments and like. The display ads may not be as repetitive as on TV, but TV can hardly put out classified ads, matrimonials, wanted ads, job announcements, property sale and car sale and the like. Television cannot announce company meetings and carry detailed speeches of company chairman. It can at best carry motivational ads on new capital issues, but it cannot put out ads on jobs in any significant manner. Is it possible to imagine young hopefuls sitting by their TV sets and lapping up notices of job opportunities ? But you can see them checking out ads in newspapers, in a friend's house or in a library if their own paper has not carried it.

The print medium is a medium of record, and what it publishes remains there for some time. It is possible to refer to it even after a gap of time. So, TV cannot hope to take away from the newspapers ads of the kind in which there is no scope for colour, nor need for demonstration of a product as in consumer advertisements. It is this area where the print medium will continue to enjoy a distinct advantage until, of course, some more technological advance comes up with new devices (hopefully not, the papers would say.) Much of this advantage will go to the big papers, which are already reaping it in a big way.

But the decline in the proportion of the press in total advertising will become steeper if TV has more and more channels, both indigenous and foreign. The competition even among the TV channels is so strong that some of them are shedding their inhibitions about liquor ads. There is, of course, the big question of the size of the overall advertisement budget. It has gone up substantially in recent years because of the coming in of multinationals trying to sell their products to Indian consumers, and the general growth of the economy.

The foreigners are in the consumer market in a big way; some of them were already here, like Hindustan Lever, and others have entered the country in the past few years of liberalisation. Already as many as six of the top ten advertisers of DD are multinationals, including marketing companies which often sell goods made by multinational companies. If the liberalisation trend continues and if the economy keeps growing at about five per cent or more, the advertising cake can only become bigger. No wonder the big newspapers are the biggest supporters of the liberalisation process.

But one may ask : will the papers not be affected by the rising trend of TV watching? In other words, will not the newspapers decline in circulation ? At what point will a daily newspaper become redundant ? We have seen how even in advanced countries where the literacy level is very high, almost a hundred per cent, the TV habit has led to the closure of many papers, even the big newspapers. Advertisements and circulation are closely related, and if ad revenue falls this would both be an indication of decline in circulation and, by reducing the resources at the disposal of the paper, cause a fall in circulation too.

In the advanced countries the TV is largely free of government control and the viewer has the satisfaction of getting a more or less complete picture of the day's happenings and multifaceted presentation of different points of view, with visuals and interviews with the main characters of the day's drama, as only TV can. This has helped TV replace the common man's newspaper. On the other hand, the local paper, announcing the daily sales in the big department stores and supermarkets (full-page ads of price slashes in big type) is of interest to the housewife.

The white-collar worker has neither the time nor the need for a newspaper. If at all, he browses through a magazine while commuting to and from office. The serious-minded reader and the intellectual, the researcher and the journalist, would certainly buy a serious-minded paper if it can support itself with adequate advertisements and is backed by a dynamic management.

Indian TV has yet to reach that stage where it leaves the viewer more or less completely satisfied about the day's coverage, so that he would not feel the need for his paper next morning. When that stage will arrive is a difficult question to answer, but the alluring options now being offered to the TV viewers, and which are being lauded by the leading English newspapers, give the audience much to enjoy and learn.

DD is also throwing open its gates fairly wide and if autonomy becomes a reality and there are options and alternatives in informative and educative programmes as well as entertainment, TV can certainly look forward to the day when both the entertainment-seeker and the discerning viewer who mixes his entertainment with information may be assured of satisfaction.

The TV medium has not only arrived; it is also full of potential and the variety it offers, with strong emphasis on entertainment, cannot be matched by the print medium. The electronic media in India had long suffered from lack of competition which is the soul of good programmes, as much as competition is the soul of a good newspaper seeking to keep ahead of its rivals in bringing to readers the news first, along with interesting and entertaining features. The foreign electronic media may have sophistication but, contrary to what some of our English newspapers propound, their newscasts are, by and large, not relevant to the Indian situation biased as they are in favour of the United States, other Western nations and Pakistan in its endless quarrels with India.

Newspapers cannot hope to compete with the TV medium in the area of entertainment but newspapers can be close to the people and their lives. If some children die of defective vaccine being administered, the local press can convey the tragedy vividly. Radio and TV can do it even more effectively but neither radio nor TV have become sufficiently local, and the foreign media just do not care for such developments except carrying a few visuals on the day of the happening.

Therefore, serious newspapers with an all-India appeal can still offer features, comments, interpretative and investigative reports that no TV channel, however autonomous it may be, can hope to do. Local newspapers seeking to reflect the events in their region can also pose a challenge to the entertainment-oriented TV medium if they know how to do it.

7

Freedom at Last

The British-owned *Pioneer* of Allahabad was an early instance of Indianization of newspaper ownership. Under the editorship of F.W Wilson, an able and vivacious journalist the *Pioneer* made good progress in circulation. But he was a thorn in the side of the bureaucracy and the management terminated his services. After this the newspaper's fortunes declined and in the early 1930's the proprietors sold the paper to some Indian landlords and businessmen of the United Provinces.

The process of Indianization was stimulated by the negotiations for the transfer of power that began as the war drew to a close. Like the owners of many plantations and industrial units, the British proprietors of newspapers decided to sell their interests and repatriate the proceeds; they feared that restrictions might be imposed by the government of a free India on the remittance of foreign exchange. Bennett Coleman sold the *Times of India* to Seth Ramakrishna Dalmia, a leading industrialist who had interests in banking and airlines. The Madras *Mail* also changed hands. The *Statesman* too eventually came under Indian management after independence.

Dawn of the Freedom

Partition was the other, and gruesome, side of the medal of independence. The Hindu-Muslim riots set off by the Muslim League's 'direct action' on 16th August 1946 made it impossible for many Hindu-owned newspapers to function in Pakistan; and for *Dawn to* continue publication in Delhi. Prominent among newspaper counterparts of the refugees who fled to India from West Pakistan were the, *Tribune* of Lahore which shifted first to Ambala and subsequently, to Chandigarh; and the Urdu *Pratap* and *Milap* which moved from Lahore to Delhi.

More far-reaching than these physical displacements were the psychic effects of partition. The scenario in post-partition India was that though the eligible voters among Muslims had voted almost to a man for the Muslim League and its two nation theory in the 194546 elections, most of them stayed back in every Indian province except Punjab. Gandhiji and Nehru wanted that the millions of Muslims who chose to remain in India after the creation of Pakistan should be able to live in safety and dignity, irrespective of how Hindus were treated in Pakistan. This was a high morality of unilateral right doing, far above the ordinary human morality of reciprocal obligation. Not many could rise to that height.

A curious feature of the newspaper scene in the post partition years was that several Hindu-owned Urdu newspapers campaigned against, Urdu, and for Hindi. Urdu was perceived as a symbol of the Muslim domination of India prior to British rule, and of the re-establishment of Muslim rule in the western and eastern wings of the sub-continent in 1947 as the result of partition.

Many Muslims for their part, and for long, had looked upon Urdu in the same way as a symbol of Muslim supremacy. When the government of the United Provinces passed an order on 8th April 1900 to the effect, that law courts and government offices should entertain petitions written not only in Urdu but in Hindi in Devanagari script, many Muslim politicians objected and held protest meetings. They said it would lower the status and prestige of Urdu.

If the post-partition campaign against Urdu in a section of the Indian Press betrayed pique, Urdu was soon to attract much solicitude from politicians, both Muslim and non-Muslim, many of whom are moved not by genuine concern for Muslims and for the language which they regard as theirs, but by calculations of the number of Muslim votes they could gain by espousing Urdu as 'the language of the minority'.

Another psychological effect of the vivisection of India in order to create an Islamic State was the feeling generated among some Hindus that what remained of India should, logically, be a Hindu State. A prominent exponent of this view was Seth Ramakrishna Dalmia, who urged that India should be proclaimed a liberal religious State. He said in the course of a statement in July 1950, published prominently by the Times of *India:* "The only right course for saving the country from economic collapse, ending refuge distress, establishing cordial relations with Pakistan and assuring complete protection to the Muslims in India is to declare India a liberal religious State, which is beyond doubt the wish of an overwhelming majority of India's citizens." He expressed regret that "though the country had not recovered from the shock of the tremendous human tragedy created by the influx of East Bengal refugees, the outbreak of the Korean war has diverted the attention of Government to international politics. Neglecting the country's most urgent domestic problems, all are busy speculating about the possibilities of a third world war."

The suggestion that India should be a religious State, even if a liberal one, was directly opposed to the thinking of Jawaharlal Nehru, educated in England and nurtured in rationalism and Marxism. He had been unhappy with Gandhiji's description of the ideal State as Ram Rajya because of its evocation of India's Hindu heritage. Nehru must have been irked also by the dig at his propensity to interest himself at least as much in the problems of the world as of India. The Prime Minister's aversion to Seth Dalmia was to be a factor in the formation of India's first Press Commission and in the framing of its terms of reference.

Independent Print Media

There were two aspects of the operations of Reuters in India as a limb of the British empire. One was its total control of the flow of news from and to India, and the other was its dominant role in news gathering and distribution within India.

An early instance of bias in reports of world events supplied by Reuters to Indian newspapers related to the Russian revolution of 1917 and subsequent events in the Soviet Union. In an article that Jawaharlal Nehru wrote for the *Hindu* (3rd April 1928) on his return from a visit to Russia the previous year, he said: "It is right that India should be eager to learn more about Russia. So, further information has been largely derived from subsidised news agencies inimical to Russia, and the most fantastic stories about her have been circulated. The question most frequently asked me has been about the alleged nationalisation of women!" Nehru went on to pour ridicule on the fictitious 'Riga correspondents' who sat in London or Paris and concocted stories denigrating the infant Soviet State.

News sent out from India by Reuters to the rest of the world tended to be governed by Britain's imperial interests. The viewpoint of the Muslim League, after it became separatist and implacably hostile to the Indian National Congress, was enthusiastically projected abroad, as will be seen from the following instance.

When the Congress Working Committee met at Bardoli during December 1941, C. Rajagopalachari persuaded the Committee to revive the offer made by it earlier, in July 1940, to support the war effort if the British government agreed to recognise India's independence at the end of the war and to form immediately a provisional national government. At this point the British Viceroy, Lord Linlithgow, decided to use reuters to publicise abroad the Muslim League's objections to the Congress proposal.

The historian S. Gopal writes: "The Viceroy, having no wish to cooperate with the Congress, disliked the Bardoli resolution. He therefore saw to it that Reuters cabled the full text of Jinnah's statement criticising the resolution, and urged Amery to give the statement the fullest weight in Britain and use it in the United States. 'If, under pressure from liberal quarters in the U.K., Rajaji and his friends were able to stifle me in their close embrace, I feel quite sure that the Mahatma would emerge once again upon the stage to give the *coup de grace* to British influence in India'.

Then, in the spring of 1942, there was, a, gaffe about the supposed death of Subhas Chandra Bose in an aeroplane accident. Bose had effected a dramatic escape from house detention in January 1941, and made his Way to Germany to canvass aid for India's freedom struggle in the belief not shared by Mahatma Gandhi, Jawaharlal Nehru and the great majority of the nationalist leadership that imperialist Britain's enemies should be regarded as India's friends. The whole country was shaken with grief. The Congress president and Gandhiji sent telegrams of condolence to the aged mother of Bose. When the allegedly dead Indian leader broadcast a talk from Radio Berlin, Reuters tried to disclaim responsibility for the report.

More grave was the failure of Reuters to make known abroad the firm opposition of the Congress leadership to the plans of Subhas Bose to liberate India with German and Japanese assistance. Mahatma Gandhi wrote in *Harijan* of 26th April 1942: "It is folly to suppose that aggressors can ever be benefactors. The Japanese may free India from the British yoke, but only to put in their own instead. I have always maintained that we should not seek any other power's help to free India from the British." Again, Viceroy Linlithgow cabled to Secretary of State Amery a summary of a report, intercepted by Intelligence, of an interview with Gandhiji on 15th May 1942 of a group of Bombay Congressman led by the former Chief Minister, B.G. Kher.

The report, sent by Sharaf Athar Ali, a Communist, to P.C. Joshi, then secretary of the Communist Party of India, quoted Gandhiji as telling Kher (who had asked whether civil disobedience at that point would not mean help to the Japanese): "Oh, no. We are driving the British (out). We do not invite the Japanese. I disagree with those who think them liberators. Chinese history points that out. In fact I believe that Subhas Bose will have to be resisted by us. Subhas has risked much for us; but if he means to set up a government in India under the Japanese, he will be resisted by US."

The Viceroy, who had got Reuters to cable Jinnah's anti Congress statement, did not organise similar publicity for these anti-Axis views of Mahatma, Gandhi. The Viceroy apart, if Reuters had performed properly its duty as a world news agency, the British Press and public opinion would not have been as grossly misinformed as they were: "In the London Press, libellous propaganda was made by publishing on the front page of certain newspapers a huge headline, 'GANDHI'S INDIA-JAP PEACE PLAN EXPOSED!' The 5th August 1942 issue of the London *Daily Sketch carried* a photograph of Miss Slade (Mira Behn) with the caption, 'ENGLISH WOMAN GANDHI'S JAP PEACE ENVOY!' Punch cartoons were unspeakable. The London *Daily Herald, too was* clotted by the contagion."

Reuters' monopoly of news flow from and to India was a matter of concern to many members of the Indian and Eastern Newspaper Society. Reuters responded to this in its own fashion. At a meeting of the Society in New Delhi on 15th February 1943, F.R. Jones of the Reuters' office in Bombay suggested that "if members desired an additional service they might as well get it from the Associated Press of America through Messrs Reuters Ltd. for an additional fee." Objection was raised on the ground that it would merely be a new Reuters service specially charged. Amritlal Seth of *Janmabhoomi* urged that a competitive service to Reuters was necessary in the interest of newspapers.

The end of Reuters' dominant role in the gathering and distribution of news within the country became inevitable with the British decision, after World War II, to withdraw from India.

Transfer of proprietorship of the Associated Press of India to Indian newspapers had been urged by Arthur Moore of the *Statesman* during the four years of his presidentship of the Indian & Eastern Newspaper Society from its inception in 1939. A liberal who believed in unimpeded flow of information, he also pressed for the abolition of the monopoly clause in Reuters' contract with Indian newspapers which bound them not to utilise any competing world news agency, and for a reduction in the Reuters subscription rate in consonance with the lowered Press cable rate.

Arthur Moore questioned the stand taken by Reuters that the issue of the transfer of API's ownership to Indian newspapers should await the end of the hostilities. Referring to the change in ownership of Reuters in October 1941 when publishers of the London newspapers, organised in the Newspaper Proprietors Association, came in and held an equal number of shares with the Press Association comprising publishers of the provincial newspapers of Britain, Moore said: "If it could be possible for the main body of Reuters to change hands in wartime, it should not be impracticable to effect a change of ownership of the Associated Press under the same conditions."

With the pressure mounting, over the years, for transfer of control of domestic news to Indian newspapers, Reuters thought of a way to ensure at least the continuance of its exclusive distribution of foreign news in India. The expedient thought of was to make the Indian successor to API a partner in Reuters. The new approach was embodied in a draft resolution that was presented at the 21st general meeting of IENS held in Bombay in mid-December 1943: "The Society is of the opinion that the time has arrived for a further and direct discussion of the question of Indian newspapers securing representation in Reuters' central organisation and assuming the management of their Indian concern (Eastern News Agency, which distributed foreign news) and of the API. With a view to the formulation of definite proposals thereon, the Society suggests:

(a) the deputation of two representatives of the Society to visit London, if necessary, for such discussion; and
(b) pending the final fulfilment of these objectives, the establishment of closer association between Reuters and API."

The terms that Reuters initially offered to Indian newspapers would have retained the cream of the profits, as well as control, for Reuters. These terms were acceptable to the British-owned newspapers represented in IENS. Unlike the All India Newspaper Editors' Conference in which the editors of both Indian and British owned newspapers took a common stand as professional journalists against restrictions on publication of news ever since they first met in November 1940, IENS was an association of newspaper publishers and a divergence in approach was not surprising. The story of Reuters' one-sided formula has been told by A.S. Bharatan, who became the first general manager of Press Trust of India which eventually took over API:

> "Reuters' attitude in the early stages was based on the belief that they could part with the minimum and hold on to the maximum. After prolonged discussions a scheme emerged under which Reuters were to retain full control of the foreign news service and transfer the internal news agency, API, to the new Indian company. The annual income of these

> two agencies was in the proportion of two-to-one... This amounted to transferring a deficit-making agency to the Indian company and keeping the profit-making part in Reuters' own hands."

Even the Indian newspaper publishers among the members of IENS were divided in their approach to the question. Eventually the following resolution was adopted: "The IENS is indebted to Mr. Sadanand and Mr. Goenka for the proposals put forward by them for organising a news service owned by newspapers in the country. The Society has in the past strongly expressed the view that steps should be taken by the newspapers in India to acquire complete control of the API and an interest in the Reuters services in the country, with a view to reorganising them on cooperative lines. To put forward concrete proposals to this end, the Society hereby appoints the following subcommittee: the president (H.W. Smith of the Times of *India), K.* Srinivasan, S. Sadanand, and Ramnath Goenka."

The name Press Trust of India for the new agency emerged during discussion at a meeting of this Press Agency Sub Committee held at Madras in February 1946. The company was incorporated at Madras on 27th August 1947, within two weeks of Independence Day. The salient features of PTI's constitution as amended from time to time are:

(i) No distribution of profits to shareholders. Any profits are to be applied entirely to expanding the range and improving the quality of PTI's services to its media and non-media subscribers.

(ii) Membership is restricted to owners of newspapers published in India and subscribing to one or more of the agency's services.

(iii) To ensure the integrity, independence and freedom from bias of PTI's news service, no person can hold more than 1,000 shares of the company, and no member is entitled to more than five votes in all.

(iv) In order to guard and promote the wider public interest, there is provision for the appointment of up to, four Directors unconnected with the newspaper business.

Meanwhile, rapid political developments in the subcontinent made Reuters give up its old approach of dictating terms to IENS. It agreed to a total transfer of its operations in India, and invited an Indian newspaper delegation to visit England and negotiate an agreement under which PTI would become a shareholder in the main Reuters organisation. The members of the IENS delegation-K. Srinivasan, Devadas Gandhi, Sadanand, Goenka and C.R. Srinivasan-assembled on 20th May 1948 in London for the negotiations, which dragged on for thirty days.

In the meanwhile, Prime Minister Nehru made a critical reference to Reuters in the Indian parliament on 12th March, 1948. He said in reply to a question that the news agency had not fully and correctly covered the speeches of Indian representatives in the United Nations Organisation. He also said that the Government were aware that Reuters gave different versions of the news relating to Kashmir, in India and Pakistan.

The Prime Minister finally announced that the Government had decided to discontinue, after due notice, the arrangement for the supply of Reuters news, on payment, to government offices in India and for use in the broadcasts of All India Radio. Yet it was a favourable nod from the Indian Government in mid-1948 that eventually resulted in the acceptance by IENS of the draft agreement with Reuters that the delegation led by K. Srinivasan brought from London. Did the Nehru government hope that PTI, by entering into partnership, could reform Reuters from within?

Anecdotes of Various Nature

Kasturi Srinivasan's biographer writes: "The delegation was a divided house right from the beginning. Sadanand and

Goenka were both strongly antagonistic to Reuters and preferred an arrangement with an American news agency instead. Devadas Gandhi, who was not particularly opposed to Reuters, was still of the view that prior commitments had been made with the Associated Press of America and it would have been much better if an agreement had been arrived at with that agency. C.R. Srinivasan was the only member of the delegation who stood by Kasturi Srinivasan all the time.

> "The main points for negotiation were the terms for the transfer of API to Indian ownership, and the basis on which Reuters should supply world news to PTI. In regard' to the latter, two alternatives had been suggested: one, bulk purchase of news from Reuters on a seller-buyer basis without PTI becoming a partner of Reuters; and the other, a partnership in Reuters on terms similar to those that had been obtained by the Australian and New Zealand Associated Presses. But the Reuters sub-committee throughout pressed only for the conclusion of a partnership arrangement and consequently no other proposition was canvassed during the negotiations."

Sadanand and Goenka, however, preferred bulk purchase of news by PTI from Reuters, without entering into partnership. The Indian delegation's mandate was that four signatures were necessary for it to conclude any agreement. Since this majority was not forthcoming, the delegation returned with a draft agreement. Its main features were as follows:

> On taking up 12,500 shares, PTI would nominate one Director and one Trustee of Reuters.. Apart from the share capital, PTI would bear its portion of the running costs of the organisation. The day PTI took its shares, API would be transferred to PTI for a value to be agreed to by the auditors of both parties.

PTI would operate as a national news agency in India and would be responsible for providing Indian news to Reuters, transmitting news outside India at Reuters' cost. Reuters might, send correspondents to India on special occasions in consultation with PTI, and while in India these would be under the discipline of PTLPTI would set up an Indian Desk in London and its Chief Representative there would be responsible for the contents of the world news service sent to India by Reuters. He would advise Reuters' Managing Editor on this, as well as on the use of incoming Indian news, and be under the discipline of Reuters.

The Indian Desk would take over from Reuters the despatch of news services to Ceylon, Burma, Pakistan, Malaya and also certain Far Easter countries. The PTI Director on Reuters would have special responsibility for the contents of the service to these countries.

The area from Cairo in the west to a point eastwards to be fixed in consultation with the Australian Associated Press would be called the Indian Zone. Subject to the general responsibility of Reuters' Board, the primary responsibility of collecting news and supervising the work of correspondents in the zone would vest in PTI. A number of correspondents nominated by PTI would be added to the Reuter set-up in the zone. Reuters would introduce Indian journalists at the executive level into their world news organisation.

A PTI man would be appointed in New York to cover the United Nations, and another would be appointed in Washington.

PTI would have exclusive use of Reuters news in India for the Press as well as the radio. PTI could sell its own news anywhere outside and should consult Reuters if it intended to sell the service to a competing world agency.

The scene shifted to India. At a four-day general body meeting of IENS in Bombay which began on 21st July 1948, the president of the Society, Tushar Kanti Ghosh, read out a letter received by him from Sardar Patel. In the course of this letter the Home Minister, who also held charge of. Information & Broadcasting, said that "having regard to the totality of the circumstances and taking a broad view of the agreement, I feel it is demonstrably in the interests of India and should be accepted." The agreement was endorsed by the Society and formally announced on 21st September 1948.

PTI had to raise funds quickly for buying the shares of Reuters. It issued 10,000 debentures of Rs. 100 each, carrying interest at 4 1/2 per cent. Sardar Patel, with whom Bharatan had good rapport, helped by persuading the ruler of Baroda to buy a large portion of the debentures. PTI remitted the money, and became a partner of Reuters with effect from 1st February 1949. Reuters' Agreement of Trust was suitably amended.

The PTI Board appointed C.R. Srinivasan as its Trustee and Devadas Gandhi as Director of Reuters. Ramnath Goenka was appointed as alternate Director. PTI took over the operations of API on lst February 1949.

What nullified the potential of the partnership agreement for PTI emerging as a major player on the world news scene was PTI's lack of resources to deploy correspondents to cover adequately the zone of operations allotted to it. The newspaper publishers who owned PTI were interested in securing the staple of news at the cheapest possible rate, supplementing it with their own correspondents in some of the world capitals. Even these few correspondents posted abroad sent home as many of them continue to do news letters rather than spot news.

The publishers did not share the vision that had impelled Jawaharlal Nehru to say at the Allahabad session of the All India Newspaper Editors' Conference on 16th February 1946: "I should like the owners of all newspapers present here to think of starting your own foreign news service. A number of newspapers could combine for the purpose and appoint their agents. I would particularly like them to go to places which are not sufficiently covered by other agencies-in South East Asia, the Middle East and the rest of the world."

PTI was without a correspondent in Moscow till 1963, and except for a two-month visit in 1949 by M. Sivaram, there was none in Peking till November 1980. It had, a maximum of only five correspondents at any time in the whole Indian zone, making do with, stringers at other places. The tenuous presence of PTI men was compounded by PTI's misjudgement in making Bombay-which did not have direct communication links with the capitals in the Indian zone-the controlling centre. It would have been more appropriate to give operational control of the Indian zone to the Chief Representative in London.

To direct the Indian Desk at the headquarters of Reuters in London, the PTI Board chose as its Chief Representative G Parthasarathi, who had been assistant editor of the *Hindu* since 1936. K. Gopalan, a senior member of the staff from the API days, was assigned to assist him. They found on arrival, in April 1949, that the 'Eastern desk' which was supposed to select and edit the news file of the world service that would go out to India and to a large number of other Asian countries consisted of six men who, except for one person, were professionally mediocre: "Five had no knowledge of Indian conditions and even Indian geography.

The sixth had a distant acquaintance with India by virtue of his having been a sub editor on the Statesman of Calcutta about twenty years ago. But he was long past the age of retirement." It was only after a personal discussion in Bombay, during a visit to India by Parthasarathi that PTI's management was persuaded to strengthen the Indian desk by replacing three of the Englishmen by Indians.

Meanwhile the Englishmen on the Indian desk presented problems not only of ignorance of the region they were expected to serve but of political prejudice imbibed over years of work in Reuters. When dealing with despatches from the

United Nations the English sub-editor, Gopalan says, tended to apply as before "the British news agency treatment of five hundred words to the British delegate, hundred to the American and twenty words to say that 'the Iraqi, Pakistani, Egyptian and Indian delegates also supported the motion' or some such thing." In, addition to its work of processing for the Indian zone the Reuters world service which was "eighty per cent British in concept and content " the Indian desk contributed to coverage from the Indian and Asian viewpoint of international events in London like the conferences of Commonwealth Prime Ministers.

The posting of D.P. Wagle at New York led to better coverage of United Nations proceedings. From Indonesia, N. Rajamani who had close links with Dr. Soekamo and other nationalist leaders did some fine reportage. When talks opened at the Hague on the political future of Indonesia, Reuters initially relied entirely on the ANP news agency of Holland. The Indian desk sent a special correspondent, on PTI account, to the Hague to ensure that justice was done also to the Indonesian nationalist viewpoint in Reuters despatches.

These limited gains were more than offset by another factor which militated against the partnership arrangement from the start, namely the conflict between India and Pakistan which were the two most important countries-at any rate at that time-of the zone allotted to PTI. Indo-Pakistan hostilities were in full swing when the PTI-Reuters agreement was being negotiated, a ceasefire coming into effect only, at the end of December 1948. Altaf Hussain, president of the Pakistan Newspaper Editors' Conference, stated in Karachi on 8th March 1950 that Pakistan "has never accepted and will never accept" the position of being treated as a part of the Indian zone mentioned in Reuters' agreement with PTI. When there was a massive exodus that year of members of the minority Hindu community from the eastern wing of Pakistan (now Bangladesh) to India, PTI sent two correspondents to Dacca.

Both were arrested by Pakistan authorities. Reuters, instead of helping to find a practical solution to the problem of news blackout in a situation of widespread human distress, sent its general manager to conduct negotiations with the Eastern News Trust of Pakistan for the operation of a separate Pakistani beam by Reuters. This new beam would additionally cover several countries which were already included in the Indian zone under the agreement with PTI which had come into force only the previous year.

Another irritant for the Indian partners of Reuters was the posting of a British correspondent in New Delhi on a regular basis, whereas the partnership agreement had visualised that "Reuters may send correspondents from headquarters to India on special occasions in consultation and in cooperation with the PTI." When the four-year partnership agreement expired at the end of 1952, it was not renewed. Instead, PTI entered into a contractual relationship with Reuters as between buyer and seller for the supply of the Reuters news and commercial service to PTI and for the supply of the PTI service to Reuters. This was what Sadanand and Goenka had urged from the beginning.

With the ending of the unequal partnership in Reuters, PTI became free to augment its sources of foreign news, including pictorial coverage, through arrangements with other international news agencies besides Reuters.

Kasturi Srinivasan had told his colleagues of the All India Newspaper Editors' Conference in October 1942 that the Indian Press could not be fully free till the country became free. But it soon turned out that, in certain respects, each State is like every other, whether it be alien and autocratic or native and democratic, capitalist or socialist. None of them will tolerate attempts at subversion through sedition and violence, or the disclosure of State secrets.

Sadanand's *Free Press journal* learnt this to its cost. When Indian ratings of the Royal Indian Navy mutinied in Bombay in February 1946 against racial discrimination, "*FPJ* stood foursquare behind the R.I.N. boys of 'Talwar' and other ships and establishments and allowed them the full use of *FPJ* columns to air their grievances, even though the R.I.N. mutiny came at a time when the Congress had started negotiations with the British Cabinet Mission and frowned on the mutiny. *FPJ* went a step further. It employed two of the R.I.N. boys sacked by the Navy and pilloried the authorities editorially. This was something Sardar Patel could never forgive."

As the war ended and it become clear that India's independence could not be long delayed, Sadanand made plans for starting an Indian international news agency with the same during-do that he had shown in organising the Free. Press of India news agency in the late 1920's. He visited Cairo, London and New York during 1945-46 and entered into agreements with American and other news agencies and individual journalists to launch the Free Press of India World Service. The project ended in smoke when the *Free Press Journal* disclosed in September 1947 that Indian naval and land forces were being moved towards Junagadh. The Muslim ruler of that overwhelmingly Hindu majority State on the Gujarat coast had acceded to Pakistan; and while the people demonstrated in protest, the Nawab was preparing to bring in outside armed support.

The story of the movement of Indian forces was broken by B.C. Dutt, who was working on the FPJ and the afternoon *Free Press Bulletin.* He recalls: "Through the grapevine I still maintained with the navy, I heard a startling piece of news. Ships and some army units were heading for Junagadh by sea and land. Natarajan (the editor) could not doubt the authenticity of the news, as I had managed to smuggle out a carbon copy of the movement order."

The story was banner-headlined in the *Free Press Bulletin* on a Saturday and the news agencies sent it on teleprinter for the Sunday papers which carried it on the front page. On

Monday morning the editor, S. Natarajan, called B.C. Dutt and told him how angry Sardar Patel, Home Minister, who was also in charge of Information & Broadcasting, was: "He is furious that we published news about the armed forces without official clearance. The phone almost burnt up by the time he hung up on Sadanand last night."

The Indian government denied to Sadanand the lease of teleprinter lines and other facilities he needed, though he had placed a large order for teleprinters. This was the beginning of his financial decline and serious ill-health. He died in 1953, a heroic and tragic figure in the history of Indian journalism.

8

Post-independence Scene

India's experience over the post-independence years has demonstrated the need, if a free Press is to flourish, not only for a constitutional guarantee of Press freedom but, equally, for those in authority to honour the spirit of the Constitution and not merely go by its letter. The importance of the second requirement is illustrated by the difference in the fortunes of the Press during the prime ministership of Jawaharlal Nehru and of some of his successors.

Best Stage

Though the Indian Constitution does not expressly guarantee freedom of the Press, the Supreme Court has held in successive judgements that freedom of the Press is covered by, and is an essential part of, freedom of expression which is guaranteed by Article 19. This occurs in Part III of the Constitution which enumerates the citizens' Fundamental Rights that are enforceable by appeal to the High Courts and the Supreme Court. A controversial amendment of this Article, relating to freedom of expression, was effected by the first amendment of the Constitution, in 1951, in Jawaharlal Nehru's time.

The provisions relating to freedom of expression had initially read as follows in the Constitution of republican India that came into force on 26th January 1950: It initially read as follows:

> "19. (1) All citizens shall have the right (a) to freedom of speech and expression;
>
> (2) Nothing in sub-clause (a) of clause (1) shall affect the operation of any existing law in so far as it relates to, or prevent the State from making any law relating to libel, slander, defamation, contempt of court or any matter which offends against decency or morality or which undermines the security of, or tends to overthrow, the State."

In the light of this, several laws which sought to abridge the right to freedom of the Press in the interests of public order came to be challenged before various High Courts. In one such case a special bench of the Patna High Court held by a majority that "if a person were to 90 on inciting to murder or other cognizable offences either through the Press or by word of mouth, he would be free to do so with impunity".

The possible consequences of this court decision were so serious that the government thought it necessary to amend Article 19 (2). But the actual amendment went beyond providing for the protection of public order. The clause as amended by parliament in 1951 read:

> "(2) Nothing in sub-clause (a) of clause (1) shall affect the operation of any existing law, or prevent the State from making any law, in so far as such law imposes reasonable restrictions on the exercise of the right conferred by the said sub-clause in the interests of the security of the State, friendly relations with foreign States, public order, decency or morality, or in relation to contempt of court, defamation or incitement to an offence."

It will be seen that three grounds were added: public order, incitement to an offence, and friendly relations with foreign States on the other hand, the requirement that restrictions imposed should be 'reasonable' made any restrictive laws justiciable.

Of the three additional grounds, the one relating to friendly relations with foreign States was patently questionable. For instance, under a law made in terms of the amended Article 19 (2), could criticism of American policy in Korea, or of totalitarian dictatorship in the Soviet Union, or of the ill treatment of the Hindu minority in Pakistan become punishable? Prime Minister Nehru said in the course of the parliamentary debate on the constitution amendment that the amended 19 (2) was only an enabling clause which empowered parliament to frame legislation in case the need arose. He gave an assurance that it was not the intention of the government to prevent criticism of its foreign policy. While there has been no legislation in this respect so far as the Press is concerned, the Cinematograph Act does empower the government to deny or withdraw certification of a film for exhibition on the grounds enumerated in Article 19 (2) as amended.

The Press Information Bureau of the Government of India announced in a release on 20th July 1981 that the censor certificate issued to the English film 'Midnight Express' had been withdrawn. A notification issued in this connection said that the film contained scenes of brutality and debased human values and showed the government, the people and the judicial system of Turkey in an unfavourable and tendentiously adverse light. According to the notification, the exhibition of the film was likely to affect "our friendly relations with Turkey" and thus contravened the provisions of the Cinematograph Act.

Age of Independence

After the constitution amendment, as before, there was no lack of criticism of Jawaharlal Nehru's foreign policy in a section of the Press. Kashmir was the first issue on which he was faulted, particularly for his reference of the matter to the United Nations. Among the critics was Khasa Subba Rau (1896-1961) publisher and editor of the English weekly *Swatantra* of Madras, who was as fearless as a journalist as he had been as a freedom fighter. His column 'Sidelights' and 'Sotto Voce' by Vighneswara (pen name of N. Raghunatha Iyer, for long years chief leader writer of the *Hindu)* were looked forward to week after week.

Khasa wrote in *Swatantra* of 10th September 1949: "The folly of the rash rush to the United Nations over the Kashmir issue will be apparent if it is studied in the light of the entirely different attitude adopted by the Government of India over the Hyderabad Issue. The Government of India never swerved from the view that the settlement of the Hyderabad dispute was their own domestic concern in which outside powers would not be allowed to interfere... Pandit Nehru is now surprised at the letter to himself and the Premier of Pakistan written about Kashmir by President Truman and Mr. Attlee, which he has rightly characterised as intervention. But what is surprising is that he should be so surprised. Pandit Nehru invited the intervention which he now resents."

The weekly *Thought* of Delhi was prominent among critics of Jawaharlal Nehru's China policy, as of his policy towards the Soviet Union. India was among the first countries to recognise Communist China following the 1949 revolution, though its leaders called Nehru and his colleagues 'running dogs of imperialism' Nehru was unhappy when Chinese troops invaded Tibet (though he was to recognise Tibet as 'a region of China' in April 1954). During the crisis touched off by the war between North and South Korea, India voted in favour of United Nations action against North Korea but resisted the condemnation of China as an aggressor by the General Assembly of the United Nations, in order not to enlarge the area of hostilities. It is in this context that the verbal exchange between *Thought* and Jawaharlal Nehru during 1951, narrated below, has to be viewed.

Press Trust of India, after consulting the Indian government, decided in November 1949 not to put out a report received from its correspondent M. Sivaram, who had visited Communist China, about the massive preparations under way for Chinese entry into the Korean war. With a tight censorship in force on the Communist-controlled mainland, Sivaram had necessarily to cable his story from Hongkong. Following, are extracts from Sivaram's message:

> This is the first uncensored despatch out of Communist China from Sivaram , PTI staff correspondent who returned to Hongkong tonight after a two-month assignment in Peking Communist China has completed preparations to throw half a million crack troops into the battle for Korea 'even at the risk of a major war, PTI learned on reliable authority in Peking. The leaders of the Chinese People's Republic, according to this authority, intervened in Korea deliberately and fully prepared to face the consequences and after having secured, so it is understood, pledges from the Soviets of assistance in the event of reverses in the campaign to roll the United Nations forces down the Korean peninsula this winter.

This authority added that a secret Chinese-Soviet deal to halt 'imperialist aggression' was concluded last month before the Chinese People's Liberation Army 'volunteers' crossed into Korea.

From all parts of China today the finest units of the Chinese Communist Army and the best available military equipment are being rushed to Manchuria, while the entire nation is being geared for war through an intensive propaganda campaign...

The official Chinese Press is filled with lists of university students and professional men, model workers and combat heroes who have volunteered to fight in Korea...

Communist China, observers believed, was gambling on two possibilities- persuading the United Nations and the world that there was no official Chinese military intervention in Korea or, alternatively, depending on the reluctance of the United Nations and of the powers fighting in Korea to expand the sphere of hostilities and thus probably precipitating a major war involving Soviet Russia as well."

A year and a half later, the above report of Sivaram's was discovered and published by *Thought.* It said in an editorial note: "The Press Trust of India, losing their nerve at an Indian journalist's daring to paint a picture different from that officially prescribed by Mr. Nehru, referred the message, before releasing it, to the Foreign Affairs Subcommittee of the Cabinet. Mr. Nehru and Mr. N.G. Ayyangar, it is believed, favoured suppressing it; Sardar Vallabhbhai Patel and Mr. Rajagopalachari considered that it should not be Concealed from the Indian public and the world's press.

The dissenting views were conveyed to the Press Trust of India, who decided on suppression. Reuters abided by this suppression, and a message sent by an Indian journalist to the Indian public was released for publication only in Australia, where it had little effect. Where Chinese Communist censorship failed, Mr. Nehru's censorship temporarily succeeded."

On the matter being raised in the Lok Sabha by the leader of the opposition, Dr. Syama Prasad Mookerjee, Prime Minister Nehru denied that the Foreign Affairs Committee of the Cabinet had discussed the report sent by the PTI correspondent, but in effect confirmed that PTI suppressed the message on official advice. Nehru said: "In regard to this message. I enquired today and the Secretary General sent a note to me. What happened was this: that a representative of the, PTI went over some time to our foreign office and consulted the Secretary General there about it. I shall use his own words (it is absurd to talk of censorship): 'On receipt of this message Mr. so and so of the PTI saw me and sought my advice as to whether or not it would be helpful. I told him that I did not think it would, and he went away.

It was for him to decide to publish it or not.' Then so and so advised his General Manager accordingly. He decided not to publish it. I did not know anything about this message at all. But a number of messages appeared round about this time, a little before and a little after, in the Press from the PTI correspondent about conditions in China. Some of the messages seemed to me not to be quite balanced judgment... It seemed to me particularly unfortunate that anything that the correspondent wrote should have been written not from China itself but after coming to a place like Hongkong which is a very peculiar place today, a hotbed of the opponents and enemies of the Chinese Government. Hon. Members may remember, long ago there was a place on the Russian border--Riga--from which all kinds of messages came." (*Parliamentary Debates,* I June 1951, Vol. 12, Part 11).

Thought said in a concluding comment (8th June 1951) on the Prime Minister's statement in parliament: "If Mr. Bajpai (the Secretary General) acted entirely on his own initiative, as the Prime Minister at one point of his speech suggested, then he was wrong in taking so grave a step without authority. But if he was carrying out the policy of the Prime Minister and the Government, he was only doing his duty, and the Prime Minister and the Government were wrong to have framed such a policy."

V.K. Krishna Menon, close friend of Jawaharlal Nehru, was Defence Minister at the time that India's relations with China changed from the euphoria of the 'Hindi-Cheeni Bhai Bhai' slogan popularised by the Indian government in the early 1950's. The acerbic Defence Minister was a target of sustained criticism by a section of the Press which regarded him as a crypto-Communist. Prominent among political leaders who felt that Krishna Menon was unduly soft in relation to the two Communist powers was Acharya J.B. Kripalani. He said in the course of a Foreword written in December 1959 to a compilation of writings in *Thought* about China: "The nation has to congratulate itself that, at long last, it is recognized that Red China is red in tooth and claw and its aggression is a challenge to the nation. Yet it was ominous that the Defence Minister in his speech said that it was difficult to define aggression, which even the UNO had not been able to do for years.

It may be difficult to define aggression even as it is difficult to define pain. But surely the man who suffers from pain does not fail to feel it simply because he cannot define it. It would appear that our Defence Minister does not feel the pain of foreign aggression as do the overwhelming majority of his countrymen... Anyway, it is all to the good that the Prime Minister, in spite of the doubts of his Defence Minister, considers Red China's excursions in our territory as aggression and as such a challenge to the nation."

Following the humiliating reverses suffered by the Indian army, ordered by the political leadership into a war along the Himalayan border for which it was wholly unprepared, Jawaharlal Nehru was constrained to drop Krishna Menon from the Cabinet. This was after an initial downgrading of Menon, from Defence to Defence Production, failed to satisfy angry critics within the Congress parliamentary party. During this time, Jawaharlal Nehru's critics, in the Press and in political parties including his own could have been muzzled through censorship, or physically jailed, by invoking Emergency powers. But such measures were foreign to his nature.

The Etiquettes

In contrast, the Press was to be brought under rigid censorship, and the country's news agencies subjected to extralegal arm-twisting, under the emergency rule of Prime Minister Indira Gandhi during 1975-76.

Jawaharlal Nehru had entertained high hopes for his daughter and did his best to train her, beginning with the correspondence course he conducted in order to afford her and a wider reading public, glimpses of world history. The process of grooming culminated in her being chosen as Congress president in 1958. After Nehru's death in 1964, Indira Gandhi joined the Union Cabinet as Minister of Information & Broadcasting. Following the sudden death of Prime Minister Lal Bahadur Shastri at Tashkent, she was elected as leader of the Congress parliamentary party and became Prime Minister in January 1966.

After a hesitant start during which she found that her decision to devalue the rupee, though inescapable on economic grounds, was politically unpopular, she decided to chart her course as a radical dedicated to the removal of mass poverty. She shook herself free of the provincial Congress barons, known as the Syndicate, and cultivated the Left within and outside the Congress. Communists supported her programme of bank nationalization and abolition of the princes' privy purses. With this support she got elected as President of India an Independent candidate, V.V. Giri, defeating the Congress nominee Sanjiva Reddy whose candidature had been sponsored earlier by Indira Gandhi herself among others. The split in the Congress that ensued had profound consequences for the Indian Press.

Several newspapers with a large circulation, some of them owned by entrepreneurs who had interests in other branches of industry and trade, opposed bank nationalization. Big newspapers therefore came to be regarded as 'bad', with the corollary that small newspapers, many of which looked to advertising and other support from the governments at Delhi and in the States were 'good'.

The initial mood of elation in the Leftist Press at the triumph of Indira Gandhi as well as its subsequent doubts are brought out in the following extract from an article by Aruna Asaf Ali, publisher of the *Link* magazine (from 1958) and the daily Patriot (from 1963) till January 1993: "I was thrilled when I came to know that Indira had made up her mind to challenge the conservative forces in the Congress. I went to her and said that her decision to oppose the Syndicate's bid for the Presidency was a historic step which would lead to far-reaching changes in the party and in the country... Indira Gandhi became the heroine of Link House, and so she remained through the stirring years of bank nationalization, abolition of the princes' privy purses, and the liberation of Bangladesh.

"Indira Gandhi's initiatives of the early 1970's antagonized the Rightist, communal and disruptive forces. Lawless agitations were fomented by a motley combination of political groups, encouraged by hostile foreign forces intent on -toppling her and destabilizing India. To arrest this dangerous trend, Indira Gandhi proclaimed a state of internal emergency. This step was supported in the initial stages by me and my colleagues of the Left. But there emerged a few months later some distortions of the emergency regulations. Well-meaning but unimaginative and harsh measures were adopted, to promote family planning and carry out slum clearance for instance, which alienated large sections of the people."

In the wake of an adverse verdict in June 1975 by a single-member bench of the Allahabad High Court, which held Prime Minister Indira Gandhi guilty of electoral malpractice in the 1971 elections to the Lok Sabha, Indira Gandhi persuaded the then President, Fakhruddin Ali Ahmed, to proclaim a state of internal emergency. The action was strictly in accord with the letter, though it was not in the spirit, of the Constitution. Article 352 read at that time as follows:

> "352 (1) If the President is satisfied that a grave emergency exists whereby the security of India or of any part of the territory thereof is threatened, whether by war or external aggression or internal disturbance, he may, by Proclamation, make a declaration to that effect.
>
> (3) A Proclamation of Emergency declaring that the security of India or of any part of the territory

> thereof is threatened by war or by, external aggression or by internal disturbance may be, made, before the actual occurrence of war or of any such aggression or disturbance if the President is satisfied that there is imminent danger thereof."

In the words of Arun Shourie, "Democratic constitutions are framed on the premise that citizens and politicians will abide by their spirit. The determined usurper thus has no difficulty in finding articles, clauses-the letter--to stab the spirit. The morning after the Reichstag fire Hitler goes to the aging Hindenburg and gives him a highly coloured account and persuades him to issue an Emergency Decree. The Emergency Decree is issued under Article 48 of the Weimar Constitution."

With the Fundamental Rights suspended for the duration of the emergency and the judiciary thus put out of action, the executive ran amuck in relation to the Press. Electric supply to newspaper establishments on Bahadur Shah Zafar Marg, where most of the capital's dailies are located, was cut off during the night of June 25-26,1975, so that they could not report truthfully or comment freely on the events culminating in the proclamation of emergency.

From 1st February 1949 when the Reuters' subsidiary API began to function as the Indian Owned Press Trust of India, it had the stimulus of competition to supplement the self-motivation of its employees. But the United Press of India, closed down in 1958 because it was financially unviable.

Soon, however, a number of newspapers came together to sponsor a new agency, the United News of India. It started operations on -21st March 1961. Observers have pointed to a number of factors that might have impelled the sponsoring newspapers to take this initiative. One is the desirability, in the words of the First Press Commission in its report (1954), of there being "at least two news agencies, each competing with the other and also acting as a corrective to the other". Another was, as an analyst put it, "the desire of the larger newspapers to have a second competing agency on which they could fall back in the event of PTI, where working journalists had begun to unionise themselves, becoming strike-bound." A third factor that has been cited is the anxiety of the then Chief Minister of West Bengal, Dr. B.C. Roy, and others to find alternative employment for the hundreds of employees who were thrown out of work when the Calcutta based UPI closed down.

The emergence of UNI in 1961 meant the revival of competition after a three-year interval during which PTI was the only English-language wire news agency in the country. The desirability of competition as a stimulus to keen journalistic effort Was demonstrated by each agency on a number of occasions. The last occasion, however, was a few hours before an event which made competition in news gathering irrelevant, namely the clamping of censorship on the Press on 25th June 1975. Tarun Basu describes- UNI's scope in these words:

> "Staffers made a beeline for the police stations. Their efforts did not go unrewarded. Amid signs of frenetic activity at the Parliament Street police station at 2 a.m., a black Ambassador drew up with an occupant that was all too familiar. As tough-looking guards tried to shield the frail figure of Jayaprakash Narayan, we made a dash for the car. *Vinashakale Viparita Buddhi* (madness takes hold as the end nears):, these historic words of J.P. were to be on the front pages of every newspaper which managed to come out next morning.

What was done in the name of an emergency, in the 28th year of India's freedom, exceeded in coarseness anything done to the Press by alien rulers during the colonial period: from governor-general Wellesley's Regulations of 1799 and the Vernacular Press Act of 1878 to the restrictions imposed during World War II. With suspension of the constitutional guarantee of Fundamental Rights, the brute force of the State (ultima ratio regum, title of an anti-Fascist poem by Stephen Spender) took over.

The Defence and Internal Security of India Rules were invoked to clamp a censorship more rigorous than what the British rulers enforced during World War II. Truthful reporting even of the proceedings of Parliament, and of the highest courts of the land, became impossible. M.A. Jinnah, in his early phase as a liberal and a nationalist, condemned in 1936 the action taken by the British authorities, under the Indian Press (Emergency Powers) Act of 1931 against *Abhyudaya* of Allahabad-founded in the 1920's by Pandit Madan Mohan Malaviya for publishing a speech of Pandit K.K. Malaviya in the Central Legislative Assembly. Jinnah said: "It is the privilege of the newspaper to have the proceedings published, and so long as they are true, fair and faithful faithful it is not liable to action."

Of the same liberal view as the early Jinnah was Feroze Gandhi who, as a Congress back-bencher, in the Lok Sabha, was a Leftist and an advocate of nationalization much before his wife Indira was to assume that role. He introduced as a non official Bill, and got enacted by Parliament in 1956, a law to protect newspapers from legal action on grounds of libel etc. for the publication of truthful accounts of parliamentary proceedings.

Among, three Press laws, which Prime Minister Indira Gandhi got enacted during the emergency, through Presidential ordinances issued on 8th December 1975 which were subsequently endorsed by parliament during January-February 1976, was one repealing the Feroze Gandhi Act. During the debate on this Bill the proceedings were blacked out at the time and were made public only in 1977, Hiren Mukherjee of the C.P.I. said in the Lok Sabha on 27th January 1976: 'We all know that it is not normal to oppose government legislation at the introduction stage, but on this occasion I am constrained to do so because this is a Bill we shall oppose from A to Z. The reason is that, quite gratuitously, government has cope forward with,, legislation which strikes at the roots of parliament functioning in an efficient manner and responsively to the needs of the country... We do not want a captive parliament. The people of our country have a right to know what is being done inside parliament.'

The next day Hiren Mukherjee went on to twit the, Indira Gandhi Regime about its patronage of pliant capitalists: "They are coming to term with them, people like K.K. Birla, who are coming to control not only their own papers but the *Indian* Express group also. They are treated as socially conscious capitalists with whom they are beginning to join hands. They are punishing decent, honest, independent reporting by putting up here a censorship apparatus."

P.G. Mavalankar (Independent) said: "Unfortunately, radio and television are departments of the Government of India. Therefore, only the Press remains As a free agency... I would suggest to the Minister and to all others, that a free Press is inevitably an extension of a free Parliament. If you take away the free Press, the Parliament does not remain a free Parliament... The record (of parliamentary proceedings) may have everything for the future historians, but people of the present generation will not know what is taking place in Parliament."

Bhupesh Gupta, C.P.I. member, said in the Rajya Sabha on 3rd February 1976: "It pains me that today... the Feroze Gandhi Act is sought to be assassinated by the very people who used to be his friends... Twenty years have passed since that law was enacted. Would there be any Vivian Bose Enquiry Committee report published, even if ;it had been laid on the Table of the House, if there had been no Feroze Gandhi Act? It would not have been possible because Dalmia had enough money to threaten defamatory action and prevent publication. What would have happened to the Mundhra case which led to the appointment of the Chagla Commission, the report of which was again published? Sir, many of the disclosures made courageously by Feroze Gandhi himself in the Lok Sabha in 1957 and in later years would not have seen the light of day, as far as the public is concerned, had there been no protection given by the Act he had conceived and piloted, and got passed. Sir, this is a shameful Bill."

A second repealing legislation enacted-during the emergency abolished the Press Council of India that had been established in 1966. The actual and proximate reason for this action was that the Press Council seemed likely to pronounce against K.K. Birla, proprietor of the *Hindustan Times* and a supporter of the emergency regime, in a case concerning his treatment, of the editor, B.G. Verghese.

The ostensible reason given in the 'statement of objects and reasons, was that, the Press Council had not been able to frame a code of conduct for the Press, Erastmo de Sequeira (Bharatiya Lok Dal) said in the Lok Sabha on 28th January 1976: 'In 26th years we have not been able in this House to codify our own privileges... I say that if the Press Council has not been able to draft a code a conduct for the Press, it probably 'faced' precisely the same difficulties as we find with reference to the codification of our privileges, and these are difficulties which we should, more than anybody else, understand. This Bill is one in a series of measures which can end up only in one direction, towards the destruction of democracy."

P.G. Mavalankar probed the reason for the repeal: "Is it because the Press Council did not toe the line of the Government since it declared the 'internal emergency? Is it because the Press Council did not want to go all the way with the Government and approve of what it has done with regard to suppression of freedom of the Press through censors and all kinds of other controls? Did the Minister want the Press Council to say that they were good?"

In the Rajya Sabha, Dr. K. Mathew Kurian (CPI-M) asked "whether it is not a fact that the B.G. Verghese case was very much in the mind of the Government when this Bill was drafted." Dr. T.N. Singh (Congress-Organisation) said: "I often wonder whether we have not already reached a stage where India is not a democracy but a dictatorship."

In addition to repealing the Feroze Gandhi Act and the Press Council Act, the emergency regime got legislation enacted for 'Prevention of Publication of Objectionable Matter'. The Act would have placed censorship on a permanent footing unless, of course, struck down by the higher judiciary after the end of the emergency and the restoration of Fundamental Rights. (The Act was repealed by the new parliament that emerged from the elections held in March 1977 in which the Congress party led by Indira Gandhi, and she herself, were defeated. The Press Council and protection of publication of parliamentary proceedings were also restored.)

Section 5 of the 1976 Press Act empowered a District Magistrate to direct that any matter relating to a particular subject or class of subjects may not be published for a period of two months. Krishna Kant, opposing the Bill in the Rajya Sabha, said on 4th February 1976: "Apparently there is no bar on continuing the censorship for successive two-month periods by issuing fresh orders. This is a provision which puts precensorship on a permanent basis on the statute book of India."

The definition of objectionable matter covered defamatory writing or visible representation relating to the President-of India, the Vice President and the Prime Minister. Though listed last according to formal protocol, it was the Prime Minister who was principally sought to be protected. As Dr. Mathew Kurian of the C.P.I (M) put it: "This Bill has the primary objective of protecting the Prime Minister from public criticism." He referred to the threat to trade union activity implied in the Bill's prohibition of incitement "to interfere with production, supply and distribution of food and other essential commodities or with essential services" and urged members of the C.P.I. to get rid of their 'confusion' that 'progressives' were occupying "the pinnacles of power in the ruling party".

T.N. Singh said that "if Gandhiji were to be reborn, he would be put behind the bars and his *Harijan* would not be allowed to be published." Umashankar Joshi, renowned poet, warned that terror "breeds cowards on one side and sycophants on the other". Referring to the effect of the legislation on artists, writers, cartoonists and musicians, he said, "Future historians would say that British rule ended up in, releasing the creative energies of the people of our country even under conditions of political subjugation and economic exploitation, but that free India found it necessary to choke these energies."

Krishna Kant quoted a Nigerian journalist who had said in London: "African newspapers which were vigorously in the vanguard of the nationalist struggle for independence now have relatively less freedom to publish under the indigenous African governments they helped to found than they did under White colonialists." Krishna Kant asked: "Is it not an irony that India, the citadel of parliamentary democracy in the midst of the growing darkness of dictatorship in Asia and Africa, is now following these countries instead of giving them a lead?"

In the Lok Sabha, Saroj Mukherjee (C.P.I.M) compared the provisions of the 1951 Press Act framed by Rajaji as Union Home Minister, following the amendment of Article 19, to establish that the 1976 legislation was worse. Whereas under the Rajaji Act it was for a sessions judge to decide on imposition of security on a press, etc., such powers were now given to district magistrates. More than one speaker referred with nostalgia to Jawaharlal Nehru's democratic temper. Satyendra Narayan Sinha (Congress-Organisation) recalled Nehru's ringing words while addressing the A.I.N.E.C. on 3rd December 1950 in New Delhi: "I have no doubt that even if the government dislikes the liberties taken by the *Press* and considers them dangerous, it is wrong to interfere with the freedom of the Press.

By imposing restrictions you do not change anything; you merely suppress the public, manifestation of certain things, thereby causing the idea and thought underlying them to spread further. Therefore, I would rather have a completely free press with all the dangers involved in the, wrong use of that freedom than a suppressed or a regulated press."

Role of Commissions : Jawaharlal Nehru had strong likes and dislikes, and could be impulsive in utterance. As will be seen presently, both these traits were in evidence in connection with the formation of India's first Press Commission in 1952. This Commission made certain proposals that were well-intentioned but could have proved damaging to the growth and liberty of the Indian Press. Nehru refrained from pushing them through.

Nehru was allergic to Seth Ramakrishna Dalmia, the new proprietor of the Times of India because Dalmia was a capitalist and an advocate of a religious State and of cow protection. Another irritant was that Dalmia had four, wives. Polygamy was legal at that time for Hindus, as it continues to be for Indian *Muslims.* Dalmia did not justify or advocate polygamy; an obituary carried by the Statesman on 27th September 1978, on Dalmia's death at the age of 85, said that he "once expressed a desire to write a book on the evils of polygamy."

Dalmia extended the range of the Bombay-based Times of India as a carrier of his views by launching an edition in India's capital in January 1950. The Statesman of Calcutta had opened a Delhi edition in 1930. *National Herald* of Lucknow wished to do so too (though the ambition was to be realised only in March 1968). Uma Shankar Dikshit (managing director of National *Herald* from 1957 to 1971) writes: "With the emergence of free India in 1947, Pandit Jawaharlal Nehru decided that the National *Herald* should be published from Delhi. He thought that the national government needed a powerful organ for promoting its policy of Five Year Plans building up a strong and growing public sector and the other progressive policies of socialism and secularism in a democratic set-up." Dikshit adds: "Pandit Nehru did not want his name as Prime Minister to be associated directly or indirectly with the job of raising funds for establishing and running the National *Herald,* (in Delhi). He depended on his colleagues and associates to acquire the needed finances, and Rafi Ahmed Kidwai did act the role in good measure."

It would thus appear that Nehru's objection was not to multiple editions of newspapers, or to money as such, but to the kind of ideas which money power enabled Dalmia to -propagate. The Prime Minister said in the course of his speech at the annual meeting of the All India Newspaper Editors' Conference on 17th September 1952 in New Delhi: "What exactly is the Press? Whatever it may be, the money involved, the owner and proprietor of that money, are major factors. Does the freedom of the Press ultimately mean freedom of the rich man to do what he likes with his money through the Press? Normally speaking-and I speak with all deference-high standards and high intelligence are not allied with large quantities of money. A person with a large amount of money need not necessarily have high cultural standards or high literary standards or any high standards at all, though, he may have the knack of making money.

Therefore, the freedom of the Press may come to mean the freedom of persons who have a knack of making money and that, after all, is not such a noble thing." M. Chalapathi Rau, who was for long years editor of National *Herald* during and after the Nehru era, recalls: "There was a minor sensation when the National *Herald* was to restart publication (November 1945). 'Nehru received through intermediaries the offer of a crore of rupees from Seth Ram. Krishna Dalmia to start a chain of newspapers. Nehru rejected it outright... Later Nehru was to describe him as that 'ugly man with an ugly, face, ugly mind and ugly ears'. The appointment of a Press Commission was announced by the government on 23rd September 1952, a week after the Prime Minister's address to the A.I.N.E.C.

If Dalmia's ownership of the *Times of India* and the advent of its Delhi edition was the main internal factor that spurred the establishment of a Press Commission in India, an external stimulus was the formation in 1947 of Britain's first Press Commission by the post-war Labour Government. There is an unmistakable resonance between the terms of the British and the Indian commissions, though the state of the industry in India, with newspapers having pitifully small circulations, was far different from conditions in industrially advanced countries like Britain.

The Ross Commission in Britain (194749) was required "to inquire into the factors affecting the maintenance of the independence, diversity and editorial standards of newspapers and periodicals, and the public's freedom of choice of newspapers and periodicals, nationally, regionally and locally, with particular reference to:

(a) the economics of newspaper and periodical publishing and distribution;
(b) the interaction of the newspaper and periodical interests held by the companies concerned with their other interests and holdings, within and outside the communications industry;
(c) management and labour practices and relations in the newspaper and periodical industry;
(d) conditions and security of employment in the newspaper and periodical industry;
(e) the distribution and concentration of ownership of the newspaper and periodical industry, and the adequacy of existing law in relation thereto; and
(f) the responsibilities, constitution and functioning of the Press Council."

The mandate for the Indian body was: "The Press Commission shall enquire into the state of the Press in India, its present and future lines of development and shall in particular examine:

(i) the control, management and ownership and financial structure of newspapers, large and small, the periodical press and news agencies and feature syndicates;

(ii) the working of monopolies and chains and their effect on the presentation of accurate news and fair views;

(iii) the effect of holding companies, the distribution of advertisements and such other forms of external influence as may have a bearing on the development of healthy journalism;

(iv) the method of recruitment, training, scales of remuneration, benefits and other conditions of employment of working journalists settlement of disputes affecting them and factors which influence the establishment and maintenance of high professional standards;

(v) the adequacy of newsprint supplies and their distribution among all classes of newspapers and the possibilities of promoting indigenous manufacture of (a) newsprint and (b) printing and composing machinery;

(vi) machinery for (a) ensuring high standards of journalism and (b) liaison between Government and the Press; the functioning of Press Advisory Committees and organisations of editors and working journalists.; and

(vii) freedom of the Press and repeal or amendment of laws not in consonance with it."

A demand from journalists' trade unions was a common factor accounting for the formation of the Press Commissions in Britain and India. The Ross Commission said in its report, in an introductory section: Me demand for a Royal Commission was initiated by the National Union of journalists. It came before the House of Commons on 29th October 1946, when two Members, both journalists, moved the following motion:

> 'That, having regard to the increasing public concern at the growth of monopolistic tendencies

in the control of the Press and with the object of furthering the free expression of opinion through the Press and the greatest practicable accuracy in the presentation of news, this House considers that a Royal Commission should be appointed to inquire into the finance, control, management and ownership of the Press.'

"The opponents of the motion, among whom also were several journalists, argued that its supporters had failed to make a prima facie case. It was suggested that they were actuated by political prejudice and by a desire to limit the freedom of the Press, or of that part of it which opposed the Government. There was nothing approaching a monopoly in the ownership of newspapers... A Royal Commission could, produce no important information about the ownership of newspapers that was not already available; if it found inaccuracy or distortion, it could do nothing about them; if it suggested legislation, it would open the way to government control; whatever' it did, its mere existence would throw unjustified doubt on the integrity of the Press. The House divided, and on a free vote the, motion was carried by 270 votes to 157."

In contrast to the division of opinion in Britain, both among journalists and the public, in India the climate of opinion at that time among the English-educated intelligentsia was strongly influenced by Prime Minister Jawaharlal Nehru's commendation of socialism understood as public ownership in key areas and government regulation of private enterprise.

The Press Commission was headed by a former Judge of the Supreme Court and its members included a distinguished economist, journalists, and public men covering the political spectrum from liberal to socialist. It included :

Justice G.S. Rajadhyaksha (Chairman), Dr. C.P. Ramaswami Aiyer, Acharya Narendra Deva, Dr. Zakir Hussain, Dr. V.K.R.V. Rao, P.H. Patwardhan, T.N. Singh, Jaipal Singh, J. Natarajan, A.R. Bhat, M. Chalapathi Rau.

These disparate personalities recommended with one voice governmental intervention in the economics of newspaper publishing in order purportedly to facilitate the expression of diverse viewpoints, while they turned a blind eye to the total monopoly exercised by the party in power at the centre over the news and views broadcast by All India Radio.

This can be understood only in the context of the belief then prevalent that State ownership and governmental regulation would conduce to promotion of the public good. There was little fear of the manipulative use of state power by the political party and its leaders for the time being in power. It wag later that the Indian scene began to resemble the situation that obtained in Britain in the early decades of the 20th century, about which G.K. Chesterton wrote: "The mere proposal to set the politician to watch the capitalist has been disturbed by the rather disconcerting discovery that they are both the same man. We are past the point, where being a capitalist is the only way of becoming a politician, and we are dangerously near the point where being a politician is much the quickest way of becoming a capitalist." Over the four decades since the First Press Commission reported India has learnt the hard way that managers of publicly owned undertakings can be as venal as those of private enterprises, and that politicians in power are not immune from the temptation to misuse public office for personal profit.

A second Press Commission was formed after the fall of the Indira Gandhi government in March 1977 as the result of the sixth elections to the Lok Sabha, and the restoration of Fundamental Rights. The new government headed by Morarji Desai announced in May 1978 the formation of a Commission comprising: Justice P.K. Goswami (retired judge of the Supreme

Court); Abu Abraham; Prem Bhatia; S.N. Dwivedi; Moinuddin Harris; Ravi J. Mathai; Yashodhar N. Mehta; V.K. Narasimhan; F.S. Nariman; Arun Shourie (on whose resignation Nikhil Chakravarty was appointed); and S.H. Vatsyayan. Their terms of reference reflected concern about safeguarding the freedom of the Press:

> "The Press Commission shall enquire into the growth and status of the Indian Press since the last Press Commission reported, and suggest how best it should develop in future. It shall, in particular, examine:

(i) The present constitutional guarantee with regard to the freedom of speech and expression, whether this is adequate to ensure freedom of the Press, and the adequacy and efficacy of the laws, rule's and regulations relating to and affecting the Press;

(ii) Means of safeguarding the freedom and independence of the Press against pressures of all kinds from Government, proprietors, advertising, commercial, trade union, political or other sources, in a plural and democratic society;

(iii) Ownership patterns and the financial structure of organs of the Press with a view to ensuring editorial independence and professional integrity and the readers' right to objective news and views and comments freely expressed;

(iv) The relationship that should exist between the Government and the Press, especially with regard to access to information, accreditation, official patronage or subsidies;

(v) The structure and functioning of the existing news and feature agencies and measures necessary for their growth as strong and viable organisations that can cover news, monitoring at every level right down to the grassroots and also world news;

(vi) Relations that should subsist between different elements of the Press, viz., publishers, managers, editors and other professional journalists, etc.;

(vii) Measures necessary to raise and maintain high standards of journalism and to inculcate among journalists and newspapers a due sense of public and social responsibility corresponding to the power of the Press, its role in national reconstruction and its obligation to the readers;

(viii) Ways and means to promote the growth and development of the language and regional Press as also the periodical Press, specialised journals and syndicated services;

(ix) The economics of the newspaper industry, including ways and means of rectifying deficiencies and evolving the basis for a fair price for newspapers keeping in view legal and constitutional requirements; and

(x) The adequacy of training in communications journalism, adequacy newspaper management, printing technology and newspaper design and graphics as also the desirability and feasibility of higher learning in journalism and mass communications."

Following the fall of the Government headed by Morarji Desai, the Goswami Commission submitted its resignation on 30th July 1979, stating that "as a matter of propriety it is desirable for a Commission to tender its resignation on a change of government. This enables the new government to view afresh the subject of continuance of the Commission in all its aspects."

The Information Minister, Purushottam Kaushik, in the new government headed by Charan Singh, replied to the Chairman of the Commission: "Government appreciate the sentiments which have prompted you to write this letter. They have considered the matter and would like you and the members of the Press Commission to continue with the work."

When, following the fall of the Charan Singh government and the elections held in January 1980, the Congress party led by Indira Gandhi returned to power, the Goswami Commission once again offered its resignation. This time it was accepted. Vasant Sathe as Information Minister in the Indira Gandhi government wrote to justice Goswami: "I am happy to note that during the course of the short period the Commission has been in existence, it has done valuable work by going round to different centres in the country, interviewing a large number of witnesses and collecting a mass of data and information.

The new Government would like to continue the Commission based on a more comprehensive set of terms of reference. This, you will kindly appreciate, will be possible only if the Commission is reconstituted. It is in this context that the Government has regretfully decided to accept your resignation as well as the resignation; of your colleagues."

The terms of reference of the Commission, reconstituted with justice K.K. Mathew as Chairman, were announced on 24th July 1980:

> "The Press Commission shall inquire re into the growth and status of the Press since the first Press Commission reported and suggest how best it should develop in future. It shall, in particular, examine and make recommendations on:

1. The role of the Press in a developing and democratic society;
2. The present constitutional guarantee with regard to the freedom of speech and expression, whether this is adequate to ensure freedom of the Press; adequacy and efficacy of the laws, rules and regulations for maintaining this freedom;
3. Constitutional and legal safeguards to protect the citizen's right to privacy;

4. Means of safeguarding the independence of the Press against economic and political pressures and Pressures from proprietors and management;
5. Role of the Press and the responsibilities it should assume in developmental policies;
6. The Press as an industry, a social institution and a forum for informed discussion of public affairs;
7. Ownership patterns, management practices and financial structures of the Press; their relation to growth, editorial independence and professional integrity;
8. Chain newspapers; links with industry, their effect on competition and on the readers' right to objective news and free comments;
9. Economics of the newspaper industry, newsprint, printing machinery and other inputs for newspapers;
10. Advertising-government and private, educational and commercial;
11. Government-Press relations and the role of official agencies;
12. Relations that should subsist between-different elements of the Press, namely publishers, managers, editors and professional journalists and others;
13. Growth of small and medium papers and of the language Press;
14. Development of the periodical Press and specialised journals;
15. News coverage and news values; structure and functioning of news agencies and feature agencies; flow of news to and from, India;
16. Training of professional manpower; steps to improve professional standards and performance; research in, journalism and mass communication;
17. Journalism as a means of better mutual understanding

in the context of proposals for a new international information order; and

18. Perspective of newspaper development."

The final composition of the reconstituted Commission was: justice K.K. Mathew, retired Judge of the Supreme Court (Chairman); justice Sisir Kumar Mukherjee, retired Judge of the Calcutta High Court; P.V. Gadgil, author and journalist; Ishrat Ali Siddiqui, Editor, *Qaumi Awaz,* Lucknow; Rajendra Mathur, Chief Editor, *Nai Duniya,* Indore; Girilal Jain, Editor, *Times of India,* Bombay; K.R. Ganesh, former Union Minister of State; H.K. Paranjape, economist and former member,. Monopolies and Restrictive Trade Practices Commission; Ranbir Singh, Editor, *Milap,* Delhi; Prem Chand Verma, President of the All India Small and Medium Newspapers' Association and former member of the Lok Sabha; and Justice A.N. Mulla, retired Judge of the Allahabad High Court And former member of the Lok Sabha and the Rajya Sabha.

There was a sharp cleavage of views as between the Chairman and six members of the Commission, on the one hand, and four other members, namely S.K. Mukherjea, Rajendra Mathur, Girilal Jain and H.K. Paranjape. The majority of seven, broadly speaking, favoured governmental regulation of newspaper ownership and management, while the minority of four were opposed to it. The report of the Mathew Commission is remarkable for the lengthy joint minute of dissent, which is virtually a separate minority report, rejoinder thereto, reply to rejoinder, and other comments.

Surveyed in this section are, the proposals made by the First Press Commission, several of which were endorsed and further elaborated by the majority of the Second Press Commission but opposed by the minority, for regulation of newspaper ownership and management. (Proposals similar to these were considered and commented on also by one or more of the three Press Commissions of the U.K.) The various views on each proposal, and the response of successive Indian governments, are reviewed below.

The Rajadhyaksha Commission, conceded (pp. 271-272) that the defects of newspapers are not invariably linked to the form of ownership: "We agree that the shortcomings to which we have drawn attention are not peculiar to any particular form of ownership... There has been evidence about newspapers whose ownership was vested in a political party, where the profit motive was not the dominant one, which indulged in misrepresentation of political opponents. There have been cases of small newspapers, owned by individuals or groups or partnerships, indulging in scurrilous and offensive publications... There has also been evidence about a newspaper, whose ownership is kept within a family, which has set up high traditions of stability and objectivity in journalism... There may also be cases where trustees of newspapers become tyrants, or cooperative ownership may become coercive, particularly if those in control do not have a proper sense of values. Whatever the forms of ownership, the character of a newspaper will depend on the character of the editor and the proprietors and not on the form of ownership."

Despite this, the first Press Commission went on to commend voluntary transfer of the control of a newspaper by its owners to a public trust: "A proposal was put before us that all newspapers, big and small, should be compelled by legislation to come under the Trust form of ownership or control. While we do not recommend any compulsion of the type suggested, we do regard the Trust form of ownership as the most desirable... We would welcome in India this trend which the Royal Commission on the Press in the United Kingdom has described as one of the most interesting developments of the last 25 years."

The Ross Commission had said in its report of 1949: "A trust does not necessarily convert a newspaper from a commercial to a non-commercial concern, or give it quality which it did not previously possess. For these reasons we do not consider that it would be effective or appropriate to put any pressure on proprietors by fiscal inducements or otherwise to adopt either trust ownership or any of the arrangements whose purposes are similar. A trust can be, however, a valuable means, of preserving qua quality where quality already exists. We accordingly welcome the action of public spirited proprietors who have taken such steps as lie in their power to safeguard the character and independence of their papers; and we hope that the number of papers so protected will grow."

Though the First Press Commission did not recommend compulsory delinking of newspaper ownership from other business interests, it gave sufficient arguments in favour of delinking to encourage the government in the post-Nehru years to initiate legislation for the purpose. "It would be ideal", the Rajadhyaksha Commission had said, "if the proprietor of a newspaper has no other interests." (page 273 of Report). The Commission also gave numerous suggestions for diffusing widely the ownership and control of newspapers.

These ideas of delinking, and diffusion came to be discussed widely in the wake of the Congress split of 1969 and the nationalisation of banks by the Indira Gandhi government which lost its majority but ruled with Communist support. When Indira Gandhi emerged strong from the mid-term elections to the Lok Sabha in 1971 and formed a new government, a Bill was drafted for amending the Companies Act so as to incorporate provisions for delinking newspaper companies from other business interests.

Another approach to securing the same end, of emasculating the most influential section of the Press, was embodied in a draft Bill prepared in July 1974 following discussions between the then Minister of information & Broadcasting and the Law Minister. Its aim was to interpose by law a Board of Control between the proprietors and the editorial staff in order in the words of a note prepared in the Ministry of I & B" to ensure editorial freedom and the newspaper's social responsibility". The draft Bill required every big newspaper company, in general meeting, to specify succinctly its editorial policy. The functions of the proposed Board of Control included the following:

> "The Board of Control shall, if it is of opinion that the editorial board is not giving proper effect to the editorial policy, or that the views expressed in the big newspaper per by the editorial board are in conflict with the editorial Policy or are prejudicial to the interests of the big newspaper company or are against the public interest, advise the editorial board...
>
> If the editorial board omits or refuses to act in accordance with the advice tendered by the Board of Control, that Board may advise the big newspaper company to so reconstitute the editorial board as to ensure that due effect is given by it to the editorial policy.
>
> Notwithstanding anything contained in any contract or in any law (other than this Act) in force for the time being, a big newspaper company may, if advised by the Board of Control so to do, terminate the contract of service of the Editor-in-Chief or any other member of the editorial board."

Though the Bills of 1971 and 1974 were not proceeded, with, the threat of legislation on such lines continued to hang over the head of the Press like the legendary sword of Damocles.. Then came the emergency and censorship in mid-1975 which knocked the Press down flat. It remained supine till the emergency regime was voted out in the March 1977 elections.

The majority of members of the Second Press Commission, formed by Indira Gandhi following her return to power in January 1980, were moved by an even deeper distrust of private enterprise and correspondingly greater faith in State regulation than the members of the first. The majority report said: "It is precisely because the business men owning or controlling big newspapers have not acted on the advice of the First Press Commission, of creating trusts for their management, that we are obliged to seriously consider the question once again and seek other remedies... We think that in the interest of the public it is necessary to insulate the Press from the dominating influence of other business interests. We propose the enactment of a law making it mandatory for persons carrying on the business of publishing a newspaper to sever their connections with other businesses to the extent indicated hereinafter...

In the first instance it should be enforced in the case of all persons who are in a position of controlling the publication of one or more daily newspapers, with the same or different titles, in one or more languages, the circulation of which, taken singly or cumulatively, exceeds one lakh copies per day... If the shares of a newspaper company are not readily purchased by eligible persons from the open market, such shares should be acquired and held by an autonomous body or agency to be specified by the legislation till they are purchased by eligible persons."

This amounted to a recommendation for the nationalisation of big newspapers if their capitalist owners do not succeed in off-loading their shares to their employees or to other 'eligible persons'. (The Rajadhyaksha Commission had recommended nationalisation only in the case of the Press Trust of India news agency. Though the Mathew Commission in the majority report affirmed that "the legislature is competent to enact the proposed law under Article 19 of the Constitution", the Congress (Indira) Government headed by Rajiv Gandhi was apparently not sure on this point. An 'action taken' report on the recommendations of the Second Press Commission, laid on the table of parliament on 14th May 1986, said: "The Government appreciates the recommendation made by the Commission but feels that in view of the legal, constitutional and other complexities involved, the matter may be referred to an expert committee for examination and report."

Events since 1982 have served to underline the skepticism voiced by the minority of the Second Press Commission about State regulation of the newspaper industry: "The majority seem to think that mercantile winds are blowing over the Press more furiously than they do elsewhere. Is it true that the democratic managers of our political system are trustees unaffected by industrial and mercantile conditions? All the ills to which the press is allegedly heir have a more virulent counterpart in the political system. Not all our politicians are delinked from money-bags, nor are they delinked from votes because of which they have to pander to the aspirations as well as the bigotry and parochial interests of the electorate... Of course, this parallel does not absolve the Press; the parallel has been drawn only to point out that there are no panaceas." (Page 227, Report of Second Press Commission.)

The Rajadhyaksha Commission recommended that the total space allotted to advertisements in daily newspapers should not exceed 40 per cent of the printed area. "We expect", they said, "that when newspapers are forced either to reduce the number of pages or to increase the price of each copy, there would be a strong temptation to condense news and editorial matter so as to accommodate all the advertisements that they have booked. As a consequence, the ratio of advertisement space to reading matter would increase. We are of the opinion that it should be kept within the definite limit that we have prescribed."

On the subject of revenue from advertisements, the Ross Commission in the U.K. had said in its report (1949): "As long as newspapers are sold to the public for less than they cost to produce, they will need a supplementary source of income. Of the various possible sources of income, the sale of their space to advertisers seems to us to be one of the least harmful. The income to be feared is that which comes from a concealed source and can be earned only by the sale of the editorial columns... The publication of advertisements should not be regarded, moreover, as a departure, under pressure of economic necessity, from the proper function of a newspaper. It is an essential part of the service which the newspaper renders to the community, valuable alike to commerce and industry and to the general public."

On the proposal for a news-to-advertisement ratio and or a tax on newspaper revenue from advertising, the Ross Commission said: "During the war some national advertising was diverted from the mass-circulation papers, by the contraction of their space, into the provincial papers; and it has been suggested to us that if this state of affairs could be preserved, the small papers would be assisted both directly by increases in their own revenue and indirectly by a reduction of the revenue, and consequently of the competitive advantages, of the large national papers.

It has therefore been proposed that a limit should be set either to the amount of advertising a newspaper of a given size may carry, or to the amount of advertising revenue it may earn. We do not think that these proposals would necessarily achieve their ostensible object; in normal circumstances their effect might merely be to drive advertisers to use other media than the Press... The limitation of revenue might necessitate either an increase in the price of newspapers or a reduction of the amount spent on producing them, and possibly of the quality of the service given to the public." The 2nd (Shawcross) Commission also rejected the proposals for a statutory limit on the proportion of space devoted to advertising, or a levy on the advertisement revenue of newspapers graded according to the size of their circulation, or a duty on the advertising revenue of newspapers with over $2 million of such revenue.

In India, however, the Second Press Commission endorsed the proposal made by the Rajadhyaksha Commission for a law to regulate advertising space. On the ground that newspapers with a small circulation needed to carry a larger proportion of advertising on account of their lower advertisement tariff and fewer number of pages, the Mathew Commission recommended that the news-to-advertisement ratio should be fixed at 60-40 for big, 50:50 for medium and 40:60 for small newspapers.

Another major recommendation of the First Press Commission was legislation to fix a minimum price of newspapers depending on the number of pages offered to the reader. "A paper with a large circulation" it was argued, "because of its lower cost of production per copy enjoys certain advantages over other papers with smaller circulation. Similarly, a paper with large capital resources behind it is free from certain handicaps which affect another paper with limited capital. Papers of long standing, which have been able to build up a large and stable volume of advertisement revenue, are in a very advantageous position as compared to others who have just entered the field.

It is true that such economic advantages and handicaps exist in a number of industries but their presence in the newspaper industry is not, in our opinion, conducive to the even and healthy development of the press. Newspapers serve as media for the free exchange of information and of ideas. The proper functioning of democracy requires that every individual should have equal opportunity, in so far as this can be achieved, to put forward his opinions. We feel that to fix a minimum price at which papers of a particular size can be sold would be the most effective measure to bring about this end."

An attempt was made during Jawaharlal Nehru's prime ministership to give effect, through legislation, to the Rajadhyaksha Commission's recommendations for enforcing a price-page schedule and a new news-to-advertisement ratio. Parliament enacted the Newspaper (Price and Page) Act in 1956. The Daily Newspapers (Price and Page) Order was issued in 1960, under the Act, fixing the number of pages that could be published by a newspaper according to the price charged. However, both the Act and the Order were struck down by the Supreme Court in *Sakal Newspapers v. Union* in 1962 as being violative of Article 19.

The Nehru Government left the matter at that. The Prime Minister did not think of amending the Constitution in order to get over the Supreme Court's judgement. An amendment of the Constitution is precisely what the majority of the Second Press Commission suggested in 1982. Though only one out of the seven members constituting the majority--namely the Chairman himself-had a judicial background, they opined that the. *Sakal* case had been incorrectly decided by the Supreme Court and merited a review. The majority of the Mathew Commission said: "Even if an amendment of the Constitution is required to give effect to our proposals regarding price page schedule and news-to-advertisement ratio, We are of the view that such an amendment will not destroy or damage the basic structure of the Constitution.

No doubt Article 19 (1) (a) has been held to be a basic structure of the Constitution; but a law prescribing a, price-page schedule or news-to-advertisement ratio is not a measure which will destroy or damage, that freedom; on the contrary, its object being promotion of competition and prevention of monopoly, the law will advance freedom of speech and expression. Shri Girilal Jain, Rajendra Mathur, S.K. Mukherjea and HK Paranjape are opposed to the prescription of price-page schedule and news-to-advertisement ratio."

It is noteworthy that at two places the majority of the Mathew Commission give the game away. They say (p.156 of the Report): "While arriving at this view (prescription of a price-page schedule with a news-to-advertisement ratio) we have not been oblivious of the fact that those papers which are today attracting a disproportionately large, amount of advertisement revenue are utilizing it to a certain extent for improving their quality and subsidising the selling price for the benefit of the readers." Again, "We are conscious that the newspapers which will come within the ambit of the proposed legislation are all quality newspapers rendering good service to the community."

The 'action report' tabled in parliament by the Rajiv Gandhi government said: ""The observations made by the' Press Commission and the arguments given in support of the constitutionality of the recommendations made by them are noted. In view of the decision of the Supreme Court and the present legal position, an expert committee may be set up to go into the question of working out a price-page schedule and news-to-advertisement ratio." This was in May 1986. There the matter stands.

The majority of the Mathew Commission were so fearful of proprietorial interference with editorial autonomy, even after the compulsory delinking of big newspapers from big industry, that they proposed the interposition of trustees to protect the editor from rough advances by the proprietor or the management. One of the members remarked in the course of discussion of this proposal that, it was as quixotic as the notion of interposing a trustee between husband and wife; it is a different matter that this member, as a loyal supporter of the Congress (I), eventually voted with the majority. The view of justice Mathew and his colleagues of the majority was as follows: "To provide an effective safeguard against proprietorial or managerial interference in editorial independence, there should be legislation for interposition of a board of trustees between the management of a large daily newspaper and its editor. The legislation should be applicable in the first instance only to daily newspapers with a circulation of over one lakh copies. The policy of every such newspaper should be clearly laid down in writing.

The function of the boards of trustees would be to ensure that full effect is given to the policy of the newspaper and to act as umpire in disputes between the editor and the management of the newspaper... They (trustees) should be appointed by the managements of the newspapers themselves in consultation with and with the approval of the Chairman of the Press Council and the Chief justice of the High Court or the Chief justice of India, as the case may be, depending upon the area of circulation of the newspaper concerned. In the event of a difference of opinion between the Chairman of the Press Council and the Chief justice on the choice of the members submitted to them by the management of a newspaper, the view of the Chief Justice should prevail."

This recommendation seemed to the Rajiv Gandhi government to go too far. The action report tabled in parliament in May 1986 said: "It is not clear what responsibility would be cast on such a board (of trustees) in the running of the newspapers and how the proposal could be implemented in a practicable manner. It is also noted that even organisations on which, among others, editors were represented had expressed themselves against the proposal. The recommendation is not, therefore, accepted."

On the citizens' right to information, which was one of the terms of reference, the Mathew Commission recommended repeal of Section 5 of the Official Secrets Act of 1923 and its replacement by provisions suited to reconciling the vital interests of the State with the right of the people to know the affairs of the State affecting them. This recommendation was rejected by the Rajiv Gandhi government. The 'action taken' report said tersely: "Not considered necessary as the existing provisions in law seem to be adequate."

Worth pondering in this connection are the comments of two American writers Edgar and Schmidt in the course of writings by them, in the 1970's, on 'The Espionage Statutes and Publication of Defense Information':

> "Statutes aimed at protecting defense secrets from disclosure must deal with cloak-and-dagger spying, with the fidelity of government employees to executive policies of secrecy and, most troublesome of all, with the rights and duties of journalists and

> the rest of us to engage in or refrain from discussing matters that may be critical to informed democratic policy choices... The press rarely tested the limits of its right to publish; secrets were kept because people in and out of government with access to military and diplomatic secrets shared basic assumptions about national aims. The Vietnam war changed all that. The radical perspective of I.F. Stone ('Every government is run by liars and nothing they say should be believed') became an accepted premise in reporting about the war. The Pentagon Papers dispute symbolized the passing of an era in which journalists could be counted on to work within understood limits of discretion in handling secret information."

The writers cited, in support of their plea for greater freedom to publish, the view of President Kennedy expressed retrospectively that the *New York Times* should have, in the public interest, published the information it had gained about the American 'Bay of Pigs' plan for the invasion of Cuba.

It is noteworthy that, perhaps due to the chastening effect of the March 1977 electoral verdict following the period of emergency and censorship, the Press was left free of legislative intervention for more than eight years from January 1980 when Indira Gandhi returned to power. There was once again a confrontation when the Rajiv Gandhi government introduced in parliament in August 1988 a Defamation Bill.

It placed the onus on the person accused of having made a defamatory statement to prove the truth of the statement and to establish also that the statement was made for the public good. Section 13 created a new class of offence called criminal imputation, which the Minister piloting the Bill described as "ark aggravated form of defamation calling for punishment": Punishment was provided also for aggravated those printing or engraving and selling defamatory matter.

The Defamation Bill was brought forward after disclosures and allegations in the Press about kick-backs received by or on behalf of Prime Minister Rajiv Gandhi and/or the Congress (I) from Nobel Industries of Sweden in a contract for the purchase of the Bofors gun for the Indian Army. This scandal was to cost Rajiv Gandhi dearly: as leader of the Congress (I) he could secure for his party less than 40 per cent of the popular vote in the elections held for the Lok Sabha in November 1989, as against the unprecedented share of' about a half of the votes that the party received when he led it in the December 1984 elections within Weeks of his succeeding his assassinated mother as Prime Minister. The difference was due to absence of the sympathy factor that had been at work in 1984, as well as to the adverse impression created by the Bofors scandal.

The Defamation Bill was hurriedly introduced by the Rajiv Gandhi government in the Lok Sabha on 29th August 1988 and was passed the next day. In a remarkable display of unity, newspaper employees, who had been looking to the government for securing improved wages and working conditions, joined hands with their employers in demonstrations all over the country against the Defamation Bill as an attack on Press freedom. The rallies-were climaxed by a march in the capital along Raj Path to Parliament House in which newspaper publishers marched alongside representatives of the All India Newspapers Employees Federation, the Indian Federation of Working Journalists, National Union of journalists and the Editors' Guild.

Doubtless recalling the ruling party's experience in 1977, when the voters' verdict was in part against the emergency regime of Press censorship, Prime Minister Rajiv Gandhi thought it wise to drop the Defamation Bill. It was not proceeded with in the Rajya Sabha. When all manner of allegations were made against persons prominent in public life during the securities scandal of 1993 involving banks and commercial undertakings, in the public sector and the private, many in the ruling party must have recollected the Defamation Bill with nostalgia and wished that it had been enacted and brought into force.

Another Bill pertaining to the Press that was initiated during Rajiv Gandhi's tenure as prime minister, but was abandoned, was an amendment of the Press and Registration of Books Act. Introduced in December 1988, the Bill sought to empower district magistrates to carry out inspection checks of newspaper establishments to verify circulation claims, and to increase the amount of fine that could be levied on newspapers for violation of the Act from Rs. 500 to Rs. 5,000. The amending legislation would also have permitted cancellation of the concessional rate of postage for newspapers if they consisted mainly of advertisements.

After decades since the coming into force of India's republican Constitution, guaranteeing freedom of expression subject to certain limitations, have thus witnessed, as it were, a swing of the pendulum between the spirit and the letter of Article 19.

The long and arduous battle for independence came to an end on August 15,1947, when India after partition became free from alien rule. As the country rejoiced and celebrated the historic event, a jubilant press joined its countrymen in hailing the advent of freedom for which it had fought shoulder to shoulder with the nationalist forces and made enormous sacrifices in men and material, braving the cruel persecution of the colonial rulers. In a striking editorial, *The Hindu* described the ship of freedom which had reached port thus: "After a century of storm and stress, the ship of Indian freedom has come into port.

Battered heavily by wind and sea, scarred and seamed in many a fierce encounter with embattled hosts, she has suffered grievous losses and has had to jettison much precious cargo. She is not spice and span as we had pictured her in the morning time of our hopes, it is on the whole a sad home coming. There are treacherous shoals about and the pilot is more than a little weary. But she is a brave little ship for all that, for she carries the high hopes and ambitions of 400 million. On her proud mast-head there broods, like the spirit of peace, the white soul of India....India embarks on the endless adventure of freedom, crippled and maimed in the sight of the world. She is, however, a great believer in the healing touch of time and in the magic of natural affinities."

In the first flush of freedom, the press rode with the current and was sympathetic and cooperative with the new national government which was faced with a deluge of problems plunging the country into strife and bloodshed and instability. A section, however had not got over the hangover of colonial rule and indulged in fanning communal passions and hatred and in scurrilous writing. Sensational journalism became a fashion with some and the country's interests ceased to be paramount. A Bengali editor is quoted by a writer as having confessed that he adopted a communal policy "because playing down riots and disturbances curbed his sales."

"Even the news boys", the editor is quoted as having said, "refuse to touch my paper if my rivals report a larger number of deaths than I do." The leaders who were running the government and who had established complete rapport with the press during the freedom struggle were now saddened that the press as a whole was not with them in meeting the challenges faced by the new-born government. They seemed to behave, the leaders thought, as an opposition force as they did during the British regime when the need was to play a constructive and cooperative role.

Frank Moraes, editor of the *Times of India*, referred to the attitude of Indian editors in the early years of Independence and said: "In the early years of independence, Indian editors had to make up their minds on what attitude they should adopt vis-a-vis Nehru's newly established government.... I decided after some reflection and consultation that since Nehru was faced virtually with no opposition in Parliament and since a democratic government could not effectively express itself in the absence of an opposition, the press should take it upon itself to function as an unofficial opposition outside Parliament, exercising that role with responsibility and circumspection."

Writing on the same subject *The Hindu* felt that even barely a year after freedom was achieved the suspicion and distrust which clouded the relations between the alien government and the nationalist press "continued in a very perceptible manner under the Free India Government." The Hindu said in the new circumstances the "Press may be expected to take a more detached as also a more responsible view of its obligations on the one hand to the government of the day, and on the other to the people as a whole, opposing official policy when it must, supporting it when it can and at all times bringing instructive opinion to bear from different angles on all important issues so that the people may decide with full knowledge."

Jawaharlal Nehru was one of the earliest in the government to voice his displeasure against the press. He had a dig at editors when addressing the All-India Newspapers Editors Conference in 1952, he said: "Of course, it is hardly proper to use the word 'wise' in connection with newspapers. There is no reason why newspapers should not have at least some small bit of leisured thinking and wisdom hidden away in a corner if not in the leading article always." Nehru asked: "For whom do we want press freedom—for the writer or for the owner to coerce his employee to write against his conscience?" Seven years later, in 1959, in speeches in Chandigarh and Bombay, Nehru again attacked the press, questioning the bonafides of the editors. He said it had been taken for granted that editors of Indian newspapers could not be expected to realise or speak the truth when discussing certain aspects of state policy. He recalled Stanley Baldwin's (British prime minister) remark about newspapers that they enjoyed power without responsibility and said there were no great editorial personalities in India who could stand up to newspaper owners and to advertisers. In another speech in Delhi Nehru described the press as both the product and symbol of private enterprise and editors as its champions against state control and regulation.

N. Raghunathan, well-known journalist, made this comment on Nehru's fulminations against the press: " Mr Nehru has got into a habit of coming down with a heavy hand on the bad boys of the press. But though he is never consciously unfair, the cumulative effect of these periodical fulminations is definitely unfortunate. According to their personal predilections, people may conclude that he is inclined to be intolerant of all criticism or that the press of this country is dominated by the bad boys."

There was a touch of irony in Nehru's disparaging remarks for he was the darling of the Indian press both before and after independence. He occupied quite a considerable space in the columns of newspapers. When he was not making speeches, which were reported at length and verbatim in some papers, he was issuing statements about the party, Government and international affairs and these were treated as news of great importance. When he was not speaking or making statements, he wrote articles which were distributed to the national dailies which published them prominently. *The Hindu* wrote: "It is clear that the prime minister looks upon the press more or less as a kind of permanent opposition. He has evidently been surprised by the range and volume of criticism made newspapers of domestic policies initiated by his government and he has brought himself to think that these have been inspired by self-interest. This is pure delusion."

Sardar Vallabhbhai Patel, the strong man of the Congress and number two in the National Government, was also not happy with the status of the press after freedom. In a letter to Nehru in June 1949, he wrote: "There is an absence of understanding both in the press and in the legislature in regard to some of our foremost problems of the day. Yet there can be no stopping their writing on these subjects or making public references."

When the *Times of India* wrote an editorial critical of the government in connection with the escape from house arrest of Mir Laik Ali,ex-prime minister of Hyderabad, in March, 1950,Patel's secretary, Shanker, wrote to K. Gopalaswami, acting editor of the paper: "I saw editorial on Laik Ali's escape. I hope in calmer moments you have realised that you have rushed into print far too soon. That particular news about his keeping a beard is entirely unfounded. He did keep his moustache untrimmed but that you will agree is unlikely to be particularly noticed. I would have liked the press and Parliament to suspend judgement until there was some material to go upon.

As it is, both have reacted on sheer speculation even to the extent of involving the I.G. of Police without realising that he is not in a position to defend himself. What is worse, when statements are contradicted or proved untrue, there is no retraction or regret either on the part of the press or on the part of members of Parliament. After all, it is common prudence to allocate responsibility only after the facts have been ascertained."

In another letter on the same incident, Shanker wrote; 'The whole press seems to have reacted to it as if a great national calamity has happened. Escapes of criminals from jails where guards and rules were much more strict, are not uncommon."

C. Rajagopalachari, another great leader and the last governor-general of India, did not have a good opinion of the Indian press. Campbell Johnson, press attached to Lord Mountbatten, writes in his book, *Mission with Mountbatten* that C.R. told him "that the Indian press had a long way to go before it could achieve its full freedom. Asked what influence it had on Indian politics he said: Very little. The Congress had dominated the political scene and the press instead of providing informed criticism was nothing more than a body of political propagandists. If there was to be a change in the balance of power all that the press would do would be to follow suit and one lot of propagandists would succeed another.' He said he had told an old journalist friend of his in Madras that the essential thing for the Indian press to do was to concentrate first of all on administrative matters rather than on political formulae. Once they began dealing with things which affected the daily lives of the people they would begin to exert a genuine influence. He said he agreed with the view that Indian journalism was much nearer the American in its tendency to outspokenness and overstatement."

C.R. who as home minister, introduced the first press control bill after freedom became the victim of a controversy in the press when his candidature was canvassed for the presidentship of the Indian Republic in 1950. The press disclosed that besides C.R.., Rajendra Prasad, president of the Constituent Assembly, was also a candidate for the prestigious post. The *Lokvani*, a Hindi weekly of Jaipur in Rajasthan, published pictures of C.R. and Rajendra Prasad side by side on the front page along with a story on who was likely to be chosen president Sending a cutting of this report to C.R., a Congressman told him that Hiralal Shastri, prominent Congress leader who later became chief minister, and his followers were canvassing in favour of Prasad and against him.

Sending the letter and cutting to Patel, C.R., who was then governor-general, wrote that he did not want that the Presidency should become the subject matter of "title page propaganda". He added: "If it is true that the *Lokvani* belongs to one of Shastri's group perhaps he may be told that the picture is objectionable so that he may not repeat such stuff." Patel in his reply said that Hiralal Shastri had told him that the editor had taken the idea from the Statesman and there was no intention whatsoever to raise any controversy. C.R. sent him another press cutting, this time from the Bombay weekly, *Blitz*, with the remark: "This cutting seems to be too bad to be ignored." He asked. "Do you think we could induce Rajen Babu to do something to prevent this kind of gossip?

The *Blitz* report had said that members of the Constituent Assembly from the south who were "anxious to keep Rajaji away from Madras politics are canvassing in his favour for the Presidency while a large number of members from the north, who dislike C.R. for being too clever and crafty for an average Congressman, prefer Rajendra Prasad." The report added: "A cold and calculating politician that Rajaji is, he is in the meantime quietly consolidating his position. While pretending that he has only four trunks to pack to quit Government House, he is nevertheless spreading his roots all over the place."

In another letter, C.R. unburdened himself: "It seems as if one cannot have peace as long as one lives. Who wants this governor-generalship or presidentship or deputy prime ministership or anything else? It will not do to be depressed. Otherwise, there is plenty of cause for being thoroughly disgusted with our semi-educated folk."

Patel replying to C.R. said: "With our notions of civil liberties and freedom of the press and many impediments in the way of corrective action, I am afraid it is impossible to reform *Blitz*." Rajendra Prasad, who was approached to contradict the *Blitz* report wrote to Patel that there was nothing for him in the report to contradict "There is no allegation against me." He, however, issued a statement saying: "There is and there can be no question of any rivalry between Rajaji and myself for any post or honour. I would, therefore, warn the public not to be misled by any propaganda of this nature and request all not to indulge in it."

In a letter to Patel in September, 1949, Nehru said there was a deliberate move to keep Rajaji out of the Presidency. He mentioned the name of a newspaper owner and said he was "one of the most active agents in this business." In his reply, Patel said that a large majority seemed opposed to

Rajaji. He agreed with Nehru that the newspaper owner mentioned by him was involved in it "I do not know," Patel wrote, "when our people, particularly the press lords and the press will learn to behave with a sense of responsibility and to maintain the dignity of at least the higher offices. Instead, it seems that no person or position is sacred to them."

The Tussle **:** The whole controversy took an entirely different turn when Rajendra Prasad and Nehru fell out over the issue of presidentship and the former accused the latter of "ignoring him" and condemning him and "all that I have stood for and done during all these years in association with you (Nehru)". Nehru had suggested that Prasad should withdraw in favour of Rajaji. Upset by the tenor of Prasad's letter, Nehru asked Patel to deal with him. Patel wrote to Prasad pacifying him and Prasad apologised to Nehru and the incident was closed. In the event, Rajaji lost the battle and it was Prasad who won.

A speech by Dr. B.R. Ambedkar, law minister, reported in the National Herald in April, 1948, caused concern to Nehru and Patel. According to the report, Ambedkar attacked the Congress Government and particularly Nehru and Patel. Nehru in a letter to Patel drew attention to passages in the speech "which seem very odd to me as coming from a Cabinet minister." Ambedkar in his reply to Nehru and Patel called the press report "perverted" and that "no fair-minded man could have any objection to anything I said in Lucknow." He said his speech was devoted to answering criticism from his followers on (1) why he had been silent ever since the departure of the Cabinet Mission; (2) why he joined the Congress Government; and (3) what he proposed Congress and there was no reference to any member of the government. "The press has never been kind to me.

It has always done its best to twist facts and phrases, take them out of their context and pervert the sense of anything I have said. I fear this is what has happened to my speech in Lucknow." Referring to the report in the *National herald,* he said the correspondent could not have distorted his speech in a manner worse than he had done. "I delivered my speech in Hindustani", he said, "which is not my mother tongue. It is, therefore, possible for misreporting and misrepresenting the intention of the speaker. Added to this the press in India has had its knife in me for the last 25 years. Consequently, deliberate perversion of my speeches by the press have occurred many a time."

There was one British journalist in India whose admiration for Patel bordered on hero worship. He was Ian Stephens, editor of the *Statesman*, who guided the destinies of the British-owned newspaper at a crucial period on the eve of India's independence and after. Campbell Johnson mentions in his book that the viceroy directed that Gandhi should be referred to in court circulars as "Mahatma Gandhi" instead of the usual "Mr Gandhi" after a representation by Stephens. Stephens quit his post as he did not approve of the government's acceptance of the accession of Kashmir to India and as he would have to attack the government on this ground. He believed that Kashmir should have gone to Pakistan and he moved over to Pakistan. He detested Nehru and admired Patel.

"It is my belief", he wrote that Patel would have made a better prime minister. He and Rajagopalachari were the Congress party leaders I most admired Both understood the nature of the Muslim problem in India better than Nehru did." Had Patel been chosen, Stephens said, he "would have stayed on contentedly in India longer than I did" because of the policies he believed Patel would have pursued. "Patel was a realist", Stephens said, "with down to earth understanding of how the masses felt. He wasn't half mesmerised by them as Nehru during his brilliant speeches seemed to be." Stephens said: "It's my belief that for his own earthy Hindu reasons Patel wouldn't—had he been prime minister in October, 1947—have seized Kashmir or anyhow in Nehru's or Mountbatten's way. He knew I admired him."

Stephens carried a special dispatch on Patel and his picture on his birthday in October, 1948 in the *Statesman* and also sent him a very affectionate message of greeting. "You are a great man on your public achievements alone", he said, "but also one who in my case at any rate, as I have ventured to mention more than once, inspires—whatever political differences there may be and some will doubtless recur—an unusual glow of personal affection. Prolonged good health and happiness to you."

Thanking him for the greetings and the dispatch in the paper about him, Patel wrote to Stephens: "During all our contacts I have appreciated your frankness as much as you did mine and that is largely responsible for the personal regard which both of us entertain for each other despite political differences which at times divide us. I need hardly assure you, therefore, that I have been deeply touched by the kindness and warmth of the reference about me both in your letter and the *Statesman's* dispatch." Stephens was overwhelmed by the prompt reply and sentiments in it and he wrote back: "Nowhere but in India, I think, do busy ministers and other leading men spare so much time and trouble for outside individuals. You should not have done it. But it was quite remarkably nice of you and I am grateful."

Patel was alert in taking action on disclosure made by the press regarding administration in the states. In December, 1947, the *Indian Nation* of Patna featured a report on its front page with banner headlines that the Governor of Bihar, Jairamdas Daulatram, had resigned because "he refuses to be a silent spectator of the Congress Ministry's misdeeds." The report said that the reason for his decision was that "under his very nose, His Excellency finds widespread corruption, favouritism and muddles and he finds that owing to the Congress Ministry's attitude refusing the governor to have his say, he has to be silent spectator of all misdeeds and bunglings of the ministry."

The chief secretary to the Bihar Government in frantic telegrams to the prime minister and home minister said the government did not know the governor had resigned and for the reasons mentioned in the press report. He added: "Now as a version damaging the reputation of the Ministry has appeared in the press it is very necessary that the government here should know if it is a fact that he has resigned and that too for reasons mentioned in the report." Although Patel in his reply to the chief secretary said there was no truth in the press report regarding the governor's resignation and the reasons given, in a letter to Patel on December 23, the governor did request to be relieved early. Patel assured him that there would be no delay in relieving him.

Earlier in October in the same year there was another report about the Bihar Ministryin the *Free Press Journal* of Bombay. It alleged corruption and profiteering in regard to purchases of molasses under government permits: It said that molasses was bought at a cheap price and sold at 20 to 30 times more than the control price. In a letter to the Bihar Chief Minister, Sri Krishna Sinha, Patel said: "It is amazing that such a thing should have happened in such an unseemly fashion. If the evil is as extensive and as high placed your government could have dealt with the matter drastically before it became public."

Role of Committee : Almost the first thing the National Government did after assuming office was to set up a Press Laws Enquiry Committee which submitted its report in May, 1948. It favoured the abolition of laws specially concerning the press and the incorporation of their major provisions in the ordinary laws of the land. It supported the provisions in the Telegraph Act, Post Office Act and Sea Customs Act which provided for interception of messages and literature. It recommended the retention of the Official Secrets Act and the three sections of the Indian Penal Code, 124-A, 153-A, and 505 dealing with disaffection, communal hatred and tampering with the loyalty of the armed forces.

The government brought in the Press (Objectionable Matters) Bill in 1951 to give effect to some of the recommendations of the committee. The Bill repealed the four Acts relating to the press suggested by the committee. It gave power to the government to demand and forfeit security from a newspaper or printing press after a judicial decision. It was provided that a complaint against a paper or printing press had to be made to the' sessions judge who could, after a judicial enquiry with the help of a jury, demand security from the keeper of the press. On failure to deposit the security, the declaration under the Press and Registration of Books Act, 1867, was to be deemed to be cancelled. What distinguished the Bill from the previous press laws was that the judiciary and not the executive was to decide on the necessity for action and the nature of action to be taken.

It was explained that the Bill was intended to stop encouragement of violence and sabotage and certain other "grave offences" as also publication of matters of a scurrilous nature. Rajagopalachari, who as home minister, introduced the Bill in Parliament said: "I wish to leave behind me a law that should comprise the essential don'ts for printed stuff. We cannot afford to let people's minds be poisoned." He hoped that the press would frame its own code of professional ethics and discipline and ask the government for statutory powers to execute its decisions.

N. Raghunathan made this bitter comment on the Bill: "The Britisher at his worst did not dream of consigning the press perpetually to the status of a prisoner on parole. It was left to the Mahatma's understudy to turn Rousseau's dictum upside down and say that the press was everywhere born in chains and in India it must continue to wear a good few of them for its own good. The luxury of a free press is not for us. Everyone of the home minister's specious pleas for muzzling the press was in an earlier day denounced by him and his fellow paladins as an affront to common sense and a sin against the light. The sabotage that the August patriots so easily reconciled with their non-violent consciences owed nothing to the instigation of the press; still it did help them to climb to power. And is if not the most natural thing in the world to kick the ladder by which you rose?" The Bill which became law was allowed to lapse in 1956.

Role of Commission : A Press Commission was appointed in September, 1952 under the chairmanship of Justice Rajadhyaksha. Its terms of reference included the state of the press, working conditions, of journalists' freedom of the press and machinery for ensuring high standards of journalism. The commission, which submitted its report in 1954, recommended the establishment of a Press Council whose objects should be (1) to safeguard the freedom of the press and help the press to maintain its independence; (2) to censure objectionable types of journalistic conduct and by all other possible means to build up a code in accordance with the highest professional standards; (3) to keep under review any development likely to restrict the supply and dissemination of news of public interest and importance; (4) to encourage the growth of a sense of responsibility and of public service among those engaged in the profession of journalism; (5) to study the development in the press which may tend towards concentration or monopoly and, if necessary, to suggest remedies therefore; (6) to publish reports, at least once a year, recording its work and reviewing the performance of the press, its development and the factors affecting them; (7) to improve methods of recruitment, education and training for the profession by the creation of suitable agencies for the purpose such as a Press Institute.

The commission recommended the appointment of a press registrar who would keep a close watch on the circulation of newspapers and if he came to the conclusion that in a particular area or language, a monopoly had developed he was to bring it to the notice of the Press Council who would conduct an investigation into the existence of a monopoly and what measures were necessary, if any, to meet the situation. It suggested the fixing of minimum basic wages for working journalists, introduction of price page schedule for newspapers and the diffusion of ownership.

The commission found a considerable degree of concentration in the ownership of newspapers and warned of the danger that the tendency might develop in the future. The commission stated that outside the British-owned press, which had passed mostly into Indian hands, there were no hard and fast demarcations, no allocation of set duties. Most of the staff had been taken as sub-editors or reporters. Somewhere between editorial staff and the press, there were proof-readers. There was an editor and there were assistant editors.

Affluence was rare for newspapers. It was remarkable, said the commission, that so many good men joined the profession, more remarkable that they stayed on showing considerable adaptability. However, the transformation of the newspaper into a business enterprise had begun and the new proprietors were businessmen who did much to straighten out finances. The commission noted the declining status of the editor in the daily newspapers and said that the "growing importance of the economics of production had also contributed to bring about the gradual eclipse of the editor by the manager." To reverse the trend it suggested that the editor be vested with administrative control over his staff, that appointments in the editorial department be made in consultation with him and that all members of the staff be made to realise that they were working "towards a common goal under the leadership of the editor."

The Press Council was established by an Act of Parliament in 1965. Its first president was Justice N. Rajagopala Iyengar, who said the council had a close likeness of the reconstituted British Press Council. It was, however, unique in having statutory authority. Its power to summon and enforce attendance of persons and examine them on oath; to require the discovery and production of documents; to receive evidence on affidavits; and to issue commission for the examination of witnesses or documents were valuable aids in the conduct of investigations. Every inquiry held by the council was deemed to be a judicial proceeding and no suit or other legal proceedings lay against the council or its members in respect of anything done in good faith. The inclusion of members of Parliament on the council, said Rajagopala Iyengar, was a novel feature. The council had 28 members out of whom 20 were nominated by the various newspaper organisations.

The working Journalists Act of 1955 recognised working journalists as industrial workers as recommended by the Press Commission and empowered the government to set up a wage board to fix the minimum wage for journalists. A wage board presided over by H. V. Divatia was appointed and its recommendations were published in May, 1957. The Supreme Court, however, in March, 1958 held the recommendations invalid as they were not based on consideration of capacity to pay. An ordinance was issued in June, 1958, setting up a committee of officials to remove the defects pointed out by the Supreme Court.

The committee's report, published in December, 1958, was accepted by the government and its recommendations were passed into law. A press registrar was also appointed. The Newspaper (price and page) Act of 1956 which was passed in accordance with the press commission recommendations and whose object was to regulate prices charged for newspapers in relation to their maximum or minimum number of pages and for the space allotted for advertising matter in relation to their matters was held invalid by the Supreme Court. The court said imposing restrictions on the business aspect of a newspaper would amount to an infringement of the freedom of the press.

The Press Council Act was repealed in January, 1976, during the Emergency and the council was re-established under the Press Council Act of 1978. Some important changes were made in the new Act. A second Press Commission was set up in May 1978, under the chairmanship of Justice P.C. Goswami but Justice Goswami and his colleagues on the commission resigned in January, 1980, with the formation of a new government. The commission was reconstituted in April 1980 under the chairmanship of Justice K.K. Mathew. Its terms of reference included:

(1) the role of the press in a developing and democratic society;
(2) the present constitutional guarantee with regard to freedom of speech and expression; whether this is adequate to ensure freedom of the press, adequacy and efficacy of the laws, rules and regulations for maintaining this freedom;
(3) means of safeguarding the independence of the press against economic and political pressures from proprietors and management;
(4) role of the press and the responsibilities it should assume in developmental policies;
(5) ownership patterns, management practices and financial structures of the press; their relation to growth, editorial independence and professional integrity;
(6) chain newspapers; links with industry, their effect on competition and on the readers' right to objective news and free comments;
(7) economics of the newspaper industry.

The commission, in its report submitted in 1982, said: 'The role of the press in a developing and democratic society should neither be that of an adversary nor an ally of government. To be a mindless adversary or an unquestioning ally would be to abdicate judgment. A free press should be, in our view, a constructive critic." The commission felt that the editors should insist "on their right to have the final say in the acceptance or rejection of advertisements, specially those which border on or cross the line between decency and obscenity, legitimate claims for a product or service and the proffering of magical remedies." The editors authority, it said, should extend, not only to the contents of the advertisements but also to the proportion of space devoted to them. It wanted the discontinuance of astrological predictions in newspapers and magazines.

It said that the positive role of the press of "bringing together the diverse elements in the nation's life by emphasising those aspects which tend towards unifying the communities is as important as avoidance of objectionable communal or casteist writing. This calls for a sustained campaign to promote the concept of human brotherhood." The commission said that while the press should bring to light and extend support to genuine public grievances, it should oppose unconstitutional methods of agitation. It welcomed the trend towards investigative reporting in so far as it was oriented to social and economic issues. "But the investigative reporter should not give occasion for the criticism of lack of follow-up which is a widespread failing in the Indian Press."

The commission said that a newspaper was essentially a public utility and whatever be the precise form of ownership of newspapers, the exercise of ownership rights had to be subject to some measure of restraint and regulation. Public interest was the criterion that should regulate this activity. The commission said: "The press has a social responsibility and accountability to the public. The theory that the freedom of press knows no restraints is gone." It said in the changed situation, the freedom of the issuer of news alone is not sufficient; the freedom of the consumer must also be protected. It warned that the press should be able to resist not only external pressure but also "inducements which would undermine its independence from within. Journalists should be on guard against the temptation to enjoy favours, whether from government authorities, employers, advertisers or others."

The commission declared that the Press Council, which had functioned for 15 years had "within limits set by the legislation done useful work" and it recommended that the institution should continue. It said the council should be given powers to deny facilities of accreditation for a specified period to those editors or journalists who had been held by the council thrice to have violated the accepted principles of journalistic ethics. Also, that a newspaper would invite "sanction if it comes to the adverse notice of the council thrice, whether by way of disapproval, warning, admonition or censure." The commission said: "We are of the view that it would not be desirable to draw up a code of ethics for newspapers. Such a code could be built up case by case over a period of time."

The commission said: "The Indian press is free, but does not have a wide enough reach and it has an urban and middle class base which limits its contribution towards making the development process more widely participatory." The commission recommended enactment of legislation to curb the influence of foreign money on the press. Under the law, it proposed newspapers would be required to submit their annual accounts to the Press Council giving details of the revenue obtained from advertisements and from foreign sources and names of the top 100 shareholders with their nationality and address. It recommended the amendment of the Press Council Act of 1978 to enable the council to review the quality and adequacy of training facilities for journalists and monitoring of the performance of newspapers by the council in respect of important issues.

The declaration of Emergency in June, 1975, by the government of Indira Gandhi came as a shocking blow to the Indian press which was its greatest victim. There was a raging controversy (and it has continued even to this day) whether Indira Gandhi was justified in imposing the Emergency but there was universal condemnation of the muzzling of the press and the drastic action taken against some newspapers. In a letter to a foreign friend in March, 1971, Indira Gandhi had this to say about the Indian press: "Our own press has done everything possible to mislead the public about me personally and about my aims and objectives. Even though everything they had said about my father earlier and then about me in being proved wrong all the time, the columnists continue with their supercilious analyses. The real trouble is that they have no depth or values themselves and do not care to have contact with the people. Their judgment is circumscribed by their own limited experience, so they try to fit people into preconceived and prejudiced forms. Neither my father nor I can fit into any of these."

Describing Indira Gandhi's attitude to the press, her former Press Adviser, B.G. Verghese said: "She is very shy of the press. At the beginning, I persuaded her to hold a press conference every month. But she gave up this practice after I left. She treats the press conferences as a necessary evil. Instead of using the press as a forum, she is very evasive in her answers and tries to disclose as little as possible. In the game of journalistic hide and seek, Indira Gandhi is usually the winner. Over the years she perfected a technique which enabled her to ward off inquisitive newsmen. She was always on guard with the press and unlike her father rarely allowed herself to be provoked into emotional outbursts. In the early years of prime ministership she was wont to lose her temper and lash out at pressmen who persisted in asking awkward questions. Since then her style had matured and she fielded questions with calm and good humoured self-confidence, silencing interrogators with humorous and cryptic retorts and sometimes turning inconvenient questions back at them.

"The Indian press and especially those controlled by the Opposition had been critical and even abusive about her. But while supporting suggestions that the newspaper industry should be separated from big business, she consistently rejected proposals for nationalising the press. She believed in a free press though she is not much influenced by it. Press criticism might annoy her temporarily but she soon cooled down."

The worst form of pre-censorship was imposed on the press during the Emergency and a paper of the standing of

The Hindu had to scrap an editorial on the proclamation of the Emergency as the censor refused to permit editorials on the Emergency. The do's and dont's of unimaginative and authoritarian censorship made it almost impossible for the press to function and even factual news and innocuous comments came under the axe. J.N. Sahni wrote: "In the absence of news, the newspapers filled their columns with such vital topics" as the origin of the Ramayana and Mahabharata, the discovery of skull fossils of the ape man and the relative antiquity of Harappa and Mohenjo Daro."

Defending pre-censorship Indira Gandhi told an interviewer: "To have had to impose regulations on newspapers does not make me happy. But some journals had shed all objectivity and independence and allied themselves totally with the opposition front and done everything to spread doom and defeatism. The press was very much against us even before. Our newspapers are very much class oriented....In today's world, it is absolutely essential to eradicate poverty to the greatest possible extent in order just to keep harmony. It can't be done immediately. It can't be done totally and it should be done as much as possible and yet as soon as we bend ourselves to this task and people see we are serious, the full weight of money, economic power, the press, industry, local and foreign combines. They don't say they are against the policy. Everybody says poverty is bad, nevertheless they want to obstruct our going ahead with programmes to eradicate it. Some of the press-here and abroad-are highlighting baseless charges of corruption. We have always looked into such matters and shall deal them strictly."

The pre-censorship was imposed under Rule 48 of the Defence of India Rules "in order to maintain public order." It prohibited all categories of news, comment and rumour relating to the Emergency, to arrests and detentions unless pre-authorised in writing by an "authorised officer" from the Public Information Bureau in Delhi or by the director of information of a state government. Guidelines for the press which were issued said that "in the manner in which information is printed, published or disseminated, there can be an accretion of enormous strength to those who are posing a threat to internal security."

The press was called upon for help "in the fulfilment of the primary taks of ridding the nation of the causes of the Emergency; by suppressing news themselves through moderation, particularly in illustration and headlines; by publishing nothing to excite disaffection towards government established by law in India; nothing to promote feelings of enmity between different classes of persons in India or likely to cause the cessation or slowing down of work in any place, not anything objectionable already published in a foreign newspaper, nothing containing false allegations against leaders or denigrating the institution of prime minister; nothing to subvert the functioning of democratic institutions and nothing relating to agitations."

On July 26, 1975 editors received even more detailed instructions according to which "news was not to be published which contributes to the scare and demoralisation about the general situation or public interest in all respects as determined by the Central Government nothing which will contribute even in a remote way to affect or worsen the law and order situation; nothing which is likely to convey the impression of protest or disapproval of governmental measures." These embargoes were extended to cartoons, letters to the editor and captions.

On December 8, 1975, three ordinances were issued banning the publication of "objectionable matter", abolishing the Press Council, and removing the freedom of the press to report proceedings of Parliament. The ordinance relating to publication of objectionable matter was made into a law on January 28, 1976. Among other things it prohibited "inciting any individual or class to disaffection disharmony or ill-will or causing fear or alarm to any section of the public whereby any person may be induced to commit an offence against the state of public tranquillity." They included anything defamatory (whether by word or sign) of the president, vice-president, Speaker of the Lok Sabha, slate governors, the prime minister and all members of the Cabinet of Central and state governments or deemed to be so by them. The law gave wide powers of search and seizure to the police and other petty officials. It provided for the forfeiture of securities of press deposits as safeguard against "objectionable writing". The Press Council was abolished, it was stated, because it had "failed to curb tendentious and provocative writing."

How did the press react to these draconian laws? According to Sahni: "The year 1976 will be specially remembered for a progressive voluntary blackout by the press and a weakened submission by many editors to proprietors and to the establishment in a conspiracy of suppression. What was painful was that the readers did not show lack of interest in the stuff they read and were least concerned about the adulterated food they were being provided with. While a lot will need to be written to explain the voluntary collapse, one may say that all along money has won and the conscience of the pen has lost Reporters see things but the pen does not see. Editors know things but look ignorant. One cannot remember such transition in the behaviour and attitude of the press anywhere, at any time, so willingly and voluntarily achieved....

There have been in the past repression, suppression and brain washing but never a voluntary collapse of the mind, the desire to do more to suppress or eliminate than even demanded, the refusal to stretch censorship even to the end of the permitted teacher. In the long run, people will say, as of the daily meteorological forecasts, what the press publishes is not in accord with what happens." Sahni was bitter that "today most editors are loyal to the establishment as also to the tycoons who control the purse strings. So what we get as a result is a synthetic form of 'popular' opinion, an amalgam of conformism mixed with self-interest of the controlling tycoons."

However, there was at least one newspaper which fought grimly and with determination the assault on the press and became the special target of persecution, and vindictiveness. The *Indian Express,* with its proprietor Ramnath Goenka and editor, V.K. Narasimham wrote a glorious chapter in the battle for the freedom of the press and when the nightmare ended and the press became free again, they were hailed as heroes. All the restrictions on the press were removed when the Janata Government came to power in 1977 and the Indian press once again breathed freedom, never again to lose it. In the words of Justice Grover, president of the Press Council, "The Indian press today is as free as in any other free country in the world".

The freedom of the press is guaranteed in Article 19 (1) of the Constitution which protects freedom of speech and expression. Although the guarantee is not in the same language as in the First Amendment to the Constitution of the United States where press freedom is specifically mentioned, the Supreme Court of India has held that the freedom of the press is included in the concept of freedom of speech and expression. In 1951, the Constitution Act (First Amendment) Provided for reasonable restrictions being imposed on the exercise of press freedom in the interest of the security of the state, friendly relations with foreign states, public order, decency or morality or in relation to contempt of court, defamation or incitement to an offence. By the Constitution Act of 1963 (16th Amendment), the words "sovereignty and integrity of India" were inserted before the words "security of the state."

In the case *Express* Newspapers Vs Union of India the Supreme Court held that freedom of the press was an essential part of the right of freedom of speech and expression. The court also observed in that case that the fundamental right to freedom of speech and expression enshrined in Article 19 (1) (a) of the Constitution was based on the provisions of the First Amendment to the Constitution of the U.S.A. In another case, Romesh Thapar Vs the State of Madras, the Supreme Court held that the freedom of speech and expression included freedom of propagation of ideas and that freedom was ensured by the freedom of circulation. In Brij Bhushan Vs the State of Delhi the court said that the imposition of pre-censorship on a journal was a restriction on the liberty of the press which was an essential part of the right to freedom of speech and expression declared by Article 19 (1) (a).

The Press Commission said the expression "freedom of the press" carried different meanings to different people. Some people stressed the freedom of the editor to decide what should be published in the paper. Some others emphasised the right of the owners to market their publications. The commission said; "The press as a medium of communication is a modern phenomenon. It has immense power to advance or thwart the progress of civilisation. Its freedom can be used to create a brave new world or to bring about universal catastrophe." The commission pointed out that a citizen was entirely dependent on the press for the quality, proportion and extent of the news supply. In such a situation, the exclusive and continuous advocacy of one point of view through the medium of a newspaper which held a monopolistic position was not conducive to the formation of healthy public opinion.:

> "The assumption in a democratic set up is", the commission said, "that the freedom of the press will produce a sufficiently diverse press not only to satisfy the public interest by throwing up a broad spectrum of views but also to fulfil the individual interest by enabling virtually everyone with a distinctive opinion to find some place to express it."

The commission noted that with the revolution in communication technology on the one hand and the newspapers' development of an antipathy to ideas which were opposed to their commercial interest on the other, the operation of a market place of ideas had ceased to exit. "The constitutional issue generally is whether the expression already uttered should be given the shelter of Article 19 (1) (a)."

New Developments : But what of those ideas which are unacceptable to the media and which do not find access therein? The usual answer is that Article 19 (1) (a) "guarantees freedom of the owner to do as he chooses with his media. This answer stressed the view that a newspaper is emphatically the private property of the owner who sells a manufactured product at his risk; a newspaper owes nothing to the public which grants it no franchise. Thus, the constitutional imperative of free expression becomes the very instrument for repressing competitive ideas. The freedom guaranteed by Article 19(1) (a) must be reviewed in this light."

The commission said a realistic view of Article 19 (1) (a) "has to recognise that the right to expression is somewhat thin if it can be exercised only at the sufferance of the managers of mass communication." "Self-censorship by the press," it said, "is practically as great a menace to the freedom of expression as government censorship. The whole point of a free press is that ideas deserving public hearing and the decision as to which ideas deserve that hearing shall not rest solely within the editors and owners.... The widest possible dissemination of information from as many diverse and antagonistic sources, as could be ensured, alone will secure public welfare and the constitutional guarantee of freedom of speech and expression rests on this postulate. Article 19 (1) (a) does not sanction repression of that freedom by private interests including the press."

9

New Phase

That there has been a remarkable growth of the press in India, the daily as well as periodical press, is quite apparent and it is also supported by statistical information. The first Press Commission, which reported on the state of the press in India, soon after independence in 1954, noted that "there has been a rapid growth in the number and circulation of daily newspapers in the country both in English and in the Indian languages". The commission in paragraph 47 of its report spoke thus of the daily papers but there had been more or less a similar growth in the case of the weeklies and other periodicals too.

The commission had special studies done of the circulation of the dailies according to which 330 dailies had a total circulation of 2.5 million copies. There was no organisation of the Registrar of Newspapers, RNI, then in existence (in fact, one of the concrete recommendations of the commission led to the establishment of that office in 1956), the RNI's figures now show a steady trend in subsequent years, and in fact, a fast growth in the recent years.

Slow Development

This decadal study, except for the latest period, confirms that the Indian press has advanced at a fast pace, considerably faster than the population which, of course, is growing. It also shows that after 1976 the growth has been all the more remarkable and the importance of monthlies in Indian life has somewhat diminished as the dailies and the weeklies have been gaining ground and even fortnightlies, which had a hesitant start, have maintained a fairly high growth rate.

Significantly, India is rapidly approaching the UNESCO norm of ten newspaper copies for 100 persons for the developing nations. There are now more than eight copies per 100 persons although we have to travel a considerable distance before the figure of 10 copies of dailies can become a reality. Even there, the circulation of the daily papers is upwards of 40 per cent of the total for all categories of newspapers. This rising trend is sure to be maintained although the growth of television has put some brakes on the expansion of the press and could become a problem for the newspaper industry in the years to come.

The changing life-style of the people affecting the preference for different periodicity of publications is reflected in the slower growth rate of the circulation of monthlies which, in fact, declined after rising steadily until 1986. Curiously, the number of monthlies has been growing gradually, from 2,352 to 7,857 in 1986 and 9,837 in 1993. This would mean that while the publishers put their faith in the monthlies, the readers could not afford to wait for a whole month and instead chose fortnightlies of which there were quite a few attractive ones in different languages. The dailies have maintained their supremacy while the weeklies, which in 1956 were even ahead of the dailies in terms of circulation, have kept up their second position after the daily papers.

The first Press Commission noted that the English press had the highest circulation 697,000 copies for 41 dailies, and the Hindi dailies had the second highest figure of 379,000 copies, (for the year 1952). It expressed the view that while the growth of the Indian language press would continue, the Commission was pessimistic about the prospects for the English Press. In paragraph 61, it stated, "....... it may be said that the English newspapers do not have any considerable scope of adding largely to their circulation." This forecast has been disproved by events, which have not only helped many newspapers to come up and several to spread out in different cities of India, but also their total circulation has gone up substantially. While Hindi had 41.3 percent of the circulation of all newspapers in the country in 1993 (the latest Year for which the RNI's figures are available), the English dailies had 13.3 per cent. The Hindi papers had an aggregate circulations 27.9 million, the second highest for any language was recorded by English.

The reasons are not far to seek. The literacy levels, rising rapidly in the past few years, have accounted for an upsurge in the demand for the Indian language papers, Hindi as well as other languages. On the other hand, the addition to the population of university graduates, the rise in the purchasing power of the people – there are said to be anywhere around 250 million people in India who can buy consumer durables and fast moving consumer articles advertised day in and day out on the TV and who are targeted by the multinationals operating in the country as a result of liberalisation of the economy - and last but not the least, the continuing importance of English in the government and public life are among the factors for the English Press continuing to occupy statistically and otherwise a position of vantage.

The first Press Commission had good reasons perhaps to come to the conclusion that the English Press's days were numbered or a saturation point had been reached. There was the (largely impractical) fifteen-year limit laid down by the founding fathers for English to be replaced by Hindi and perhaps in the early years after independence that was taken seriously. There could be other factors for the somewhat gloomy prediction that the English Press could not expect to add to its circulation. For example, the leading English daily of the day (which still commands a leading position today), the Times of India's Bombay edition, had not added significantly to its January-June 1952 circulation of 87,002 copies. In fact, by July-December 1953 the circulation had actually come down to 86,088 after rising slightly in the two half yearly periods in between.

The commission argued that 14 lakh people had progressed beyond the matriculation stage to intermediate; graduate or diploma level and they were already buying seven lakh copies of the English dailies. It, therefore, drew the conclusion that there was not much scope for the expansion of the circulation of the English dailies. The others who could read a paper and could afford to buy one were already taking Indian language papers. Anyway, things turned out differently and no one had serious misgivings about the continuation and prosperous existence of the English press, certainly not the people who publish the papers.

Twenty-eight years after the first Press Commission had reported, the second one, under Justice K.K. Mathew, submitted its report. The second body had a chequered history. Appointed by the Janata Government which was formed in the wake of the internal Emergency, under Justice P.K. Goswami (like Justice Mathew, a retired judge of the Supreme Court of India), it was replaced by an entirely new body after the Congress (I), under the late Mrs. Indira Gandhi, returned to power at the Centre. The first body was constituted in May 1978 and the second one in June 1980 after the chairman and members of the commission, under Justice Goswami, had resigned as soon as the new government was formed.

The second Press Commission also made a detailed study of the-state of the Indian Press. It found that India had by then the second largest number of dailies in Asia and the fourth in the world after the United States, (Federal Republic of)

Germany, and China. The circulation in 1979, according to the RNI report for 1980, covering the operations in 1979, was as much as four times the figure in 1952, 13-29 million as compared with 2.5 million in the case of the weeklies, the circulation went up from 3 million in 1956 (as in the figures quoted earlier) to 12.9 million by 1979, an increase of more than three times. As for the other periodicals the figure was up from 5 million in 1956 to 20 million.

Smooth-stage

This showed considerable progress and it was tempered by the thought that population and literacy had also gone up. Taking the growth of literacy into account, the actual rise in circulation was seven per cent for 1,000 literate persons in the case of the dailies or 57.4 copies in 1979 from 50.4 in 1960. In respect of the weeklies the increase was from 50 to 56.1 copies for 1,000 persons and in the case of the other periodicals the rise was from 80.6 copies to 88.1 for 1,000 literate Indians.

The other limitations that the commission noted for the date collected by the RNI were in respect of the number of newspapers actually in publication, as against the number registered with him, and the claims of circulation which could not be checked from year to year, given the modest machinery at the RNI's disposal for such checks and the untrue claims indulged in by many newspapers while the independent ABC's checks were confined to its membership which was small.

Briefly, the point to be made is that the registration of newspapers is not a true index of the existence of a newspaper. The number of newspapers on the list of DAVP (Directorate of Advertising and Visual Publicity) of the Central government, which places advertisements for most of the ministries except the railways, is more realistic. In 1994 that number was 5,300 while those reporting their circulation to the RNI was about 4,000. This would show that even now the old problem is continuing and the newspapers in actual publication are only a sixth or less of the total number of registered papers. But the fact that there is consistency in the number of newspapers which report their circulations and the RNI is able to check the claims of over a 1,000 papers a year now would show that there is much force in the circulation figures compiled by the RNI.

The DAVP list covers 5,000 papers. This would atleast mean that about 5,000 papers are being published as the DAVP figures are based on actual scrutiny of the published issues. Thus about 1,000 or more of the 5,300 papers on the DAVP list do not report the circulation figures to the RNI at all, the total number of copies of the newspaper available to the people may, therefore, be even more than the figure of 67.61 million arrived at by the RNI for 1993.

By 1979 as the second Press Commission analysis shows, the Indian language papers were making more headway than the English papers. The share of the English dailies came down to 22.5 per cent in 1979 as compared with 27.6 in 1952. For the first time, the Hindi press forged ahead of the its English counterpart, Hindi had a 23 per cent share as against 15 per cent in 1952. But by 1979 the prediction of the first Press Commission about the lack of scope for advancement of the English dailies was already proving way off the mark because the figure of copies of English daily newspapers had gone up from 0.697 million to nearly 3 million. For Hindi the growth was from 0.378 million in 1952 to 3.048 million in 1979. Malayalam, Marathi and Gujarati had each recorded more than a million circulation level for their dailies from under two lakhs in 1952 while other major languages had also made substantial progress. (A lakh is equal to 100,000).

Another indicator of the rise of the Indian language press was the number of dailies with individual circulation of above a lakh. In 1960, there were just two dailies to have that distinction and both were English dailies. Now in 1979 of the 30 dailies in that category, as many as 20 were Indian language dailies. The highest circulated daily was also an Indian language paper, the Bengali daily *Ananda Bazar Patrika* from Calcutta, which had a total circulation of 4,03,047 for a single edition daily newspaper. Remarkably the daily enjoys the same position today also (in 1993) but its circulation has been almost unchanged 4,58,104. It occupied the eleventh position among all the dailies but the lack of any significant progress in circulation since 1979 perhaps shows that the new arrivals on the scene, the *Aajkaal* and the *Bartaman* have prevented the *Ananda Bazar* from getting a significant share of the new readership.

The number of English dailies with a circulation of over a lakh had gone up by 1979 to 10 from two in 1960 while there were five each in Hindi and Malayalam with that circulation, three each in Marathi and Gujarati, two in Bengali and one each in Kannada and Tamil.

Novel Drifts

The RNI reports shows that there are 992 dailies in the country, including a few tribal weeklies, for which circulation data was available. Of them, 73 came in the big category, or those having a circulation of 75,000 or more, 27 mediums, or those with a circulation of more than 25,000 but less than 75,000 and the remaining 682 were small, or those with a circulation of 25,000 of less. Again, the 73 big ones were further sub-divided into those with a circulation of a lakh of copies or more and those between 75,000 and a lakh. Thus there were 45 dailies with a daily circulation of a lakh or more. These along with the other 28 falling between a lakh and the lower limit had a share of 34.5 per cent of the total circulation of all dailies. The medium had a share of 32.9 per cent and the small papers the balance 32.6 per cent.

The figures, quoted above are for 1993, the latest year for which the RNI report of 1994 is available. It showed a growth of 6.2 per cent in the circulation of Indian newspapers over the level registered for 1992 from 63,667,000 to 67,611,000 copies. The number of dailies had declined but their circulations had gone up by 6.84 per cent, perhaps indicating that the rule of survival of the fittest was operating. Between 1984 and 1993, however, the number of dailies had also risen, as much as 132.5 per cent. Again, we can a guess that the growing presence of television was forcing some of the dailies, as between 1992 and 1993, to close down.

No daily paper, not even those with multiple editions, had crossed the million mark, although the *Malayala Manorama weekly* already had achieved that distinction.

Hindi dailies had a 40.9 per cent share of the total circulation of all dailies, with 11,966,000 copies, with English following behind it at a respectable distance. The English dailies had a circulation of 3,849,000 or 13.2 per cent of the total circulation of dailies in all languages. In respect of the number of dailies published, Hindi was in the lead, followed by Urdu, Tamil, English, Marathi, Kannada, and Malayalam. The *Ananda Bazar Patrika,* as we have noted before, continued to occupy the leading position among all dailies followed by the *Times of India,* Bombay edition which had a circulation of 3,70,273, incidentally the highest for any single edition of an English newspaper. But the Malayalam daily, the *Malayala Manorama,* published from five centres, Kottayam, Kozhikode, Kochi, Thriuvananthapuram and Palakkat, held the first position among all dailies with its combined circulation of 7,18,876. The *Times of India,* having five different editions at Bombay, Delhi, Ahmedabad, Bangalore, and Patna, was not far behind with a total combine circulation of 6,41,264.

The third position again went to an Indian language daily, the Hindi *Punjab Kesari,* with three editions at Delhi, Jalandhar and Ambala and a total circulation of 6,13,129. With fifteen editions, the *Indian Express* came fourth, its combined circulation being 5,50,165 copies.

A majority of Indian Newspapers are periodicals of which again the weeklies constitute the largest single category, 11,136 out of 29,597 periodicals. There are 4,571 fortnightlies and

9,837 monthlies and 4,053 periodicals of higher periodicity mainly quarterlies and annuals. As we saw at the start of this chapter, weeklies had a high circulation of 21.38 million, or 31.6 per cent of the total circulations of all newspapers, monthlies accounted for 14.6, fortnightlies 8.6 per cent and the remaining periodicals had 1.6 per cent among them.

The linguistic diversity of India is fairly well known but even the knowledgeable may be surprised to learn that Indian papers are being published in 96 languages, including the eighteen languages listed in the Eighth Schedule of the Constitution and English. The remaining 77 include a large number of tribal languages. The largest populated state of India, Uttar Pradesh, which has a population bigger than that of most of the countries in the world, (139,112,287), naturally accounted for the largest number of newspapers, 5,131 followed by Delhi, with 4,435, Maharashtra 3,614 and West Bengal 2,896. Of the total circulation of all papers published from India, which is 67.61 million, UP claimed 10,355 million. Maharashtra was second with 8,215 and Delhi third with 7,262 million.

There is thus a virtual boom in newspapers and the boom is not only in respect of the number of papers published but also in terms of the readership they enjoy. It is justified by the high circulations achieved by a number of papers and the wide dispersal of the readership. Newspapers coming out of the metropolitan cities have naturally high circulations as they have better access to news at comparatively less cost (a newspaper from Solapur to Maharashtra would have to incur substantial expenditure to station more than one correspondent in Bombay, the state capital and at least one in Delhi, the national capital), more financial resources, better trained staff and other facilities.

It is not surprising that the papers coming out of Delhi, Bombay, Calcutta and Madras, had between them a circulation of 20.6 million, or about 30.5 per cent of the total in India.

But the point which has been made later in the book would show that much of this circulation is accounted for by sales in the vast hinterland of the neighbouring states and even a few which are somewhat remote. For example, Delhi dailies have either their own vans or those belonging to their contractors which enable them to reach their early morning editions to cities and towns at a distance of 300 to 400 kilometres by these vans or by a relay of the vans. They, of course, compete unequally with the local or regional papers, but then their circulation is not meant entirely, or even substantially for the citizens of the metropolitan cities only.

More Promotion

Transport by road has played a major part in the propagation of the dailies and periodicals. In the early years of the twentieth century and until soon after independence, railway and postal deliveries were the major means of propagation. Gradually the road vans took over and now you have a Delhi, Bombay, Madras or Calcutta paper, or from some state capitals, at your breakfast table, later if you were living 200 km away from there, and a little later if you were 300-400 km away. What the contractors do is to arrange for relays of the vans at a central point where not only the copies meant for that town would be off-loaded for further distribution by bicycle hawkers but a fresh van would cover the areas which thus constitute the hinterland of that town while the van from the metro goes back with some other fare or parcels.

The state capitals (India has 28 states and seven Union Territories, UT) excluding the four metros, which are also State or UT Capitals, account for 18.6 per cent of the circulation as they have their own papers. Other cities, outsides the state capitals with a population of a lakh or more, have between them 33.5 per cent of the circulation, the highest for any of the four groups of cities.

The fourth group covering towns with a population of less than a lakh, had 16.39 per cent of the circulation. The circulation is thus urban oriented but, as we have seen in the case of the four metros, the papers reach out to the far flung areas of the country and the spread of the newspapers can be said to have achieved a fair level of propagation, although the urban bias would still persist. Some of the cities in this third group, that is cities which are over a lakh in population other than the state capitals and from which prominent papers are coming out are :

> Jalandhar in Punjab; Ambala in Haryana; Agra, Meerut, Kanpur, Bareilly, Varanasi and Allahabad in Uttar Pradesh; Ranchi, Jamshedpur; and Dhanbad in Bihar; Siliguri in West Bengal; Jorhat in Assam; Cuttack in Orissa; Vijayawada, Visakhapatnam and Tirupati in Andhra Pradesh; Kottayam, Kochi, Kozikode and Palakkat in Kerala; Coimbatore, Madurai, Salem, Thiruchirapalli and Tirunelveli in Tamil Nadu; Pune, Nasik, Solapur, Kolhapur, Nagpur and Aurangabad in Maharashtra; Baroda, Ahmedabad, Rajkot, Surat and Bhavnagar in Gujarat; and Indore, Gwalior, Raipur and Jabalpur in Madhya Pradesh.

As we will see later in this chapter, the newspaper have spread out far into the interior and there are now district and even tehsil towns from where dailies and other papers are being published.

We have seen earlier the language-wise pattern of the number and circulation of newspapers in the years-1952, 1960, 1970 and 1979.

The spread of the, dailies and other papers to the interior of the country has been noticeable in the past two decades. The factors which contributed to it have been the gradual spread of literacy (the figure for the 1991 census is 52 per cent but since then literacy has spread further in a big way), the gradual rise in the people's purchasing power and the rise in the level of political and general awareness among the population. Combined with those factors was the fact that the papers were now available in district towns and even places like tehsil or taluka headquarters and reaching many of the bigger villages, fairly early in the day in the case of the dailies.

In the late seventies the number of newspapers on the DAVP's list we around 2,300. This has grown almost by leaps and bounds and stands, as we have seen, at 5,300. Once more we have to emphasise that the DAVP list is a good index of the number of papers in actual publication and in need of advertisements. For the small and medium papers which are not getting sufficient private advertising the DAVP advertisements are extremely important. DAVP impalement also acts as a stepping stone for getting state government and district administration ads and those of the Panchayati Raj institutions. The DAVP is a kind of measuring yard for these other authorities.

In several states like Maharashtra it is even laid down that tender notices and other advertisements pertaining to a district must be placed with the district papers or those being published in the district (even as multiple editions). All this has acted as an incentive to the growth of the district papers, dailies as well as weeklies. A few of them could be papers in name only, with no regularity and coming out occasionally to gobble up advertisements, but the large majority are genuine. In the case of the DAVP, of which the author has personal knowledge having been director of the organisation, rigid tests are applied before a paper is empaneled even in the case of the big English dailies.

What to talk of the small and medium papers even many of the big dailies care for DAVP empanelment both as a source of revenue and because DAVP advertisements like recruitment through the Union Public Service Commission (UPSC) and other Central government agencies are important for attracting readers. These advertisements are released by the DAVP. The weekly appearance of the advertisements is looked forward to by many young men and women and their parents and guardians.

Of course, DAVP has its own rates and these are generally lower than the newspapers' own commercial rates. But no discrimination is practised by the organisation in determining the rates according to a set formula. Fairness is generally observed in placement. Some newspapers still prefer to do without these ads because they would not like to practise a double rate system. The *Hindu, Eenadu and India Today* are among them.

Now we come to the publication of dailies and others being undertaken from district towns and those below that category, although the challenge and competition from the chain and multiple edition papers is a powerful disincentive.

Every district town has a newspaper and sometime more than one. This is in addition to the district editions of the big Papers and the circulation, as we have seen, of the leading dailies in the districts from their publication centres in the metropolitan cities, state capitals or major publication centres outside the state capitals which we have noted earlier. For example, in Andhra Pradesh, apart from the Hyderabad or Vijayawada-based papers, like the *Eenadu,* the, *Andhra Jyoti, Udayam, Andhra Prabha,* and the *Andhra Bhoomi,* which also cover the district towns, or have district-specific editions, there are papers like *State Times (T), Gopi Krishna* and the *Eluru Times,* (Telugu) from Eluru, Poddu from Nizamabad, which also appears from Hyderabad, *Praja Por* and *Praja Portam* from Nalgonda, *Warangal Vani* from Warangal, and *Guntur Express* from Guntur.

The major publishing centres in the state, obviously have scope for not only the leading papers coming out from there but also smaller ones. Besides the Telugu papers listed above there are English dailies like the *Hindu, Indian Express,* the indigenous *Deccan Chronicle* and the equally indigenous but slow-moving *Newstime of* the *Eenadu* group, and Urdu dailies like the *Siasat, Munsiff, Rehnuma-e-Deccan* and *Angarey.* The competition from such powerful papers notwithstanding, there are a number of Telugu papers like the *Krishna Patrika* from the twin city of Secunderabad and *Sayamkalam Patrika,* Telugu evening paper, from the capital. The city of Vijayawada, home to most leading Telugu papers, has room for smaller dailies like *Janatha* and *Praiasakthi.* Visakhapatnam, another major newspaper centre in the state, has place for smaller dailies like Vijayabhanu and *Visakha Samacharam* and Vizianagaram is home to *Grameen Vedica.*

Hyderabad has continued to be one of the major publishing centres of Urdu papers. Besides those we have referred to there are smaller ones like the *Aina-e-Hyderabad, Bhagyanagar Observer, Bhagyanagar Times, Haq Baat, Khateeb, Kamander Maheshar, Naveed-e-Deccan, Rehnuma-e-Hind, Saz-e-Deccan, Shan-e-Hind, Siasi Mahaz, Takeed, Tulway Sahir, Voice of Hyderabad,* and *Watan ki Pukar.* Hyderabad also has, an evening English daily like the *Skyline* and a Hindi daily, the *Hindi Milap.* It goes without saying that the district and smaller papers have come up and been appearing over a number of years.

In another major state, Bihar, there are more than 70 dailies including, of course, the major ones like the *Hindustan Times,* the Aj, the *Times of India, Navbharat Times, Sangam, Sada-e-Aam, Azimabad Express* and *Tanzeem* (all urdu), the *Ranchi Express* from Ranchi, *Awaz* from Dhanbad and *Udit Vani* from Jamshedpur in Hindi. There are a number of papers from Muzaffarpur, Samastipur, Bhagalpur, Khagaria, Vaishali and Saharsha and other district towns. In the state there is a tendency for the newspapers to concentrate in the capital city of Patna, although there is good dispersal also.

The old established papers like the *Aryavarta* and *Indian Nation* had been left behind in the race by papers coming in from Uttar Pradesh, like the *Aaj, The Times of India, The Navbharat Times* from Delhi and the *Hindustan Times* and its Hindi stablemate the *Hindustan*. They have lately managed to surface again. Bihar has also the distinction of having in Patna a number of important Urdu papers. Besides those there are quite a few published from the state capital and, what is more, there are some Urdu papers coming out of Bhagalpur *(Desh Bidesh)*, Muzaffarpur *(Garam Hawa)*, Samastipur *(Halate-Bihar)* and others.

In Gujarat, *Bhoomi* has established itself in Jamnagar, besides the *Nohat, Prasaran* has come up in Dohad, *Saurashtra Bhoomi* in Junagadh, *Valsad Times* (Gujarati) from Valsad, and *Naya Padkar* from Anand and *Navnirman* from Surat. These are in addition to the leading papers like the *Gujarat Samachar* and *Sandesh* with their editions from Ahmedabad, Baroda, Rajkot, Surat and Bombay (in the case of Gujarat Samachar), the *Times of India* and the *Indian Express* along with its Gujarati counterpart, the *Loksatta* and *Jansatta* from Ahmedabad, Baroda and Rajkot, which are now said to have been sold out by the *Express* group to a local concern, the *Gujarati* of Surat, the *Jai Hind* with editions from Rajkot and Ahmedabad and the *Phulchhab* from Rajkot and its sister publication Kutch *Mitra* from Bhuj.

In Karnataka, the main publication centres are Bangalore, Manipal, Dharwar (Hubli), and Belgaum. Apart from major dailies like the *Deccan Herald* and its Kannada counterpart, the *Prajavani*, the *Hindu*, *Indian Express* and *Times of India* from Bangalore, the *Sanyukta Karnataka* from Hubli as well as Bangalore *Udayavani* from Manipal, and Tarun *Bharat* (Marathi) and *Kannadama* (Kannada) from Belgaum, there are papers coming out from Chitradurga, Betgiri, Mysore, Mangalore, Hassan, Davangere, Bidar and similar places. Bangalore is home to some Urdu papers like the *Pasban* and some Urdu dailies also come out of other places in the state.

In terms of newspaper publication there is nothing to beat Kerala state where both the numbers and circulations of dailies and even weeklies are high. This is largely because of the high literacy rate and the high degree of political awareness among its people and of course, love of the mother tongue Malayalam. We will have occasion to speak of the prominent papers in different languages and states in a later chapter and Kerala's Malayalam papers will have an important place there. Here it would suffice to say that because of the strong identity of leading dailies the *Malayala Manorama, Mathrubhoomi, Kerala, Kaumudi,* and group papers like the *Chandrika, Deshabhimani, Janayugam* and *Deepika,* the growth of smaller papers in the districts has not been noticeable.

The additional reason, an important one, for this is that road and water transport in Kerala being widespread most of the towns and villages are accessible from the main publishing centres-Kozhikode, Kottayam, Thiruvananthapuram, Kochi and Palakkat.

But when you come to the Hindi speaking states of Madhya Pradesh, Rajasthan and Uttar Pradesh, you find that the growth of district papers is almost of phenomenal proportions. There are a number of major publishing centres for dailies in MP like the state capital Bhopal, Gwalior, Jabalpur, Raipur, Indore and Bilaspur, from where the Nai *Duniya, Navabharat, Bhaskar, Deshbandhu, Swadesh* and similar papers are being published. The district towns which have their own papers include Ujjain, Sagar, Katni, Korba, Morena, Balaghat, Neemuch, Datia, Ratiam, Satna, Shahdol, Sidhi, Shivpur, Chhatarpur, Ambikapur, Raigarh, Raisen, Guna, Rewa and Mandsaur. Needless to, add that some of these are more than mere district towns, some are not even district headquarters.

In Rajasthan, Jaipur, the state capital, is of course, a major centre of newspaper publication but there is much publishing activity in Jodhpur, Ajmer, Kota, Bikaner and Udaipur also. From here the leading papers of the state, like the *Rajasthan Patrika, Navjyoti, Rashtradoot,* and those which have come from other states to Rajasthan like the *Navbharat Times,* are published. But newspapers have also gradually been coming out of almost all parts of Rajasthan like the towns of Sriganganagar, Sikar, Alwar, Bharatpur, Churu, Bhilwara, Udaipur, Jalore, Bundi, Sawai Madhopur, Dholpur , Nagaur, Banswara, Jhunjhunu, Chittorgarh, Pali, Tonk, Beawar, Hindon, Gangapur, Sirohi, Dungarpur, Hanurnangarh, Jaiselmer and Barmer.

What we are talking here is about dailies only which means daily papers are being published from these far flung centres of Rajasthan. Even the major cities of Jaipur, Ajmer, Kota, Jodhpur and Bikaner are home to any number of dailies other than the big ones referred to above. It goes without saying that, as in other states most of these dailies are small in circulation and find the competition with the well established papers an arduous task.

In the country's largest populated state of Uttar Pradesh, Lucknow the state capital, Varanasi, Agra, Kanpur, Bareilly, Allahabad, Gorakhpur and Meerut, are among the main centre of newspaper publication. These are the places from which the leading dailies—*Aaj, Jagran, Amar Ujala, Pioneer, National Herald, Navbharat Times, Northern India Patrika,* Amrit Prabhat and *Swantantra Bharat,* are being brought out. But many more places, including district towns, and even smaller centres, are home to a number of Hindi dailies.

These include Sultanpur, Lakhimpur, Kheri, Etawah, Bijnor, Moradabad, Orai, Deoria, Aligarh, Rai Bareilly, Hardwar, Rishikesh, Ghaziabad, Noida (near Delhi), Unnao, Badaun, Ballia, Gonda, Mathura, Hardoi, Azamgarh, Fatehpur, Dehradun, Saharanpur, Jhansi, Basti, Faizabad, Pilibhit, Mirzapur, Mainpuri, Garhwal, Pauri Garhwal, Jaunpur, Muzaffarnagar, Hamirpur, Maharajganj, Azamgarh, Rampur, Mau, Bulandshaher, Banda, Bahraich, Haldwani, Nainital, and Sitapur.

Several of these centres have more than one paper and the major centres like Lucknow, Agra and Varanasi have besides the mainline dailies a number of other dailies. UP has several Urdu dailies too and apart from the leading ones like the

Quami Awaz, Siasat, Paigham from Lucknow and Kanpur, there are a number of Urdu dailies from these and other centres too.

In Punjab, a number of Punjabi papers have come up in different centres and places like Phillaur, Sangrur, Bhatinda, Rajpura, apart from the old established papers like *Ajit* and *Akali Patrika,* Published from Jalandhar, and the *Charhdikala* from Patiala. Punjab is one of the highly developed states in the country and has a network of roads which facilitates the supply of papers from the main centres at Jalandhar, Ludhiana and Patiala apart from Chandigarh. The *Tribune,* which had moved to Ambala after partition from its base at Lahore in Pakistan, ultimately found a permanent home in Chandigarh serving not only the Union Territory but also Punjab as well as Haryana and Himachal Pradesh and to some extent Jammu and Kashmir also. Jalandhar is also the home of the *Hind Samachar* group which branched out from Urdu Journalism into Hindi through its highly successful *Punjab Kesari* and a Punjabi paper, the *Jagbani.*

In Tamil Nadu, the leading Tamil papers, the *Thanthi,* the *Dinakaran, Dinamalar, Dinamani* as well as the comparatively recent ones like the *Malai Malar* and *Malai Murasu,* have spread out in almost all parts of the state from their bases in Madras city. So their network serves the readers throughout the state, apart from some other papers being published from places like Nagarcoil. Madras is of course, the home of the *Hindu* and the *Indian Express* and there is an Urdu paper, the *Musalman,* being published from there which is one of the old dailies in the Urdu language. The first Tamil paper, the *Swadesamitran,* which had a glorious past but had to close down, has recently been revived but it has yet to make its presence felt.

Calcutta was at once time equal to the whole of West Bengal, in terms of newspaper publication at least. Apart from the *Statesman* and the *Telegraph,* it is home to the *Ananda Bazar Patrika* and the late entrants to the field, the successful *Bartaman* and *Aajkaal,* and noted Urdu dailies like the *Azad Hind, Rozana*

Hind and *Akkas, Hindi* dailies -like the *Sanmarg* and *Vishwamitra*. There was practically nothing in the rest of the state. But now the situation is somewhat different and papers have come up in towns like Siliguri, Midnapore, Burdwan and Asansol.

In Maharashtra, Bombay has been dominating the life of the state but unlike Calcutta, not to the exclusion of enterprise in the vast hinterland. Major centres like Pune, Nagpur, Nashik, Kolhapur, Aurangabad, Solapur and some others have provided enough support and sustenance to a number of dailies. The *Times of India,* group has in Bombay its flagship, the Bombay edition of the *Times of India,* and there are other important dailies from Bombay, like the *Free Press Journal.* The *Indian Express,* two good eveningers the *Midday* and the *Afternoon Despatch* and *Courier,* leading Marathi papers the *Loksatta, Maharashtra Times, Samna* and the *Navakal,* Gujarati papers like the *Mumbai Samachar,* the *Janmabhoomi* of the Saurashtra Trust, and the *Urdu Times* and *Inqulab* The *Sakai* of Pune has branched out in other centres. The *Kesari* has done, likewise from its Pune base and the *Lokmat* of Nagpur has also expanded.

But journalism has spread far and wise in the state and besides the major centres referred to above new ones have come up in Satara, Dhule, Chandrapur, Alibag, Ahmednagar, Nanded, Malegaon, Amravati, Jalgaon, Akola, Ratnagiri, Latur, Srirampur and Parbhani.

It goes without saying that the dailies which have come up in the smaller centres, other than the metros, state capitals and the bigger cities outsides the capital cities, are mostly in the small category. But their appearance itself is a sign of the growing expansion of newspapers in India, although for them the competition from the newspapers with larger resources and better financial and other management advantages, is too strong to make out a living. What we have talked about here is only the growth of dailies. The list of periodicals, weeklies and others which have come up in the smaller towns is indeed large, larger than the list of dailies.

Bibliography

Ahuja, B.N. : *Theory and Practice of Journalism*, Surjeet Publications, Delhi, 1979.

Alfred, John : *Mass Communication in the New Millennium*, Prime Publication, New Jersey, 2003.

Apter, Michel : *The New Technology of Education*, MacMillan, London, 1968.

Aronson, James : *The Press and the Cold War*, Beacon Press, Boston, 1970.

Awasthy, G.C. : *Broadcasting in India*, Allied Publishers Private Ltd., Bombay, 1965.

Bard, F. Eraser : *An Introduction to Journalism*, The MacMillan Co., New York, 1958.

Bernard, H. W. : *Principles of Journalism: A Basic Text*, Allied Publishers Private Ltd., New Delhi, 1998.

Bhatia, A. : *Journalism in Modern India*, Asia Publishing House, Bombay, 1964.

Brank, S.M. : *Journalism Characteristics and School Learning*, Harper, New York, 1976.

Carrol, L. : *Occupational Information*, Prentice Hall, New York, 1961.

Cattell, B.B. : *Media Structure, Growth and Action*, Houghton Mifflin Co., Boston, 1999.

Chatterjee, R.K. : *Mass Communication*, National Book Trust, New Delhi, 2002.

Chauhan, S.S. : *A Textbook of Mass Communication*, Sterling Publishers, New Delhi, 2001.

Cottle, W.C. : *Interest and Personality Inventories*, Houghton Miffling Co., New York, 1968.

Cream, David : *Explaining Teaching Machines and Programmes*, Featon, San Fracisco, 1961.

Critchfield, Richard : *The Indian Reporter's Guide*, Allied Pacific Pvt. Ltd., Bombay, 1962.

Curfis, D. : *Interpretotive Reporting*, MacMillan Co., New York, 1957.

Dale, Edgare : *Audio-Visual Method in Teaching*, Dryden Rinehart and Winston, New York, 1969.

Das, R.C. : *Educational Technology*, Sterling Publishers, New Delhi, 2000.

Donald, H. : *Developmental Counselling*, The Ronald Press, New York, 1966.

Donald, Mc. : *The Art of Radio*, Faber & Faber, London, 1961.

Emery, Edwin : *The Press and America*, Prentice Hall, New Jersey, 1999.

Eve, A. A. : *Micro-teaching Theory into Practice*, Oxford, New York, 1969.

Frank, H. Krouse : *Media Technique with Youth*, Charles and Mervil, Ohio, 1990.

Gagne, R.M. : *The Conditions of Learning*, Holt Binsort and Winston, New York, 1965.

Gaur, J.S. and Saraswat, R.K. : *Mass Media*, NCERT, New Delhi, 1998.

Ghiselli, Edwin E. : *Personnel and Industrial Media*, McGraw Hill Book Co., New York, 1955.

Gunning, Robert : *The Technique of Clear Writing*, McGraw Hill Book Co., New York.

Haban, F. : *Movies that Teach*, Dryden Press, New York, 1945.

Hancock, Alan : *Planning for Educational Mass Media*, Longmans, London, 1977.

Hercleread, A.V. : *Instruction: Materials and Methods,* Mc Graw Hill Book Co., New York, 1964.

Hoppock, Rebert : *Occupational Information,* McGraw Hill Book Co., New York, 1997.

Hudson, Kenneth : *The Dictionary of Diseased English,* The MacMillan Co., Bombay, 1977.

James, S. : *Audio-Visual Materials and Techniques,* American Book Company, New York, 1959.

John, A. : *The Asian Newspaper's Reluctant Revolution,* The Iowa State University Press, Iowa, 1977.

John, Hohenberg : *The Professional Journalist,* Rinehort and Winston, New York, 1969.

Johnson, Stanley and Julian Harriss : *The Complete Reporter,* The MacMillan Co., New York, 1942.

Joseph and Jospeth : *Idyels Past and Present: An Editor's Wet Copy,* Orient Longman, Bombay, 1979.

Kaul, B.N. : *Studies in Mass Media,* Har Anand, New Delhi, 1998.

Knight, R. : *Intelligence and Intelligence Tests,* Methuen and Co. Ltd. London, 1943.

Kothari, O.S. : *Report of the Indian Education Commission, 1964-66,* Publication Divison, New Delhi, 1966.

Krug, R.E. : *Ability Testing in Developing Countries: A Handbook of Principles and Techniques,* Praeger, New York, 1972.

Laxman, N.J. : *Introduction to Media Technology,* Oxford Publishing Company, New Delhi, 2003.

Lowman, J. : *Mastering Techniques of Media,* Prentice Hall, New York, 1999.

Luhan, Mc : *Understanding Media,* Routludge, London, 1964.

Mahler, C.A. : *Media Counselling in the Schools,* Houghton Mifflin, Boston, 1969.

Matheson, Alastair : *The Communication Materials and Methods,* McGraw Hill Book Company, New Delhi, 1964.

McCully, C.H. : *The Media—Instrument of Change*, National College Record, Bombay, 2001.

Mehta, D.S. : *Mass Communication and Journalism in India*, Allied Publishers Pvt. Ltd., Bombay, 1979.

Menon, Narayan : *The Communication Revolution*, National Book Trust, New Delhi, 1976.

Miller, Care G. : *Modern Journalism*, Rinehart and Winston, New York, 1962.

Miller, Carroll, H. : *Foundations of Guidance*, Harper and Brothers, New York, 1961.

Mitchell, V. : *Reporting*, Rinehart and Winston, New York, 1960.

Mohanty, J. : *Educational Broadcasting: Radio & Television in Education*, Sterling Publishers, New Delhi, 1984.

Mojar, N.F. : *Current Trends in Mass Communication*, Deep & Deep Publications, New Delhi, 2001.

Mokam, K.B. : *Dynamics of Mass Media in India*, Deep & Deep Publications, New Delhi, 2000.

Mosan, N.N. : *Indian Education in the Emerging Society*, Sterling Publishers, New Delhi, 1982.

Moven, Kiran : *Studies in Educational Broadcasting*, Deep & Deep Publications, New Delhi, 1996.

Mujuni, J.P. : *Studies in Media Education*, Deep & Deep Publications, New Delhi, 1995.

Muni, K.W. : *Media Technology*, Deep & Deep Publications, New Delhi, 2003.

Murthy, Nadig Krishna : *Indian Journalism*, University of Mysore, Prasaranga, 1966.

Natrajan, J. : *History of Indian Journalism*, Publications Division, New Delhi, 1999.

Natrajan, S. : *A History of the Press in India*, Asia Publishing House, Bombay, 1962.

Oscar, Krisen : *Encyclopaedia of Mass Media and Journalism*, Oxford, New York, 1998.

Ottaway, A.K.C. : *Press and Society*, Routldge and Kegan Paul, London, 1962.

Oxtoby, J.S. : *Media and Cultural Environment*, Methuen, London, 1969

Page, C.M. : *Society and Media*, MacMillan, London, 1950.

Panda, K.C. : *Role of Mass Media in School Learning*, RCE, Bhubaneswar, 1978.

Parikh, R.D. : *The Press and Society*, Popular Prakashan, Bombay, 1965.

Quirk, A. : *Editor and Editorial Writer*, Rinehart & Co., New York, 1955.

Reston, James : *The Artillery of the Press: Its Influence on American Foreign Policy*, Harper & Row, New York, 1967.

Rewntreu, Desk : *Media Technology in Curriculum Development*, Harper and Row Publishers, London, 2001.

Richder L. : *Handbook of Broadcasting*, McGraw- Hill Book Co., New York, 1957.

Roland, E. : *Exploring Journalism*, Prentice Hall, New Jersey, 1958.

Sadanand, K.R. : *New Media: Memo to Educational Planners*, John, Wiley, London, [illegible].

Sahni, J.N. : *Truth About the Indian Press*, Allied Publishers, Bombay, 1974.

Schramm, Wilbur : *Big Media, Little Media*, Edward Arnold, London, 2000.

Sethi, Patanjali : *Professional Journalism*, Orient Longman, Bombay, 1974.

Shaw, David : *Journalism Today*, Harper's College Press, London, 1977.

Shelly, C. : *Fundamentals of Mass Media*, Houghton Miffin Co., Boston, 1976.

Thedore, M. : *Headlines and Deadlines*, Columbia University Press, New York, 1961.

Thorndike, R.L. : *Media Psychology and Education*, Wiley Eastern Pvt. Ltd., New Delhi, 2001.

Ullan, J. : *Technical Reporting*, Rinehart and Winston, New York, 1963.

Vedanayagam, G. : *Media Teaching Technology for College Teachers*, Sterling Publishers, New Delhi, 1989.

Viner, B. : *The Practice of Journalism*, Heinemann, London, 1963.

Warich, D. : *Modular Circula: International Encyclopaedia*, Pergamone Publications, London, 1994.

Whinnie, Donald : *The Art of Broadcasting*, Faber & Faber, London, 1961.

Willian, Charvat : *Handbook for Writers*, Prentice Hall, New Jersey, 1962.

Wolseley, E. : *How to Report and Write the News?*, Prentice Hall, New Jersey, 1961.

Zanda, B. : *Journalism as Guidance*, MacMillan Co., New York, 1998.

Zohar, B. : *Principles and Techniques of Journalism*, Vikas Publishing House, New Delhi, 1982.

Index

A

Advertisement, 22, 56, 57, 224, 225, 231, 232, 233, 240, 293, 294, 295, 296, 297.

All India Radio, 221, 233, 252, 283.

All-India Press Council, 10.

Amrita Bazar Patrika, 126, 127, 148, 157, 193, 197, 201.

Associated Press of India, 102, 249.

B

BBC, 20.

Bombay Times, 69, 143, 144.

British India, 142, 204.

Broadcast, 247, 283.

C

Cable, 206, 235, 236, 237, 248, 249, 265.

Channel, 163, 223, 233, 235, 238, 242.

Chief Editor, 288.

Chief Justice, 2, 22, 108, 159, 212, 298.

Chief Minister, 19, 108, 230, 248, 272, 306, 311.

Chief Reporter, 145.

D

Defence of India, 8, 9, 206, 321.

Doordarshan, 221, 223, 226, 232, 233, 234, 235, 237, 238.

E

Editor, 2, 3, 12, 14, 24, 33, 55, 60, 62, 63, 68, 77, 85, 88, 89, 91, 93, 95, 96, 97, 98, 99, 101, 104, 106, 108, 109, 110, 111, 112, 113, 114, 115, 116, 117, 121, 123, 124, 125, 126, 127, 128, 131, 133, 134, 135, 137, 138, 139, 140, 141, 143, 144, 145, 147, 148, 149, 151, 152, 157, 159, 164, 165, 167,

168, 182, 183, 184, 186, 189, 190, 193, 196, 201, 202, 203, 207, 208, 209, 211, 222, 226, 227, 254, 256, 257, 259, 260, 264, 275, 279, 288, 289, 291, 297, 302, 305, 306, 309, 314, 321, 323, 324.

Editorial, 44, 50, 63, 68, 89, 94, 95, 98, 100, 104, 105, 106, 108, 109, 112, 125, 131, 132, 135, 145, 146, 147, 150, 152, 159, 184, 188, 207, 208, 225, 266, 280, 284, 287, 290, 291, 293, 297, 301, 304, 305, 314, 316, 320.

Electronic Media, 20, 232, 236, 242.

Emergency Powers, 9, 16, 273.

F

FM Channel, 223.

G

General Advertiser, 2, 21.

Government of India, 9, 44, 45, 48, 51, 55, 68, 96, 102, 139, 140, 141, 142, 152, 184, 185, 193, 200, 206, 210, 263, 264, 274.

H

Hindustan Times, 16, 111, 121, 275, 340.

I

India, 1, 2, 3, 4, 5, 8, 9, 10, 13, 14, 15, 16, 17, 19, 20, 21, 22, 23, 24, 25, 28, 29, 30, 32, 33, 34, 35, 37, 38, 39, 41, 42, 43, 44, 45, 47, 48, 49, 50, 51, 52, 54, 55, 56, 57, 60, 61, 62, 67, 68, 69, 70, 74, 76, 77, 79, 80, 82, 83, 84, 86, 87, 88, 89, 90, 91, 92, 93, 94, 96, 97, 98, 99, 100, 101, 102, 103, 105, 106, 107, 108, 109, 111, 112, 113, 114, 115, 116, 121, 128, 130, 131, 132, 134, 136, 139, 140, 141, 142, 143, 144, 145, 146, 147, 148, 149, 150, 151, 152, 153, 154, 155, 156, 157, 158, 161, 163, 164, 165, 166, 167, 168, 169, 170, 171, 172, 173, 175, 176, 177, 179, 180, 181, 182, 183, 184, 185, 186, 187, 188, 190, 191, 192, 193, 194, 196, 197, 198, 200, 201, 202, 203, 204, 205, 206, 208, 209, 210, 211, 212, 213, 215, 216, 218, 219, 220, 221, 223, 225, 226, 228, 229, 232, 233, 234, 236, 237, 238, 242, 243, 244, 245, 246, 247, 248, 249, 250, 251,

252, 254, 255, 256, 257, 258, 259, 262, 263, 264, 265, 266, 269, 270, 271, 273, 274, 275, 276, 277, 278, 279, 280, 281, 282, 283, 287, 288, 289, 292, 294, 298, 300, 301, 302, 303, 304, 305, 309, 310, 312, 321, 323, 327, 328, 329, 330, 334, 335, 336, 339, 340, 341, 343, 345.

India Today, 56, 148, 238, 339.

Indian Express, 16, 19, 42, 100, 101, 105, 109, 212, 274, 323, 334, 339, 341, 344, 345.

Indian Journalism, 23, 28, 63, 64, 93, 99, 112, 114, 122, 124, 127, 133, 157, 215, 219, 230, 260, 306.

Indian Language, 12, 31, 44, 49, 51, 63, 64, 65, 69, 210, 222, 223, 230, 238, 329, 330, 332, 334.

Indian Newspaper, 20, 23, 30, 88, 134, 145, 178, 185, 197, 220, 236, 251, 252, 334.

Indian Papers, 143, 148, 191, 193, 198, 203, 208, 209, 335.

Indian Politics, 73, 88, 187, 305.

Indian Press, 1, 8, 9, 10, 11, 15, 16, 20, 23, 29, 34, 43, 60, 62, 63, 64, 65, 66, 67, 69, 107, 125, 134, 155, 174, 179, 183, 185, 187, 192, 195, 196, 200, 201, 202, 203, 210, 212, 220, 221, 223, 245, 258, 269, 273, 278, 284, 304, 305, 306, 317, 319, 323, 328, 330.

Internet, 20.

J

Journalism, 11, 12, 20, 23, 28, 36, 55, 56, 61, 62, 63, 64, 87, 93, 94, 99, 100, 103, 106, 110, 111, 112, 113, 114, 119, 122, 124, 126, 127, 131, 133, 135, 139, 142, 157, 170, 181, 183, 187, 204, 206, 214, 215, 218, 219, 222, 227, 228, 230, 260, 281, 285, 287, 289, 302, 306, 313, 344, 345.

L

Lok Sabha, 266, 270, 273, 275, 277, 283, 288, 290, 300, 322.

London, 1, 2, 21, 67, 68, 96, 97, 98, 103, 106, 135, 155, 171, 172, 175, 178, 195, 207, 208, 217, 219, 220, 246, 248, 249, 250, 252, 254, 256, 257, 259, 277.

M

Magazine, 2, 24, 28, 54, 61, 135, 213, 238, 241, 269.

Mass Communication, 39, 47, 56, 71, 180, 210, 287, 325.
Mass Media, 45, 47, 70, 71, 72, 74, 211.
Media, 20, 39, 44, 45, 46, 47, 57, 70, 71, 72, 73, 74, 82, 85, 86, 210, 211, 223, 226, 231, 232, 233, 235, 236, 237, 238, 239, 242, 246, 251, 294, 295, 325.
Media in India, 242.

N

Nai Duniya, 288, 342.
National Book Trust, 50, 51, 53.
Navbharat Times, 340, 342, 343.
Network, 44, 45, 46, 53, 236, 237, 344.
New India, 15, 205, 206, 213.
New York, 254, 257, 259, 299.
News, 1, 7, 9, 11, 15, 16, 18, 19, 20, 22, 28, 35, 43, 44, 45, 46, 55, 57, 61, 62, 72, 76, 93, 97, 102, 103, 112, 118, 133, 134, 135, 140, 144, 148, 194, 207, 210, 215, 219, 223, 224, 228, 229, 231, 234, 235, 238, 242, 246, 248, 249, 250, 251, 252, 253, 254, 255, 256, 257, 258, 259, 260, 268, 271, 272, 281, 282, 283, 284, 287, 292, 293, 294, 295, 296, 297, 302, 304, 305, 313, 316, 317, 320, 321, 324, 335.
News Agencies, 18, 20, 44, 103, 219, 246, 258, 259, 268, 271, 281, 287.
Newspaper, 2, 3, 5, 6, 7, 8, 11, 12, 13, 20, 21, 22, 23, 30, 31, 33, 35, 36, 39, 43, 45, 56, 61, 63, 65, 68, 69, 70, 87, 88, 99, 100, 101, 103, 105, 106, 107, 109, 110, 111, 113, 114, 115, 116, 117, 119, 121, 123, 125, 126, 132, 134, 135, 140, 142, 144, 145, 156, 157, 168, 174, 175, 178, 183, 184, 185, 207, 209, 213, 215, 218, 219, 220, 223, 224, 225, 226, 227, 228, 229, 230, 231, 232, 233, 234, 235, 236, 238, 240, 241, 242, 243, 244, 248, 249, 250, 251, 252, 255, 257, 258, 271, 272, 273, 279, 280, 283, 285, 287, 288, 289, 290, 291, 292, 293, 294, 295, 297, 298, 300, 301, 307, 309, 314, 315, 316, 318, 319, 321, 323, 324, 325, 328, 331, 332, 333, 334, 335, 337, 339, 340, 341, 342, 343, 344.

P

Parliament, 37, 44, 84, 108,

153, 142, 156, 163, 182, 204, 227, 252, 262, 263, 267, 272, 273, 274, 276, 292, 295, 297, 298, 299, 300, 303, 305, 312, 314, 315, 322.
Photograph, 248.
Pioneer, 14, 23, 100, 112, 143, 168, 191, 195, 208, 243, 343.
Press, 1, 2, 3, 4, 5, 6, 7, 8, 9, 10, 11, 12, 13, 14, 15, 16, 17, 18, 19, 20, 21, 22,. 23, 26, 29, 30, 31, 32, 34, 35, 36, 38, 39, 40, 41, 42, 43, 44, 45, 46, 55, 56, 57, 59, 60, 62, 63, 64, 65, 66, 67, 69, 72, 76, 82, 83, 86, 88, 89, 92, 98, 99, 100, 101, 102, 103, 104, 107, 108, 109, 111, 112, 113, 114, 116, 117, 118, 121, 122, 124, 125, 127, 129, 133, 134, 135, 136, 145, 148, 150, 151, 152, 155, 156, 157, 158, 160, 161, 165, 166, 174, 179, 182, 183, 184, 185, 186, 187, 192, 195, 196, 200, 201, 202, 203, 205, 206, 207, 209, 210, 211, 212, 213, 214, 218, 219, 220, 221, 222, 223, 224, 225, 226, 227, 228, 229, 230, 231, 232, 233, 234, 235, 237, 238, 240, 242, 245, 246, 248, 249, 250, 251, 253, 254, 258, 259, 261, 262, 263, 265, 266, 267, 268, 269, 271, 272, 273, 274, 275, 276, 277, 278, 279, 280, 281, 282, 283, 284, 285, 286, 287, 288, 289, 290, 291, 292, 293, 294, 295, 296, 297, 298, 299, 300, 301, 302, 303, 304, 305, 306, 307, 308, 309, 310, 311, 312, 313, 314, 315, 316, 317, 318, 319, 320, 321, 322, 323, 324, 325, 327, 328, 329, 330, 332.
Press Council, 10, 231, 275, 276, 280, 298, 313, 314, 316, 318, 321, 322, 323.
Print Media, 232, 237, 238, 246.
Printing Technology, 55, 56, 285.

Q

Quit India Movement, 16, 17, 79, 83.

R

Radio, 18, 44, 55, 211, 221, 225, 232, 233, 235, 237, 239, 242, 247, 252, 254, 274, 283.
Reporter, 96, 111, 145, 208, 317.

S

Star News, 20.
Statesman, 18, 61, 88, 95,

96, 97, 98, 107, 126, 130, 136, 137, 138, 139, 140, 141, 142, 161, 196, 202, 243, 249, 256, 278, 306, 309, 310, 344.

T

Television, 44, 55, 211, 225, 231, 232, 233, 234, 235, 236, 238, 239, 274, 328, 334.

The Hindu, 16, 99, 36, 62, 114, 115, 116, 117, 126, 131, 132, 133, 134, 135, 136, 143, 148, 154, 156, 157, 161, 162, 163, 165, 167, 168, 182,194, 202, 206, 207, 209, 244, 246, 263, 264, 301, 303, 304, 320, 339, 341, 344.

Times of India, 14, 19, 42, 88, 93, 105, 106, 107, 108, 109, 111, 126, 142, 143, 144, 145, 146, 147, 148, 182, 191, 192, 193, 196, 200, 201, 208, 243, 245, 251, 278, 280, 288, 302, 305, 334, 340, 341, 345.

U

UK, 47.

United News of India, 271.

USA, 18, 43, 47.

V

Video, 237, 238.

Y

Young India, 74, 76, 77, 82, 84, 209.

Yugantar, 173, 186.

Z

Zee India, 20.

❑❑❑